ediate | Philip Kerr

8/12

Straightforward

MACMILLAN

	Reading & Listening	Speaking	Writing (in the Workbook)
7A	L A radio programme about people who have met celebrities	Describing & guessing jobs	A letter of application
7B	R *Life on the other side*	Talking about your experiences of work Describing an imaginary life ***Did you know?*** Salaries in the UK	
7C	R An article about horoscopes & work R Horoscopes	Deciding what qualities are needed for different jobs	
7D	L An interview in a recruitment agency	Talking about finding a job in your town Roleplay: careers advice	
8A	R A conference programme	Talking about science fiction films Giving a thirty-second talk	A note giving instructions
8B	L A description of *Star Quest*, a TV game show	Deciding who is the best candidate for *Star Quest*	
8C	L A conversation about how to send an email	Talking about how you use computers ***Did you know?*** Computer games in the USA	
8D	L Descriptions of gadgets R *A great idea?*	Discussing & choosing gadgets on a website	
9A	L A radio programme about entertainment in London	Talking about entertainment in London & your town ***Did you know?*** Leisure activities in the UK	A review of a film
9B	R *Reality TV – love it or leave it*	Planning a reality TV show	
9C	R *Oscars night*	Talking about going to the cinema Acting a scene from *Titanic*	
9D	L Four people buy tickets on the phone	Roleplay: at the box office Describing a concert	
10A	R *The United States of animals*	Talking about pets & animals Communication activity: guessing animals	A story 2
10B	R An article about stress	Discussing stressful jobs Ranking stressful experiences	
10C	L A news report about the marathon runners, Ranulph Fiennes & Mike Stroud	Talking about how fit you are ***Did you know?*** Sport in Australia	
10D	L Two doctors' appointments	Roleplay: at the doctor's	
11A	L Two people talk about things they wanted when they were younger	Describing a favourite possession Communication activity: describing & guessing objects	A description of a favourite possession
11B	R *Office worker flip flops out of job*	Discussing clothes & appearance	
11C	R *Home comforts*	Giving a presentation on shopping in your town ***Did you know?*** Shopping in London	
11D	L A conversation in a shopping mall	Roleplay: in a clothes shop	
12A	L A news report about the American adventurer, Steve Fossett	Discussing famous explorers Planning a 'round the world' trip	An opinion composition
12B	R An email describing Trinidad carnival	Talking about festivals Describing a festival	
12C	R *English as an International Language – no problem, OK?*	Talking about the English language in your country	
12D	L Four conversations at a party	Discussing global issues ***Did you know?*** Oxfam	

1A | Family life

VOCABULARY & SPEAKING: family & friends

1 Match the words in the box to the definitions.

> aunt colleague cousin daughter
> grandfather mother-in-law pet
> ~~neighbour~~ nephew niece son
> son-in-law uncle best friend

1 neighbour

1 a person who lives very near you
2 a person you work with
3 an animal that lives with the family
4 your male child
5 your aunt's (or your uncle's) child
6 your brother's (or your sister's) daughter
7 your closest friend
8 your daughter's husband
9 your mother's (or your father's) sister

2 Work in pairs. Write definitions for the other words in the box.

3 Write the names of four people who are important to you.

  Work in pairs. Tell your partner as much as possible about these people.

Tara is my niece. She is nineteen years old and she studies at university …

READING

1 Read the article about two families. Match the photos A–D to the stories.

2 Read the article again and answer the questions.

1 Where was Gemma born?
2 When was her wedding?
3 Where is her husband from?
4 What's her daughter's name?
5 How many children are there in Judy's family?
6 What is the family home when they travel?
7 What is the youngest child's name?
8 Where was the family's first show?

A

B

Mother Love

Gemma Burford Enolengila

Gemma was born in 1978 in a quiet village in the south of England. Her mother worked in a library and her father was an accountant. When she was a student at Oxford University, she
5 travelled to Tanzania and met her future husband, Lesikar, for the first time. The couple got married in 2003. When they had a baby (a daughter, Lucia) they decided to go and live in Tanzania. 'I want my daughter to have the best life possible,' said Gemma.

10 Lesikar is a Masai and lives in a village near Arusha in the north of the country. There is no electricity in the home and they walk almost a kilometre to get water. Gemma cooks simple dinners of corn and vegetables and she washes the clothes in a bucket. There is a small primary school in the village, but Gemma and
15 Lesikar will also teach Lucia at home.

Judy Boehmer

Judy had her first child, Adam, 27 years ago. She now has four sons and seven daughters and a pet dog, Bosco, but she wants more boys. Judy and her husband, Larry, live in Atlanta,
20 Georgia, but they also have a 10-metre-long motor home. The family sometimes travels more than 40,000 kilometres a year for their work. The children do not go to school, but they study at home with their parents.

The Boehmers are a circus family and all the children take part
25 in the show. They do different kinds of juggling and Margaret, the youngest, stands on one leg in her mother's hand. The first show of the Boehmer Family Jugglers was at a theme park in Iowa in 1989, and they now perform all over America.

C

D

3 Close your book. How much can you remember about the two families?

4 Do you think that the life of these two families is good for the children? Why or why not?

GRAMMAR: questions with *to be*

We make questions with the verb *to be* by putting the verb before the subject.

Yes/No questions
Is she *married?*
Were you *at school yesterday?*

Short answers
We can answer *yes/no* questions with short answers.

Yes, I am.	*No, I'm not.*
Yes, she is.	*No, she isn't.*
Yes, he was.	*No, he wasn't.*
Yes, they were.	*No, they weren't.*

Wh- questions
We can put question words before the verb.
Where were *you born?*
What is *her daughter's name?*

> SEE LANGUAGE REFERENCE PAGE 14

1 Match the questions in column A with the short answers in column B.

A
1 Are you married?
2 Is your family very large?
3 Were you born in this town?
4 Is your father a good cook?
5 Are your parents from this town?
6 Are there many people with the same name as you?

B
a Yes, I was.
b Yes, it is.
c Yes, there are.
d No, I'm not.
e No, he isn't.
f No, they aren't.

2 Change the answers to the questions in exercise 1 so that they are true for you.

3 Rearrange the words to make questions.

1 How many people are there in your family?

1 are   family   how   in   many   people   there   your ?
2 are   names   their   what ?
3 are   how   old   they ?
4 are   hobbies   their   what ?
5 born   parents   were   where   your ?
6 family   in   is   person   the   who   youngest   your ?
7 family   holiday   last   was   when   your ?

4 Work in pairs. Ask and answer the questions in exercise 3.

SPEAKING

1 🔘 **1.1** Listen to a description of a typical English family. Put the topics in the order that you hear them.

☐ **Children**
How many children are there? What are their names? How old are they? What are their hobbies?

☐ **Family pet**
Is there a family pet? What is it? What is it called?

☐ **Food**
When does the family eat together? What is their favourite food?

☐ **Weekends and holidays**
What does the family do at the weekend? What do they do in the holidays?

1 **Parents**
What are the parents' names? How old are they? What are their jobs? What are their interests?

☐ **TV**
What are the family's favourite TV programmes?

2 Work in pairs. Think about a typical family in your country. Make notes using the questions in exercise 1.

3 Work in groups. Describe your typical family to each other.

1B | Where are they now?

SPEAKING

'A true friend is the best possession in the world.'

1 Translate the proverb above into your language. Are there any similar proverbs in your language?

2 Work in pairs. How many different ways can you complete the sentence below?

A true friend …
   … always listens to you.
   … makes you laugh.
   … knows you well.

VOCABULARY: verb collocations (friendship)

1 Put the text in the correct order.

☐ each other very often, but we **keep**
☐ good friends. We come from similar
☑ David is one of my oldest
☐ backgrounds and we **have** a lot
☐ friends. We were at college together. We didn't **get**
☐ in common. He lives in Spain now, so we don't **see**
☐ in touch by phone and email.
☐ on well at first, but later we became

2 🔘 1.2 Listen to the recording to check your answers.

3 Complete the questions with a word in **bold** from exercise 1.

1 What sort of people do you _____ on well with?
2 How often do you and your best friend _____ each other?
3 Do you _____ a lot in common with your best friend? What?
4 How do you _____ in touch with friends in other towns or countries?

4 Work in pairs. Ask and answer the questions in exercise 3.

LISTENING

1 Work in pairs. Look at the photograph. Choose one of the people in the photo and describe her/him to your partner. Your partner must decide who you are describing.

2 You are going to listen to a woman, Christine, talking to her husband about the photograph. Before you listen, read the sentences and decide if they are true (T) or false (F).

1 The two girls on the left are sisters.
2 The girl with red shoes (Christine) was fourteen years old.
3 The picture was taken in 1973.
4 The boy with the guitar (Nicholas) was Christine's boyfriend.
5 Christine is now married to Nicholas.
6 The girl with blonde hair (Helga) was in love with Nicholas.
7 Helga is Spanish.
8 Helga was Christine's best friend.

3 🔘 1.3 Listen to the conversation to check your answers.

GRAMMAR: questions with auxiliary verbs

Present simple & past simple
We make questions in the present simple and past simple with an auxiliary verb (*do/does/did*) and the infinitive. We put the auxiliary verb before the subject and we put the infinitive after the subject.

question word	auxiliary	subject	infinitive
Where	do	you	live?
What	does	he	want?
When	did	they	arrive?

Other forms
All other verb forms (for example, present continuous, *can, will*) already have an auxiliary verb and a main verb. We put the auxiliary verb before the subject and we put the main verb after the subject.

question word	auxiliary	subject	main verb
What	are	you	doing?
Where	can	we	meet?
When	will	we	know?

> SEE LANGUAGE REFERENCE PAGE 14

1 Complete the questions with an auxiliary verb from the box.

> does (x2)   did   is   was

1 What _____ your best friend's name?
2 Where _____ she/he live?
3 What _____ she/he do?
4 Where and when _____ you first meet?
5 When _____ the last time you met?

2 Work in pairs. Ask and answer the questions in exercise 1.

3 Look at the text below. Some of the text is missing. Prepare questions to ask about the missing information.

Christine Smith left school in 1976. She studied (1)_____ (*What?*) at Leeds University and then got a job (2) _____ (*Where?*). When she was in America, she met (3) _____ (*Who?*) at a party at the White House. He worked for (4) _____ (*Who?*). They started going out together and they got married (5) _____ (*When?*). They now have (6) _____ (*How many?*) children. Christine and her husband now live (7) _____ (*Where?*). She works for (8) _____ (*Who?*) and he is writing (9) _____ (*What?*). Christine wants to get in touch with (10) _____ (*Who?*) and promises to reply to all emails.

4 Work in pairs, A and B.

A: Turn to page 129. B: Turn to page 127.

Ask and answer the questions in exercise 3 to complete the missing information.

PRONUNCIATION: contractions 1

1 🔊 1.4 Listen to these contractions.

do not	→	don't
did not	→	didn't
what is	→	what's

2 Make contractions from these words.

1 does not   3 that is   5 were not
2 he has   4 was not   6 who is

3 🔊 1.5 Listen to the contractions and repeat.

SPEAKING

1 Correct the grammatical mistakes in the questions.

1 Who you did read about?
2 Is she/he be married?
3 How old she/he is?
4 How many children does she/he has?
5 Where she/he is living now?
6 What do she/he do?

2 Work in groups of four, A–D. You are going to read about the people in Christine's photo.

A: Turn to page 126.   C: Turn to page 129.
B: Turn to page 127.   D: Turn to page 131.

Use the questions in exercise 1 to find out about Christine's old friends. Who do you think Christine will get in touch with first?

DID YOU KNOW?

1 Work in pairs. Read the text and answer the questions.

FRIENDS REUNITED is one of the most popular websites in Britain. It has seven million members and more than three million people visit the site every day.
People visit the site because they want to find out about old friends. You can read news about friends from school or university. You can look at photos of these people now and you can send voice and email messages. After visiting the site, many people organize reunions with their old friends.

• Have you got a similar website in your country?
• Are you still in touch with friends from your last school?

1c | Neighbours

SPEAKING

1 Work in pairs. Ask and answer these questions about your neighbours.

- What are their names?
- What do they do?
- Where do they come from?
- Are they good neighbours? Why or why not?

READING

1 Read the magazine article. Put the information in the correct order.

- ☐ British men like the pop singer, Kylie Minogue.
- ☐ *1* Many British people would like to live next door to a gardening expert.
- ☐ Kylie lives in a fashionable part of London.
- ☐ Mr Titchmarsh's neighbours do not know him very well.
- ☐ Most people do not want to live next door to the prime minister.
- ☐ Alan Titchmarsh is a well-known British gardening expert.

2 Read the article again and answer the questions.

1 How many people voted for Alan Titchmarsh as their perfect neighbour?
2 What part of England does Alan Titchmarsh live in?
3 How old is his home?
4 Name two famous people who live in Chelsea.
5 Where does the prime minister of Britain live?

3 Which famous person in the text would you like as your neighbour?

Life

WHO WOULD YOU LIKE AS ...
a neighbour?

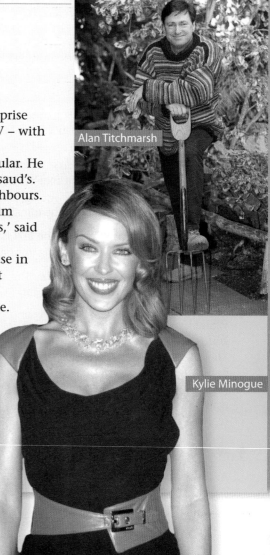

Alan Titchmarsh

Kylie Minogue

A recent opinion poll asked 1,000 people in Britain this question. The surprise winner of the poll was Alan Titchmarsh – a gardening expert on BBC TV – with 29% of the vote.

The British are very interested in gardening and Titchmarsh is very popular. He
5 is a best-selling writer and a famous TV face. He is even in Madame Tussaud's. To find out more about him, we spoke to some of Mr Titchmarsh's neighbours. We did not learn very much. 'He's a very quiet man and we don't see him much,' said one neighbour. 'We don't ask him for help with our gardens,' said another. 'He's a very busy man.'
10 Titchmarsh, a very private man, lives in an eighteenth-century farmhouse in a small village in the south of England. Like many people, he likes quiet neighbours and he is happy where he lives.

The top woman in the poll was the Australian pop singer, Kylie Minogue. 85% of her voters were men. Ms Minogue lives in fashionable Chelsea
15 in the west of London. Her neighbours include her sister Dannii, pop stars Madonna and Bob Geldof, supermodel Liz Hurley, Sean Connery and Formula One king, Bernie Ecclestone. It is an excellent place for star-spotters and Kylie Minogue fans.

The British like gardening and attractive Australian pop singers, but,
20 it seems, they do not want to live next door to their prime minister. He got only 3% of the votes in the poll. Is this because people do not want to live in Downing Street? Or is it because they do not like the prime minister?

GRAMMAR: *how* & *what* questions

We can combine *how* and *what* with other words to begin questions.

How* + adjectives/adverbs/*much/many
  How popular is the prime minister?
  How often do you speak to your neighbours?
  How many children do they have?

What* + noun/*kind of/sort of/type of
  What colour is your car?
  What time do you get up?
  What kind of neighbour is he?

⟩ SEE LANGUAGE REFERENCE PAGE 14

1 Complete the questions for the answers below.

1 How _____?
  I usually drive quite fast, especially on the motorway.
2 What _____?
  My father's hair is grey.
3 How _____?
  I know my teacher very well.
4 What _____?
  I usually have dinner at about eight o'clock.
5 How _____?
  I have six cousins.
6 What _____?
  I don't like pop music very much, but I like everything else.

2 Work in pairs. Ask and answer the questions in exercise 1.

3 You have new neighbours and you want to know more about them. Write four questions that you would like to ask. Use the prompts below to help you.

- What time … ?
- What kind of … ?
- How much … ?
- How many … ?
- How often … ?
- How old … ?

4 Work in pairs and compare your questions. Which is the most interesting question?

PRONUNCIATION: the alphabet

1 Look at the three lists of letters. In each list, the letters use the same sound. Choose a letter from the box to complete each list.

G	I	J	O	Q	R	U	W	X	Y

1 /eɪ/ A H ___ K
2 /iː/ B C D E ___ P T V
3 /e/ F L M N S ___ Z

2 🔘 1.6 Listen to the recording to check your answers.

3 🔘 1.7 Now listen to the other letters from the box and repeat after the recording.

4 🔘 1.8 Listen to a list of the six most common surnames in Britain and write them down.

5 🔘 1.9 Now listen to the recording to check your spelling.

SPEAKING

1 Make a list of five famous people from your country (film stars, musicians, politicians, sports stars, TV personalities, artists, business people).

Now put the people in your list in order
(1 = best neighbour → 5 = worst neighbour).

2 Work in small groups. Talk about the people in your list and explain why you think they would be good or bad neighbours.

Useful language

X is probably a good/bad neighbour because …
I would/wouldn't like to live next door to Y because …
I imagine that Z is very …

1D | Making contact

SPEAKING

1 Work in pairs. Discuss these questions.

- Which of the ways shown in the pictures below do you use most often to contact other people?
- Which do you prefer? When and why?

2 Think of the last three phone calls that you made.

- Who did you call? (a friend/business call?)
- Why did you call her/him? (to give some news/ask a question?)

I phoned my brother because he is not well at the moment.
I phoned my friend, Karen, because I wanted to invite her for dinner.

Work in pairs and compare your answers.

FUNCTIONAL LANGUAGE 1: phone numbers

1 🔘 1.10 Listen to a phone message and choose the best answer.

1 To listen to the menu, press
   a) **4**   b) **#**   c) **✱**

2 For general enquiries, press

   a) **1 #**   b) **2 #**   c) **3 #**

3 Kate's home phone number is
   a) 0307 775 3046   b) 0307 755 3846   c) 0307 755 3046

4 Kate's mobile number is
   a) 0477 320188   b) 0477 328118   c) 0477 321880

2 Look at tapescript 1.10 on page 133 to check your answers.

3 Work in pairs, A and B. You are going to practise saying phone numbers.

A: Turn to page 126. B: Turn to page 128.

Listen to the phone numbers your partner says and write them down.

READING

1 Read the advertisements opposite and put them into four groups.

- Accommodation
- English language lessons
- Jobs
- Making friends

2 Read the advertisements again and answer the questions.

1 What does Mary teach?
2 What is the name of the recruitment agency?
3 Where does Mike live?
4 When are the Kung Fu classes?
5 What does Patrick want?
6 How much does the room near London Bridge cost?
7 Where can you get free accommodation?
8 What languages can you practise on Thursday evenings?

3 Imagine that you are in London and you want to improve your English. Which advertisements would you choose and why?

A

Beautiful? We have a beautiful room for a beautiful person in our flat near London Bridge. £750 per month. Call David and Gavin on 0803 731886

B

Experienced teacher offers private English lessons. All levels (beginners – advanced). Mary Sharp 0307 727 2377

C

Kung Fu classes. Monday 7.30–8.30. Get fit and make friends at the same time. Stuart. Tel: 0308 783 9494

D

New friends. English gentleman would like to meet new people from all over the world. Interests: cinema, concerts, pubs, learning languages. Patrick Trotter 0906 641480

E

Notting Hill, single room in house near Underground station. No pets. £600 per month + bills. 0780 696 91134 Ask for Mike.

F

Student needed for general hotel work. Good pay and free accommodation. No experience necessary. Regent Hotel 0308 845 6921

G

Temporary work. We are urgently looking for temporary staff for shops, restaurants and offices in this area. Call now. Sayers Recruitment and Training 0870 446091

H

Thursday evening conversation classes in central London. All languages! Come and talk! Call 0278 846772 for more information.

LISTENING

1 1.11–1.14 Listen to four phone calls. Match the calls 1–4 to the advertisements A–H.

Which caller does **not** leave a message on an answering machine?

2 1.11–1.14 Listen to the messages again and answer the questions.

1 What is Davina's phone number?
2 What is a good time to call her?
3 What is Bella's phone number?
4 What is her family name?
5 What is Ruby's number?
6 Why does Sara want English lessons?

FUNCTIONAL LANGUAGE 2: phone messages

1 1.15 Listen and complete the phone messages.

This is 641480. I'm afraid there's no one to take your call right (1) _____. Please leave your (2) _____ and (3) _____ after the tone and I'll call you back.
Ah, yes, hello. Mr Trotter, my (4) _____ is Davina and I'm (5) _____ in your advertisement. Could you call me back, please? Any time before …

Stuart here. I'm not home at the (6) _____, so please leave a (7) _____ after the beep. Thanks.
Hello, good morning. (8) _____ is Bella Moor, that's Moor – M – double O – R. I'm (9) _____ about the Kung Fu classes. You can call me back on my (10) _____, that's 0447 …

2 Write your own answering machine message. Use the language in exercise 1 to help you.

Roleplay

3 Work in pairs, A and B.

A: You are going to telephone another student. First of all, decide why you want to call them. Use the language in exercise 1 and in the Useful language box below to prepare what you want to say. Listen to the message on their answering machine and then leave your own message.

B: Another student is going to telephone you. Read out the answering machine message that you have prepared and then listen to the message that your partner leaves. Write down their name, phone number and any other important information.

> ### Useful language
>
> Hi, this is …
> Hello, it's … here.
>
> I'm calling about …
> I'm interested in …
>
> Can/Could you call me back later?
>
> My (mobile) number is …
> I'm on …

4 When you have finished, change roles. Then change partners and repeat the task with other students in the class.

GRAMMAR

Yes/No questions

Questions with to be

We make questions with the verb *to be* by putting the verb before the subject.

verb	subject	
Is	*he*	*French?*
Are	*you*	*married?*

We can answer these questions with short answers.

Is he French? **Yes, he is.**
Are they married? **No they aren't.**

Present simple *to be*		
Am	I	
Is	she/he/it	married?
Are	you/we/they	

Past simple *to be*		
Was	I	
	she/he/it	at school yesterday?
Were	you/we/they	

Short answer		
Yes, No,	I	am/was. 'm not/wasn't.
	she/he/it	is/was. isn't/wasn't.
	you/we/they	are/were. aren't/weren't.

Questions with present simple & past simple

We make questions in the present simple and past simple with an auxiliary verb (*do/does/did*) and the infinitive without *to*. We put *do/does/did* before the subject and we put the infinitive after the subject.

auxiliary	subject	infinitive	
Do	*you*	*like*	*pop music?*
Does	*she*	*live*	*in London?*
Did	*she*	*enjoy*	*the party?*

We can answer these questions with short answers.
Do you like pop music? **Yes, I do.**
Does she live in London? **No, she doesn't.**

Present simple			
Do	I		
Does	she/he/it	like	pop music?
Do	you/we/they		

Past simple			
	I		
Did	she/he/it	go	to the cinema last night?
	you/we/they		

Short answer		
Yes, No,	I	do/did. don't/didn't.
	she/he/it	does/did. doesn't/didn't.
	you/we/they	do/did. don't/didn't.

Questions with other verb forms

All other verb forms (for example, present continuous, *can*, *will*) already have an auxiliary verb and a main verb. We put the auxiliary verb before the subject and we put the main verb after the subject.

auxiliary	subject	main verb
Are	*you*	*listening?*
Can	*we*	*start?*
Will	*she*	*phone?*

We can answer these questions with short answers.

Are you listening? **Yes, I am.**
Can we start? **No, we can't.**
Will she phone? **No, she won't.**

Wh- questions

We can put question words before the verb. The most common question words are: *what, which, when, where, why, who* and *how*.

What *is her daughter's name?*
Who *was your first boyfriend?*
When *did they arrive?*

We can combine *how* and *what* with other words to begin questions.

How + adjectives (*far, old, popular, tall*)
adverbs (*often, well,* etc)
much (*much money, much time*)
many (*many children, many cousins*)

How old *is Sarah?*
How often *do you travel by train?*
How many *CDs does he have?*

What + noun (colour, time, etc)
kind of/sort of/type of

What colour *is their car?*
What time *is it?*
What kind *of pizza do you like?*

FUNCTIONAL LANGUAGE
Phone messages

This is 0307 775 3046.
This is Kate Woods.
You have reached the voicemail of …
Thank you for calling …

I'm afraid there is no one to take your call right now.
I'm not home/in the office at the moment.

Please leave	*your name and number* *a/your message*	*after*	*the beep.* *the tone.*

This is a message for …
I'm interested in …
I'm calling about …

I'll call you back.
Could you call me back, please?

WORD LIST
Family

aunt *n C* **	/ɑːnt/
cousin *n C* **	/ˈkʌz(ə)n/
daughter *n C* ***	/ˈdɔːtə/
grandfather *n C* *	/ˈgrænfɑːðə/
grandmother *n C* *	/ˈgrænmʌðə/
husband *n C* ***	/ˈhʌzbənd/
mother-in-law *n C*	/ˈmʌðə(r)ɪnlɔː/
nephew *n C*	/ˈnefjuː/
niece *n C*	/niːs/
pet *n C* *	/pet/
son *n C* ***	/sʌn/
son-in-law *n C*	/ˈsʌnɪnlɔː/
uncle *n C* *	/ˈʌŋkl/
wife *n C* ***	/waɪf/

Friendship

best friend	/best ˈfrend/
get on (well) with (sb)	/get ˈɒn wɪð/
have a lot in common with (sb)	/hæv ə lɒt ɪn ˈkɒmən wɪð/
keep in touch with (sb)	/kiːp ɪn ˈtʌtʃ wɪð/
neighbour *n C* **	/ˈneɪbə/

Other words & phrases

accommodation *n U* **	/əkɒməˈdeɪʃn/
accountant *n C* **	/əˈkaʊntənt/
advert(isement) *n C*	/ədˈvɜːtɪsmənt/
attractive *adj* **	/əˈtræktɪv/
background *n C* **	/ˈbækgraʊnd/
best-selling *adj*	/best ˈselɪŋ/
blonde *adj*	/blɒnd/
bucket *n C*	/ˈbʌkɪt/
circus *n C*	/ˈsɜːkəs/
clothes *n pl* ***	/kləʊðz/
colleague *n C* **	/ˈkɒliːg/
college *n C/U* ***	/ˈkɒlɪdʒ/
concert *n C* **	/ˈkɒnsət/
contact *v* ***	/ˈkɒntækt/
corn *n U*	/kɔːn/
couple *n C* ***	/ˈkʌpl/
doll *n C*	/dɒl/
dress *n C* **	/dres/
electricity *n U* **	/ɪlekˈtrɪsəti/
email *n C* **	/ˈiːmeɪl/
enquiry *n C* **	/ɪnˈkwaɪri/
experience *n U* ***	/ɪkˈspɪərɪəns/
expert *n C* **	/ˈekspɜːt/
famous *adj* ***	/ˈfeɪməs/
fan *n C* **	/fæn/
farmhouse *n C*	/ˈfɑːmhaʊs/
fashionable *adj* **	/ˈfæʃnəbl/
find out *v*	/faɪnd ˈaʊt/
fit *adj* *	/fɪt/
flat *n C* **	/flæt/
flowery *adj*	/ˈflaʊəri/
gardening *n U*	/ˈgɑːdnɪŋ/
guitar *n C* **	/gɪˈtɑː/
hobby *n C*	/ˈhɒbi/
housework *n U* *	/ˈhaʊswɜːk/
include *v* ***	/ɪnˈkluːd/
juggling *n U*	/ˈdʒʌglɪŋ/
laugh *v* ***	/lɑːf/
library *n C* ***	/ˈlaɪbrəri/
lovely *adj*	/ˈlʌvli/
member *n C* ***	/ˈmembə/
message *n C* ***	/ˈmesɪdʒ/
motor home *n C*	/ˈməʊtə həʊm/
perform *v* ***	/pəˈfɔːm/
pink *adj*	/pɪŋk/
poll *n C* *	/pəʊl/
pop singer *v C*	/pɒp ˈsɪŋə/
popular *adj* ***	/ˈpɒpjʊlə/
practise *v* **	/ˈpræktɪs/
press *v* ***	/pres/
primary school *n C*	/ˈpraɪməri skuːl/
prime minister *n C* **	/praɪm ˈmɪnɪstə/
private *adj* ***	/ˈpraɪvət/
pub *n C* **	/pʌb/
recent *adj* ***	/ˈriːsnt/
recruitment agency *n C*	/rɪˈkruːtmənt eɪdʒənsi/
secretary *n C* *	/ˈsekrətri/
shirt *n C* ***	/ʃɜːt/
show *n C* ***	/ʃəʊ/
soap opera *n C*	/ˈsəʊp ɒprə/
staff *n U* ***	/stɑːf/
surprise *n C/U* ***	/səˈpraɪz/
temporary *adj* ***	/ˈtemp(ə)rəri/
theme park *n C*	/ˈθiːm pɑːk/
tone *n C* *	/təʊn/
traditional *adj* ***	/trəˈdɪʃn(ə)l/
typical *adj* ***	/ˈtɪpɪkl/
university *n C/U* ***	/juːnɪˈvɜːsəti/
urgently *adv*	/ˈɜːdʒəntli/
vegetable *n C* ***	/ˈvedʒtəbl/
village *n C* ***	/ˈvɪlɪdʒ/
voicemail *n U*	/ˈvɔɪsmeɪl/
vote *n C/v* ***	/vəʊt/
website *n C*	/ˈwebsaɪt/
wedding *n C* **	/ˈwedɪŋ/
winner *n C* **	/ˈwɪnə/
wonder *v* ***	/ˈwʌndə/

Abbreviations

n	noun
v	verb
adj	adjective
adv	adverb
sb	somebody
sth	something
C	countable
U	uncountable
pl	plural
s	singular

*** the most common and basic words
** very common words
* fairly common words

2A | School days

VOCABULARY & SPEAKING: adjectives with prepositions

1 Which sentences have a positive (+) meaning and which have a negative (–) meaning?

1 I was **good at** mathematics. +
2 I was **bored with** my school. –
3 I was **afraid of** the older children.
4 I was **fond of** my science teacher.
5 I was **interested in** science and technology.
6 I was **terrible at** arriving on time.
7 I was **keen on** sports and swimming.
8 I was **worried about** my grades.

2 Think about your experience of school. Change the sentences in exercise 1 so that they are true for you.

3 Work in pairs. Compare your sentences. Were your experiences similar or different?

LISTENING

1 🔊 1.16–1.18 Listen to three people talking about their school days. Match the speakers 1–3 to the topics a–c below.

a my favourite subject
b my favourite teacher
c my problems at school

2 🔊 1.16–1.18 Listen to the recording again and complete column A with a phrase from column B.

A	B
1 I never missed	a good grades.
2 I always got	b my exams.
3 I was terrible at	c my homework.
4 I failed	d lessons.
5 I never did	e most subjects.
6 I was good at	f music.
7 I didn't want to leave	g school.

3 Did you have any similar experiences at school?

GRAMMAR: past simple

1 Complete the table. Look at tapescripts 1.16–1.18 on page 134 to check your answers.

infinitive	past simple	infinitive	past simple
hate	(1) _____	study	(5) _____
listen	(2) _____	talk	(6) _____
leave	(3) _____	teach	(7) _____
love	(4) _____	try	(8) _____

2 Now put the verbs in the table into four groups.

a Regular verbs: infinitive + -ed   _listened_
b Regular verbs: infinitive + -d _____
c Regular verbs: infinitive ending in -y → -i + ed _____
d Irregular verbs   _____

> We make negatives with *didn't (did not)* + infinitive.
> **I didn't want** to leave school.
> We make questions with *did* + subject + infinitive.
> *Where **did you go** to school?*
> ***Did you like** school?*

> SEE LANGUAGE REFERENCE PAGE 24

3 Complete the conversation. Put the verbs in brackets into the past simple.

A: Where (1) _did you go_ (you / go) to school?
B: My father (2) _____ (*work*) for a multinational company and we (3) _____ (*live*) in lots of different countries, so I (4) _____ (*go*) to five different schools.
A: (5) _____ (*you / enjoy*) your school days?
B: No, I didn't. Not really. I (6) _____ (*not have*) many friends because we (7) _____ (*not stay*) long in one place. I (8) _____ (*leave*) one school after six months!
A: (9) _____ (*you / do*) well in your exams?
B: Yes, I did. Because I (10) _____ (*not / go*) out with friends, I (11) _____ (*study*) a lot in the evenings and at the weekends. I (12) _____ (*not / get*) top grades, but I (13) _____ (*get*) a place at Cambridge University.
A: What was that like? (14) _____ (*you / like*) it?
B: Yes. I (15) _____ (*think*) it was great.

4 Work in pairs. Write a similar conversation.

PRONUNCIATION: regular past simple verbs

1 🌐 1.19 When we say regular past simple forms, we usually add the sound /t/ or /d/ to the infinitive. We do **not** need an extra syllable. Listen to these examples.

open /əʊpən/ → opened /əʊpənd/
love /lʌv/ → loved /lʌvd/
try /traɪ/ → tried /traɪd/

But if the infinitive ends in /t/ or /d/, we **do** need to add an extra syllable (/ɪd/) when we say the regular past form. Listen to these examples.

want /wɒnt/ → wanted /wɒntɪd/
decide /dɪsaɪd/ → decided /dɪsaɪdɪd/

2 Put the verbs in the box into two groups: no extra syllable (NS) and extra syllable (ES).

| arrived NS | ended | hated | helped |
| needed | studied | waited | worked |

3 🌐 1.20 Listen to the recording to check your answers.

SPEAKING

1 Do you know any films or TV programmes about schools and teachers?

2 You are going to talk about a teacher that you really liked. Use these questions to help you.

- What was the teacher's name?
- What did she/he teach?
- Where did she/he teach?
- How often did you have lessons with her/him?
- What did she/he look like?
- Why did you like her/him?
- Do you remember a particular moment with this teacher?
- What happened?

3 Work in groups. Describe the teacher that you really liked to your group.

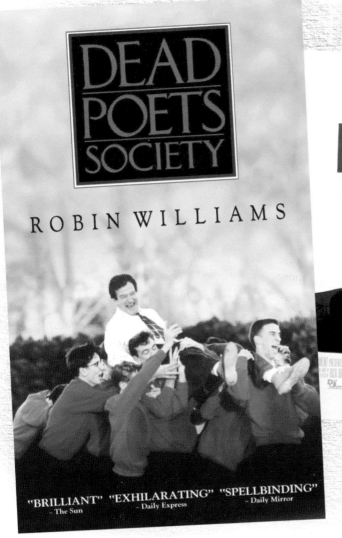

2B | Irish schools

SPEAKING

1 Work in pairs. Discuss these questions.

- Are there any big differences between the schools in your town? Are some schools better than others? If so, why?

- What is your idea of a good school?

VOCABULARY: education

1 Complete the sentences with a word from the box.

> age   certificate   compulsory
> punishment   results   sex   system

1 Some schools in England are for boys and girls and some are single _____.
2 In the English education _____, there are private schools and state schools.
3 Some subjects, like English and maths, are _____ until the age of sixteen in England.
4 English children must sometimes stay in class at break as a _____.
5 The minimum leaving _____ in England is sixteen, but most students continue for another two years.
6 There is no leaving _____ in England, but many students take 'A level' exams when they are eighteen.
7 School students in England get their exam _____ in the summer holidays after they leave school.

2 🔘 1.21 Listen to the recording to check your answers.

3 Change the sentences in exercise 1 so that they are true for your country.

READING

1 Read a magazine article about education in Ireland. Match the paragraphs 1–4 to the headings a–d below.

1 = b

a Rich and poor, boys and girls
b A success story
c School subjects
d Traditional teaching

18

Schools in Europe

This month we take a look at schools in:

The Republic of Ireland

(1) _____

Ireland now has one of the best education systems in the world. Class sizes are small, exam results are good and most children are happy to stay at school after the minimum leaving age of sixteen. It is easy to forget that the picture used to be very different.

(2) _____

5 For years, Ireland had one of the most complicated education systems in the world. There were many different kinds of school, but most of them had a lot in common. Classes were large and the teaching was very traditional. As in many countries, teachers used to hit the children if they made mistakes (the government banned corporal punishment in 1982).

(3) _____

10 Parents used to pay for their children's education and, as a result, there were schools for the rich and schools for the poor. Boys and girls went to different schools and studied different subjects. Nowadays, most schools are free and only about half the schools are single-sex. In many ways, education is now a woman's world. Girls do better than boys in their
15 exams, more girls go to university and most teachers are women.

(4) _____

At the end of secondary school, students take their final exams (the 'Leaving Certificate'). Compulsory subjects are maths, history, Irish and a foreign language. In addition, they must choose two or three extra subjects. Some of these, like Business Organization, help to prepare
20 them for the world of work. This is very different from the past when Latin, Greek and Religion used to be the most important subjects.

2 Read the article again and find one piece of information to show that each statement is true.

1 The exam results are good.

1 Ireland has a good education system.
2 Teaching in Ireland used to be very traditional.
3 Irish boys and girls used to have very different experiences of school.
4 Education in Ireland is a woman's world.
5 Irish students study many different subjects.

3 Are there any similarities between education in Ireland and education in your country?

GRAMMAR: *used to*

> We use *used to* + infinitive to talk about past states.
>
> *Latin and Greek **used to be** important school subjects.*
>
> We also use *used to* + infinitive to talk about past actions that happened many times.
>
> *Teachers **used to hit** children.*
>
> We can always use the past simple instead of *used to*.
>
> *Boys and girls **used to go/went** to different schools.*
>
> However, we cannot use *used to* for past actions that happened once.
>
> *The government **banned** corporal punishment.* (**not** *used to ban*)

> ➲ SEE LANGUAGE REFERENCE PAGE 24

1 Look at the sentences about a famous Irishman. Rewrite the sentences using *used to* + infinitive.

1 His family used to be very poor.

1 His family was very poor.
2 He lived with his grandparents.
3 He wasn't a very happy child.
4 The teachers at school hit him.
5 The other children called him 'Irish'.
6 He didn't like his school.
7 He wanted to be an artist.

Who are the sentences about: Pierce Brosnan (the actor), Bono (the musician) or Roy Keane (the footballer)? See page 128 for the answer.

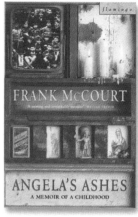

2 Look at the sentences below. Replace the past simple with *used to* where possible.

used to be
1 The writer, Frank McCourt, ~~was~~ ⋏ a teacher.
2 He wrote a book called *Angela's Ashes*.
3 He was born in New York.
4 His family moved to Ireland.
5 His family didn't have much money.
6 His father told funny stories to Frank.
7 Frank loved listening to his father.
8 Frank won the Pulitzer Prize for this book about his childhood.

3 Write six sentences about yourself when you were at primary school. Begin three sentences with *I used to …* and three with *I didn't use to …* .

PRONUNCIATION: irregular past simple verbs

1 Underline the word in the groups 1–4 below which has a different sound from the other words in the group.

1 bought	caught	found	thought
2 came	gave	made	said
3 broke	drove	lost	spoke
4 felt	knew	met	went

2 🔘 1.22 Listen to the recording to check your answers.

SPEAKING

1 Think about schools in your country now and in the past. How are they different? Make notes, using your own ideas and the ideas in the box to help you.

> computers/technology   class sizes   types of school
> the school buildings   when you can leave school
> school subjects   exams   behaviour   punishment

2 Work in pairs and compare your ideas. Are schools now better or worse than they used to be?

Schools in my country used to be very different. For example, …

19

2c | Red faces

SPEAKING & READING

1 Work in pairs. Look at the pictures A–C and describe what is happening in each one. Which of these situations do you think is the most embarrassing?

2 Read the messages from an internet discussion group for teachers and match them to the pictures.

It's the head!

I thought it was a fancy dress party ...

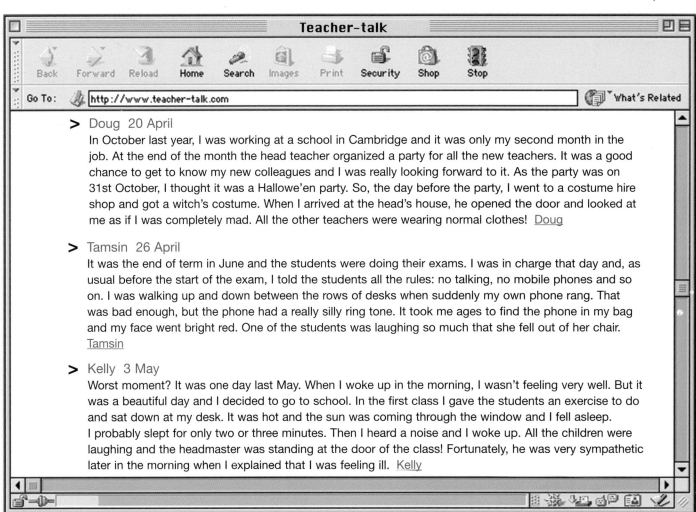

Teacher-talk

Back Forward Reload Home Search Images Print Security Shop Stop

Go To: http://www.teacher-talk.com   What's Related

> Doug 20 April
In October last year, I was working at a school in Cambridge and it was only my second month in the job. At the end of the month the head teacher organized a party for all the new teachers. It was a good chance to get to know my new colleagues and I was really looking forward to it. As the party was on 31st October, I thought it was a Hallowe'en party. So, the day before the party, I went to a costume hire shop and got a witch's costume. When I arrived at the head's house, he opened the door and looked at me as if I was completely mad. All the other teachers were wearing normal clothes! Doug

> Tamsin 26 April
It was the end of term in June and the students were doing their exams. I was in charge that day and, as usual before the start of the exam, I told the students all the rules: no talking, no mobile phones and so on. I was walking up and down between the rows of desks when suddenly my own phone rang. That was bad enough, but the phone had a really silly ring tone. It took me ages to find the phone in my bag and my face went bright red. One of the students was laughing so much that she fell out of her chair. Tamsin

> Kelly 3 May
Worst moment? It was one day last May. When I woke up in the morning, I wasn't feeling very well. But it was a beautiful day and I decided to go to school. In the first class I gave the students an exercise to do and sat down at my desk. It was hot and the sun was coming through the window and I fell asleep. I probably slept for only two or three minutes. Then I heard a noise and I woke up. All the children were laughing and the headmaster was standing at the door of the class! Fortunately, he was very sympathetic later in the morning when I explained that I was feeling ill. Kelly

3 Read the messages again and answer the questions.

1 Why did Doug's head teacher organize a party?
2 Why was Doug looking forward to the party?
3 Why did he wear witch's clothes?
4 Why was Tamsin in an examination room?
5 What was special about Tamsin's phone?
6 Why didn't she turn off her phone immediately?
7 Why did Kelly decide to go to work when she wasn't well?
8 Why did Kelly wake up?

4 Work in pairs. Describe an embarrassing experience that happened to you or someone you know.

GRAMMAR: past continuous

> We use the past continuous to describe actions in progress at a particular time in the past.
>
> *Where **were** you **working** in October last year?*
> *I **was working** at a school in Cambridge.*
> ***Was** she **feeling** ill? Yes, she **was**. / No, she **wasn't**.*
>
> We use the past simple for actions that interrupt the actions in the past continuous.
>
> *I **was walking** up and down when my phone **rang**.*

❯ SEE LANGUAGE REFERENCE PAGE 24

1 Complete the text. Put the verbs in brackets into the past simple or the past continuous.

A few days ago, I (1) _____ (*wait*) for the bus with my younger brother. We (2) _____ (*go*) home after an afternoon at the shops. A very large woman with a big shopping bag (3) _____ (*stand*) in front of us. After a few minutes, the bus (4) _____ (*arrive*). The woman (5) _____ (*get*) on the bus when she (6) _____ (*turn*) round. 'Can you help me with my bag?' she (7) _____ (*ask*) us. 'Yes, of course, (8) _____ (*say*) my brother. 'Are you going to have a baby?'

2 Look at the pictures A–C on page 20 for one minute. Then work in pairs. Turn to page 127 and answer the questions.

3 Work in pairs. Ask and answer questions about what you were doing at the times below.

- fifteen minutes ago
- one hour ago
- at six o'clock this morning
- at eleven o'clock last night
- at three o'clock last Saturday
- at this time last week

What were you doing fifteen minutes ago?
I was having a cup of coffee.

SPEAKING

1 Work in groups. First, read these sentences and decide which list they belong to.

1 Speak in front of their friends about funny things that they did when they were younger.
2 Don't say hello to their friends when they visit your home.
3 When their friends are visiting, speak with your mouth full of food.
4 Tell them (in front of their friends) to wear clothes that they do not like.

> How to embarrass your parents
> •
> •
> •
> •
> •

> How to embarrass your children
> •
> •
> •
> •
> •

2 Now discuss how parents can embarrass their children and how children can embarrass their parents. Add three more sentences to each list.

3 Present your lists to the rest of the class.

2D | Which school?

SPEAKING

1 Work in pairs. You and your partner win first prize in a competition.
Read the information and decide which city you both want to study in.

First Prize

English Study Tour for Two

Two weeks all inclusive
(flight, accommodation, school fees)

Pick the centre of your choice:

England: London • Scotland: Edinburgh
Republic of Ireland: Dublin • America: New York
Australia: Sydney • New Zealand: Christchurch
South Africa: Cape Town

VOCABULARY: school facilities

1 Look at the advertisement for an English school.
Match the words in **bold** to the definitions below.

1 = library

1 a place to borrow or read books
2 a restaurant/café in a place of work
3 money you pay for a professional service
4 place or position
5 teaching
6 that you can change
7 they have done this job a lot
8 they have professional exams/qualifications

2 List three important things for you in choosing
a language school.

3 Work in pairs and compare your lists.

VICTORIA SCHOOL OF ENGLISH
SYDNEY

The Victoria School has a central **location** near the Opera House.
Our **qualified** and **experienced** teachers provide top quality **tuition**
with **flexible** timetables. The school has an ultra-modern multi-media
centre with 20 PCs, a language laboratory and a **library**. The school
has its own **cafeteria** and an exciting social programme.
Special **fees** for international students.

LISTENING

1 💿 **1.23** A man is asking for information about a course in a French language school. Listen to the conversation and <u>underline</u> the correct information.

CLASS SIZE	10 / <u>15</u> / 20 students per class
LEVEL	Beginner / Intermediate / Advanced
TIMETABLE	Mon & Wed / Tues & Thurs / Tues & Fri 7.30 - 9.00 / 8.00 - 9.30 / 8.30 - 9.30
COURSE LENGTH	10 / 12 / 15 weeks
FRENCH CLUB	Friday mornings / Friday evenings / Saturday evenings
PRICE	£100 / £120 / £150

2 Match the words in column A with the words from column B to make phrases.

A		**B**	
1	day-time	a	activities
2	native	b	class
3	registration	c	courses
4	social	d	form
5	ten-week	e	speakers

3 💿 **1.23** Listen to the conversation again to check your answers.

FUNCTIONAL LANGUAGE: asking for information

1 Rearrange the words to make questions.

1 Please could I have some information about your school?

1 about could information have school I please some your ?
2 about could courses me tell you your ?
3 a are class how in many students ?
4 beginners classes do for have you ?
5 are classes the time what ?
6 course does how last long the ?
7 activities any are social there ?
8 fees course the much are how ?

Look at tapescript 1.23 on page 134 to check your answers.

SPEAKING

Roleplay

1 Work in pairs. You are going to plan an evening school. Use these questions to help you.

- Where is your school?
- What is it called?
- What kinds of courses does the school offer?
- Who are the teachers?
- What facilities does the school have?
- How much do the courses cost?
- What is special about your school?

2 Find another pair and work in groups of four. Find out about each other's schools.

DID YOU KNOW?

1 Work in pairs. Read the facts about the English language and discuss the questions.

- About 375,000,000 people speak English as a first language.
- About 375,000,000 people speak English as a second language.
- About 1,000,000,000 people study English around the world.
- About 500,000 people take examinations (British or American) in English as a foreign language every year.
- About 1,000,000 people go to Britain or America to study English every year.

- When and where do people use English in your country?
- Do many people in your country study English? Why do they study?
- What English language examinations do people take in your country?
- Do you know anyone who has studied English in an English-speaking country? Did they like it?

GRAMMAR

Past simple

We use the past simple to talk about past actions and states. The actions and states are finished.

*I **left** school in 1999. Then I **went** to University.*
*I **liked** rock music when I **was** a teenager.*

We often use a time expression with the past simple, for example, *yesterday, last week, in 2003*.

*I saw John **yesterday**.*
*We lived in Brussels **in 2003**.*

Affirmative & Negative		
I		
He/She/It	found	a job.
You/We/They	didn't find	

Question				
When	did	I he/she/it you/we/they	find	a job?

Short answer	
Did you find a job?	Yes, I did. / No, I didn't.

With regular verbs, we usually add *–ed* to the infinitive in the affirmative. There are three groups of exceptions.

1 When the verb ends in *-e*, we add *-d*.
   like → liked   love → loved
2 When the verb ends in *-y* after a consonant, we change the *-y* to *-ied*.
   study → studied   try → tried
3 With some verbs that end in a consonant, we double the consonant.
   plan → planned   stop → stopped
   Other verbs in this group include: *admit, chat, control, drop, nod, occur, refer, regret, rob, transfer* and *trap*.

Many common verbs have irregular past forms.
   eat → ate   go → went   leave → left

Used to

We use *used to* to talk about past states and past actions that happened many times.

*My family **used to live** in Rome.*
*We **used to go out** for a meal every Saturday.*

We can always use the past simple instead of *used to*, but we cannot use *used to* for actions that happened only once.

*We **used to live** in Rome. = We **lived** in Rome.*
*My family **moved** back to London in 1995.*
Not *~~My family used to move back to London in 1995~~.*

Affirmative & Negative			
I			
He/She/It	used to	like	school.
You/We/They	didn't use to	walk to	

Question				
Did	I He/she/it You/we/they	use to	like walk to	school?

Short answer	
Did you use to like school?	Yes, I did. / No, I didn't.

Past continuous

We use the past continuous to describe actions in progress at a particular time in the past. We often use the past continuous to describe the background situation of a story.

*It was the end of term and the students **were doing** their exams.*

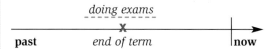

We often use the past simple and past continuous together. We use the past simple for actions that interrupt the actions in the past continuous.

*I **was walking** into class when my phone **rang**.*
(First, I walked into class. Second, my phone rang.)

We cannot normally use stative verbs, in the continuous form. See page 44 for a list of common stative verbs.

*She **knew** that he was happy.*
Not *~~She was knowing he was happy~~.*

Affirmative & Negative			
I	was		
He/She/It	wasn't	talking	on the phone.
You/We/They	were weren't		

Question				
When	was were	I he/she/it you/we/they	talking	on the phone?

Short answer	
Were you talking?	Yes, I was. / No, I wasn't.
Were they working?	Yes, they were. / No, they weren't.

We make the past continuous with *was/were* + infinitive + *-ing*. If the infinitive ends in a consonant + *-e*.

~~live~~ → living

With some verbs that end in a consonant, we double the consonant. See the list of verbs in group 3 in the past simple above.

FUNCTIONAL LANGUAGE

Asking for information

(Please) could I have some information about … ?
Could you tell me about …, (please)?
How much is/are … ?
What time is/are … ?
How long does/do the … last?
Do you have … ?
Is there a … ?
Are there any … ?
How many … are there?

WORD LIST

Adjectives with prepositions

afraid of ***	/ə'freɪd əv/
bored with **	/'bɔːd wɪð/
fond of *	/'fɒnd əv/
good at ***	/'gʊd ət/
interested in ***	/'ɪntrəstɪd ɪn/
keen on **	/'kiːn ɒn/
terrible at **	/'terəbl ət/z
worried about *	/'wʌrɪd əbaʊt/

Education

cafeteria *n C*	/kæfə'tɪərɪə/
certificate *n C **	/sɜː'tɪfɪkət/
compulsory *adj* *	/kəm'pʌlsəri/
computer *n C ***	/kəm'pjuːtə/
course *n C ***	/kɔːs/
desk *n C ***	/desk/
education system *n C*	/edjʊ'keɪʃn sɪstəm/
examination (exam) *n C ***	/ɪgzæmɪ'neɪʃn/
experienced *adj* *	/ɪk'spɪərɪənst/
fail (an exam) *v ***	/feɪl/
fee *n C **	/fiː/
get a place (at university)	/get ə 'pleɪs (ət juːnɪ'vɜːsəti)/
grade *n C *	/greɪd/
headmaster *n C*	/hed'mɑːstə/
headmistress *n C*	/hed'mɪstrəs/
headteacher *n C*	/hed'tiːtʃə/
homework *n U *	/'həʊmwɜːk/
language	/'læŋgwɪdʒ
laboratory *n C*	ləbɒrət(ə)ri/
leaving age *n C*	/'liːvɪŋ eɪdʒ/

leaving certificate *n C*	/'liːvɪŋ sə'tɪfɪkət/
lesson *n C ***	/'lesən/
location *n C **	/ləʊ'keɪʃn/
mixed sex *adj*	/mɪkst seks/
multi-media centre *n C*	/mʌlti 'miːdɪə sentə/
native speaker *n C*	/neɪtɪv 'spiːkə/
pass (an exam) *v ***	/pɑːs (ən ɪg'zæm)/
private school *n C* (corporal)	/'praɪvət skuːl/
punishment *n U *	/'pʌnɪʃmənt/
pupil *n C ***	/'pjuːpl/
qualification *n C *	/kwɒlɪfɪ'keɪʃn/
registration form *n C*	/redʒɪ'streɪʃn fɔːm/
result *n C ***	/rɪ'zʌlt/
single sex *adj*	/sɪŋgl seks/
social programme/ activity *n C*	/'səʊʃlprəʊgræm æktɪvəti/
state school *n C*	/steɪt skuːl/
subject *n C ***	/'sʌbdʒɪkt/
term *n C ***	/tɜːm/
timetable *n C*	/'taɪmteɪbl/
tuition *n U*	/'tʃuːɪʃn/
university *n C ***	/juːnɪ'vɜːsəti/

School subjects

art *n U ***	/ɑːt/
biology *n U*	/baɪ'ɒlədʒi/
Greek *n U*	/griːk/
history *n U ***	/'hɪstri/
Irish *n U*	/'aɪrɪʃ/
Latin *n U*	/'lætɪn/
mathematics (maths) *n U*	/mæθə'mætɪks/
music *n U ***	/'mjuːzɪk/
religion *n U ***	/rɪ'lɪdʒ(ə)n/
science *n U ***	/'saɪjəns/
technology *n U ***	/tek'nɒlədʒi/

Other words & phrases

accent *n C *	/'æksənt/
actually *adv ***	/'æktʃuəli/
anyway *adv ***	/'eniweɪ/
artist *n C **	/'ɑːtɪst/
as usual	/əz juːʒuəl/
(fall) asleep *adj **	/ə'sliːp/
ban *v *	/bæn/
behaviour *n U ***	/bɪ'heɪvjə/
borrow *v **	/'bɒrəʊ/
brilliant *adj *	/'brɪljənt/
care (about sb) *v ***	/'keə/

club *n C ***	/klʌb/
choose *v *** (multinational)	/tʃuːz/
company *n C ***	/'kʌmp(ə)ni/
competition *n C ***	/kɒmpə'tɪʃn/
complicated *adj **	/'kɒmplɪkeɪtɪd/
embarrass *v*	/ɪm'bærəs/
enjoy *v ***	/ɪn'dʒɔɪ/
exciting *adj **	/ɪk'saɪtɪŋ/
fancy dress costume/ party *n C*	/fænsi 'dres kɒstjuːm/pɑːti/
flexible *adj *	/'fleksəbl/
flight *n C ***	/flaɪt/
fun *adj*	/fʌn/
funny *adj ***	/'fʌni/
government *n C ***	/'gʌvnmənt/
great *adj ***	/greɪt/
in addition	/ɪn ə'dɪʃn/
in charge (of)	/ɪn 'tʃɑːdʒ/
(all) inclusive *adj*	/ɪn'kluːsɪv/
minimum *adj/n **	/'mɪnɪməm/
miss (a lesson) *v ***	/mɪs/
mobile phone *n C*	/məʊbaɪl 'fəʊn/
of course *adv ***	/əv 'kɔːs/
organize *v **	/'ɔːgənaɪz/
painter *n C*	/'peɪntə/
provide *v ***	/prə'vaɪd/
row *n C ***	/rəʊ/
rule *n C ***	/ruːl/
shopping bag *n C*	/'ʃɒpɪŋ bæg/
stupid *adj **	/'stjuːpɪd/
sympathetic *adj*	/sɪmpə'θetɪk/
ultra-modern *adj*	/ʌltrə 'mɒd(ə)n/
witch *n C*	/wɪtʃ/
worry	/'wʌri/
(about sb/sth) *v ***	

3A | Flatmates

VOCABULARY: *house & home*

1 Do you live in a house or a flat? What do you like most about your home? Discuss and compare your answers in pairs.

2 Complete the sentences with *house* or *home*.

1 What is your _home_ town like?
2 At what age do people usually leave _house_ in your country?
3 How do you feel when you are away from _home_?
4 Is your mother a _house_ wife or does she have another job?
5 How much _home_ work does your teacher usually give you?
6 What time do you usually get _home_ in the evenings?
7 Who does most of the cleaning and the other _house_ work where you live?

3 Work in pairs. Ask and answer the questions in exercise 2.

PRONUNCIATION: /h/

1 Find two words in the box that do **not** begin with the sound /h/.

happy	holiday	honest	hotel	who
hospital	home	house	what	whole

2 🔘 1.24 Listen to the recording to check your answers.

3 How well can you say the sentence below?

> In Hertford, Hereford and Hampshire hurricanes hardly ever happen.
> (from the film *My Fair Lady*)

4 🔘 1.25 Listen and repeat.

LISTENING

1 You are going to listen to two friends talking about their home life. Ali lives with his parents and two brothers. He wants to go to live with Charlie, who shares a flat with four friends.

Look at the statements below. Who do you think is speaking: Ali (A) or Charlie (C)?

1 There's nothing to eat.
2 I get no peace and I can't do any work.
3 There's no space in the house.
4 We don't go to bed early.
5 I can't have any friends in the house.
6 The kitchen is a bit dirty.

2 🔘 1.26 Listen to the conversation to check your answers.

3 🔘 1.26 Listen to the conversation again. Choose the best definition for the phrases below.

1 Grim!
   a) That's bad!   b) That's good!

2 It's driving me mad.
   a) It makes me angry.   b) It makes me sad.

3 I don't want to put you off.
   a) I don't want to encourage you.
   b) I don't want to discourage you.

4 Work in pairs. Discuss these questions.

- What do you think Ali should do?
- What are the advantages and disadvantages of living at home when you are a student?
- Do most students live at home in your country?

GRAMMAR: countable & uncountable nouns with *some, any* & *no*

> ### Countable nouns
>
> We can count countable nouns (for example, *one problem, two problems*). They have both a singular and plural form.
>
> *There's a new **problem**.*
> *He's got **problems** at home.*
>
> ### Uncountable nouns
>
> We cannot count uncountable nouns. (We cannot say *two ~~homeworks~~*.) They only have a singular form.
>
> *I have to do my **homework**.*
>
> ### *Some, any & no*
>
> We can use *some, any* and *no* with both countable and uncountable nouns.
>
> ### *Some*
>
> We usually use *some* in positive sentences.
>
> *We've got **some** cousins.* (countable)
> *I'm going to get **some** food.* (uncountable)
>
> ### *Any*
>
> We usually use *any* in negative sentences and questions.
>
> *I can't have **any** friends.* (countable)
> *I can't do **any** work.* (uncountable)
> *Have you got **any** better ideas?* (countable)
> *Do you have **any** time at the weekend?* (uncountable)
>
> ### *No*
>
> A positive verb + *no* has the same meaning as a negative verb + *any*.
>
> *There are **no** problems.*
> = *There **aren't any** problems.* (countable)
> *I get **no** independence.*
> = *I **don't get any** independence.* (uncountable)

⊙ SEE LANGUAGE REFERENCE PAGE 34

1 Are the nouns in the box countable (C) or uncountable (U)?

> bread *U*   brother *C*   cash   food
> friend   independence   money
> parent   peace   sofa   space

Look at tapescript 1.26 on pages 134–5 to check your answers.

2 Choose the correct words to complete the dialogue.

Mum: What's the (1) *problem / problems*, Ali? You look really unhappy at the moment.

Ali: There's (2) *any / no* problem, Mum.

Mum: Yes, there is. What's the matter? (3) *Is / Are* your teachers at college giving you a lot of (4) *homework / homeworks*?

Ali: No, it's not that. But you know I've got (5) *any / some* very important exams in two weeks …

Mum: Yes?

Ali: Well, I can't find the (6) *time / times* to study. I don't get (7) *any / no* peace in my room with the others there. It's really hard to work.

Mum: I'm sorry. I know what you mean. There really isn't (8) *any / some* space in the house when we have guests, is there?

Ali: Mum – I'm thinking of moving in with (9) *any / some* friends.

Mum: Oh, you can't do that! I know, I've got (10) *an / some* idea. Why don't you do your (11) *work / works* with me in the living room?

3 Work in pairs, A and B.

A: Turn to page 127. Look at the picture of Charlie's bedroom.
B: Turn to page 129. Look at the picture of Charlie's bedroom after a party.

How many differences can you find?

*Are there **any** people in your picture?*
*There are **some** bottles on the table.*
*There's **no** food in this picture.*

SPEAKING

Roleplay

Hey! Are there any clean glasses in this flat?

1 Work in groups of three to five. You share a flat with the other students in your group. There are some problems and no one is really happy.

Read your role card and decide what you want to say to your flatmates. At the end of the discussion, make a list of four rules for the flat so that everyone is happy.

No smoking in the flat.

A: Turn to page 126.   D: Turn to page 128.
B: Turn to page 129.   E: Turn to page 130.
C: Turn to page 131.

You are sitting in the living room with your flatmates. Student C begins the discussion.

There are some things I want to talk about …

3B | Another country

READING

1 On a piece of paper, write everything that you know about Scotland. You have two minutes.

Now work in pairs and compare your ideas.

2 Read the magazine article and choose the best summary.

1 An American man becomes interested in where his family came from.
2 An American man goes to a conference about Scotland.
3 An American man returns to his family's home town in Scotland.

3 Read the article again and put the sentences a–f in the gaps 1–6.

a And they also told me about the communities of Scots living abroad.
b I already have my ticket.
c my grandmother worked for President Roosevelt.
d Scottish bankers, Scottish businessmen, in politics, in the arts, in education – everywhere you look there's a Scot.
e There are, for example, 75 places called Hamilton around the world.
f They went to Australia, Canada, America and New Zealand.

4 Find these words in the article and choose the best definition.

1 *conference* (line 6)
 a) a large meeting where people talk about one subject
 b) a short conversation
2 *origin* (line 15)
 a) a place where you go on holiday
 b) the place that you come from
3 *settled down* (line 17)
 a) got married and stayed in a place
 b) sat down
4 *strange* (line 24)
 a) normal or ordinary
 b) not normal
5 *reunion* (line 29)
 a) wedding
 b) meeting people again after a long time

Scots Abroad *by Ted Hamilton*

I always knew that I had a Scottish name, but I always thought of myself as American. I never thought about my name. I was born, like my parents and grandparents before them, here in Lexington, Kentucky. My father was in the Marines and (1) ____ Not many
5 families are more American than us.
Then, two weeks ago, I went to a conference of whisky producers here in Lexington. I counted 245 names on the conference programme and many of them were Scottish. I also met two brothers called Hamilton and they never stopped talking. They told me about the Hamilton clan
10 (the Scottish word for family) and about the Hamilton tartan. They told me about the first Lord Hamilton, who married the daughter of King James II of Scotland. (2) ____ (The brothers came, would you believe it, from a place called Hamilton in Canada.)
Apparently, five million people live in Scotland, but there are more
15 than 30 million people of Scottish origin around the world. Many Scots went to live abroad in the nineteenth century to find land and jobs. (3) ____ They settled down, had families and some of them gave their names to their home towns. (4) ____
Here, in the state of Kentucky, it seems that most of the people you
20 meet have some Scottish origins. We came here poor, but we are everywhere now. (5) ____ How many of them are like me, I asked the Hamilton brothers. How many know almost nothing about their origins? To my surprise, I learnt that I was probably the only one. The Hamilton brothers thought I was very strange.
25 But after the conference I was a changed man. Now, most days, I go to the Hamilton Family website and chat with James and David, the brothers from Ontario (and a hundred others). Yesterday, I got my first copy of a magazine called *Scots Abroad*. I am also waiting for the tartan scarf that I ordered online. And next summer, there is a reunion of
30 Hamiltons in Edinburgh Castle. (6) ____

SPEAKING

1 Work in pairs. Discuss these questions.

- Did many people leave your country in the past? Why did they leave? Where did they go?
- Do many people from your country live abroad?
- Do you know anybody who lives abroad? If so, why did they go?
- What do people from your country miss when they are abroad?

GRAMMAR: *some, many & most*

> We can use *some*, *many* and *most* with or without *of*.
> **Some of** *them gave their names to their home towns.*
> **Most of** *the people you meet have* **some** *Scottish origins.*
> **Many** *Scots went to foreign countries.*
> **Most** *days, I log on to the website.*
>
> | *not many* *some* *many* *most* | *of* | *the, my, his*, etc + plural noun *(people)* *them* *us* |
> |---|---|---|
> | *not many* *some* *many* *most* | | + plural noun *(Scots, days)* |

> ➤ SEE LANGUAGE REFERENCE PAGE 34

1 In four of the sentences below the word *of* is missing. Insert *of* where necessary.

1 Many the passengers on the *Titanic* were leaving for a new life in America.
2 Most the Scots in America came in the nineteenth century.
3 Most Afro-Americans live in the southern states and the industrial cities.
4 Some US cities, like Boston, have big Irish communities.
5 There aren't many places in California that do not have a Spanish-speaking community.
6 Some the first immigrants to America were Dutch.
7 Not many the new immigrants to America come from Western Europe.
8 There are many Koreans and Japanese in LA.

2 Make true sentences using the phrases in the table.

Not many Some Many Most		people in this country people in this town students	are difficult to understand. are married. are very interesting. arrive late.
	of	the students in this class my friends my work colleagues our English lessons	don't have much money. drive a nice car. have a job. like their work. live near here. need English at work. speak two or three languages.
		us	

3 Work in pairs and compare your answers.

DID YOU KNOW?

1 Work in pairs. How much do you know about the United Kingdom?

- Write the capital cities on the correct places on the map.
- What do you know about the different countries in the United Kingdom?

Great Britain is the island of England, Scotland and Wales. The United Kingdom is Great Britain and Northern Ireland. The flag of the United Kingdom is called the Union Flag.

Capital Cities of the UK

Cardiff • London
Belfast • Edinburgh

3c | Home town

VOCABULARY: towns

1 Look at the words in the box.

> art gallery   bar   bus   cinema   crime
> flat   house   library   metro   nightclub
> park   pollution   restaurant   studio   theatre
> traffic   tram

Put the words into these groups.

- public transport
- types of accommodation
- nightlife, culture
- other

Can you add any other words to the groups?

2 Imagine that you are going to live somewhere new. Which things are most important for you?

READING

1 Imagine that you are going to live in Montreal. Read the webpage. Choose which area (Verdun, Outremont or Old Montreal) you would prefer to live in. Why?

Work in pairs and compare your answers.

2 Read the webpage again. Which part of Montreal do the sentences refer to: Verdun (V), Outremont (O) or Old Montreal (OM)?

1 = OM

1 There are a lot of cars.
2 It doesn't cost a lot to live here.
3 It has the best places to eat.
4 It isn't dangerous.
5 It's a good place for outdoor sport.
6 There isn't much to do in the evening.
7 There are a lot of cultural activities.
8 There isn't much cheap accommodation.

living

Back   Forward   Reload   Home   Search   My   Images   Pr

Go To: http:// www.livinginmontreal.com

livinginmontreal.com

- Home
- Mini guide
- Choosing an area
- **Find out from the people who live there**
- Public transport
- Eating
- Health
- Services

Harbor and waterfront

Verdun

We live down by the river. It's a poor area and there's a lot of crime, but the shops are good and there are a few good restaurants. The shopping area is not very attractive, but it is changing. Public transport is excellent and we're near the city centre. In the summer, Verdun is the place to be. The river here is really beautiful and you can have picnics in the park. There isn't enough nightlife for us, so we go to the area near the university for that. Accommodation is cheap!!
BRIGITTE GOFFIN & BERNARD YIP (students)

Want to know more? Click here

Outremont

Outremont has many advantages. The best restaurants in town, the most beautiful park and the biggest houses. You feel safe here. You meet interesting, important people and it's good for business. There are not many Japanese restaurants and we do very well. When we're not working, we like having a coffee outside one of the cafés. We don't have much time to enjoy the area, but we like going up to the park at Mount Royal sometimes. The only problem, really, is that you need to speak French in this part of town (and we don't!).
K.INAMOTO (restaurant owner)

Want to know more? Click here

Marie Reine du Monde Cathedral

Old Montreal

True, there are too many tourists and there's too much traffic. The metro doesn't take you into the centre of Old Montreal. There is a little crime in the area, but not too much. But why am I being so negative? Old Montreal is the **only** place to be. There are a lot of good bars and restaurants. There are excellent museums (if you like that kind of thing), an IMAX cinema, an interesting park to go rollerblading in the summer or ice-skating in the winter. What more do you want? Just one big problem: not enough cheap flats. I found the last one!

Mr. J. B. LAZARIDIS (computer programmer)

Want to know more? Click here

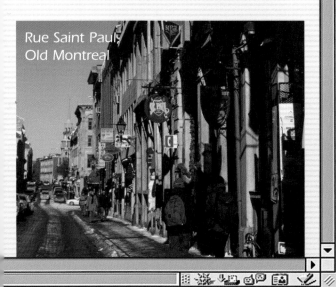

Rue Saint Paul, Old Montreal

GRAMMAR: quantifiers

1 Look again at the text about Montreal. Find the expressions in the table below and complete the examples with nouns from the text.

quantifiers with plural countable nouns	quantifiers with uncountable nouns
too many _tourists_	too much _traffic_
a lot of _____	a lot of _____
many _____	not much _____
not many _____	a little _____
a few _____	not enough _____
not enough _____	

> SEE LANGUAGE REFERENCE PAGE 34

2 Here is some more information about these places. Choose the correct expression to complete the sentences.

Verdun
1 There are a *lot of / much* cheap flats.
2 There are *not many / not much* hotels for tourists.
3 There are a *little / a few* big factories.

Outremont
4 There's *not many / not much* crime.
5 There are a *lot of / too much* French speakers.
6 There is *not many / not much* unemployment.

Old Montreal
7 There are *too many / too much* cars.
8 There are *many / too much* things to do for children.

3 Write six sentences about your town. Use a different quantifier in each sentence.

SPEAKING

1 Turn to page 127 and complete column A.

2 Work in pairs. Ask questions about your partner's town. Write the answers in column B on page 127.

Useful language

What is the name of your town?
How much ... is there?
How many ... are there?

3 Compare your answers.

If you described the same town as your partner, did you have the same answers?

If you described a different town, which town is the better place to live?

3D | Lost!

Speaking

1 Read the information about the city of Newcastle.

2 Work in small groups.

Are there any towns or cities in your country that are similar to Newcastle? In what ways?

Bilbao is near the sea. It also has a famous football team ...

Official name:	Newcastle-upon-Tyne.
Location:	North-east England. On the River Tyne, 13 km from the North Sea.
Population:	Approximately 200,000.
History:	Old Roman town. 19th century industrial centre (ships, coal).

A lively city with good nightlife.
Centre for contemporary art.
Interesting place to visit.
Famous football team.
Beautiful countryside.

Vocabulary: places in a town

1 Label the map below with the words in the box.

> art gallery   bars and restaurants   bridge   castle
> bus station   cathedral   church   ~~library~~
> opera house   shopping centre   stadium   train station

2 Are the statements below true (T) or false (F)?

1 The art gallery is opposite the library.
2 The bars and restaurants are near the river.
3 The cathedral is opposite the stadium.
4 The opera house is next to the castle.
5 The shopping centre is between the art gallery and the bus station.
6 There is a metro station not far from the stadium.

3 Do you have these places in your town? Where are they?

Newcastle City Centre

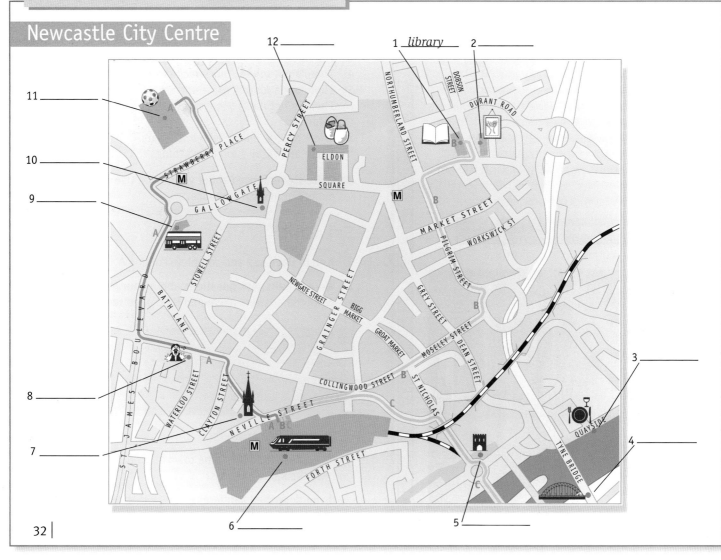

12 _____   1 _library_   2 _____

11 _____

10 _____

9 _____

8 _____

7 _____

6 _____   5 _____   4 _____   3 _____

LISTENING

1 🔘 **1.27** Listen to a conversation in Newcastle train station. Choose the correct words to complete the sentences.

1 Mary is saying *goodbye / hello* to Emma and Lucy.
2 The men want to go to the *shopping centre / stadium*.
3 Emma finds it *difficult / easy* to give directions.
4 Her aunt *helps / doesn't help*.

2 🔘 **1.27** Listen again and follow Mary's directions on the map. Which route did she describe: A, B or C?

FUNCTIONAL LANGUAGE: directions

1 🔘 **1.28–1.30** Stuart and Tony are in front of the castle. Listen to three more conversations. Which speaker gives the best directions to the stadium?

2 🔘 **1.31** Listen to extracts from conversations 1–3 again and complete the sentences.

1 _____ straight on.
2 _____ the first street on the right.
3 _____ past the station.
4 _____ the bridge.
5 _____ to the end of the road.
6 _____ the first street on the left.

3 Match the phrases in exercise 2 to the pictures.

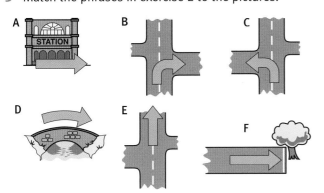

A | B | C
D | E | F

4 Work in pairs, A and B. You are at the train station in Newcastle.

A: Choose a place you want to go to. Ask B for directions.
B: Look at the map and give A directions.

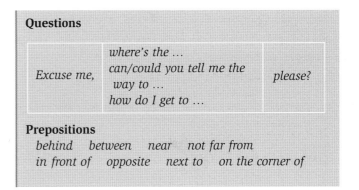

Questions		
Excuse me,	*where's the …* *can/could you tell me the way to …* *how do I get to …*	*please?*

Prepositions
behind   between   near   not far from
in front of   opposite   next to   on the corner of

PRONUNCIATION: *to*

1 🔘 **1.32** Listen to the pronunciation of the word *to* (/tə/) in the middle of these phrases.

• interesting place to visit
• difficult to give directions
• next to the castle

2 Look at tapescript 1.27 on page 135. There are five examples of *to* in the middle of a phrase. Find them and underline them.

3 🔘 **1.33** Listen to the recording to check your answers.

4 Practise saying the phrases with the short pronunciation of *to* (/tə/).

GRAMMAR

Countable & uncountable nouns

Countable nouns
Most nouns in English are countable. We can count them. They have both a singular and plural form for example, *one house, two houses*.

> *It's a new house.*
> *He's got two houses in London.*

A small group of countable nouns has irregular plurals (*child/children, man/men, woman/women, foot/feet, tooth/teeth, mouse/mice*).

Uncountable nouns
Some nouns are uncountable. We cannot count them. For example, we cannot say *two ~~homeworks~~*. They only have a singular form.

> *I want to do my homework.*

Some nouns can be both countable and uncountable. The uncountable noun refers to the thing in general; the countable noun refers to a particular example of it.

> **Crime** *is a problem in many cities.*
> (uncountable: crime in general)
> *Sherlock Holmes solved hundreds of* **crimes**.
> (countable: particular crimes)

Determiners

Some & any
We use *some* and *any* to describe an indefinite quantity of something. We can use *some* and *any* with both countable and uncountable nouns.

We usually use *some* in positive sentences.
> *I've got* **some** *biscuits.* (countable)
> *He's going to buy* **some** *milk.* (uncountable)

We usually use *any* in negative sentences and questions.
> *Mark doesn't like* **any** *vegetables.* (countable)
> *I haven't got* **any** *money.* (uncountable)
> *Have you got* **any** *apples?* (countable)
> *Do you have* **any** *advice for me?* (uncountable)

No
We use *no* with both countable and uncountable nouns. A positive verb + *no* has the same meaning as a negative verb + *any*.

> *There are* **no** *biscuits.* = There aren't any biscuits.
> (countable)
> *I have* **no** *time.* = I don't have any time.
> (uncountable)

Quantifiers
We can use quantifiers before a noun to show how much of something there is.

quantifiers with plural countable nouns	quantifiers with uncountable nouns
too many *a lot of* *many* *not many* *a few* *not enough*	*too much* *a lot of* *not much* *a little* *not enough*

> *There are* **too many** *tourists in this town.*
> *I know a* **few** *good restaurants near here.*
> *We do* **not** *have* **much** *time.*

We do not usually use *much* in affirmative sentences. We use *a lot of* instead.

> *There's a lot of work to do.* Not ~~There's much work~~.

Some, many & most
We can use *some, many* and *most* with or without *of*.

Not many Some Many	of	my friends the students them	live at home.
Most		students	

> **Some of** *my friends are working.*
> **Most of** *the people I know are very interesting.*
> **Many** *people spend their holidays abroad.*
> **Most** *days, I do some homework.*

FUNCTIONAL LANGUAGE

Directions

Excuse me, | where's the … / can/could you tell me the way to … / how do I get to … | please?

behind
between
in front of
near
next to
not far from
on the corner of
opposite

Cross the bridge road.
Go past the …
Go straight on.
Go to the end of the road/street.
Take the first/second street on the left/right.

WORD LIST

House & home

(be) away from home	/əweɪ frəm 'həʊm/
get home	/get 'həʊm/
home town	/həʊm 'taʊn/
homework n U *	/'həʊmwɜːk/
housewife n C	/'haʊswaɪf/
housework n U	/'haʊswɜːk/
leave home	/liːv 'həʊm/

Towns

accommodation n U **	/əkɒmə'deɪʃn/
art gallery n C	/'ɑːt gæləri/
bar n C ***	/bɑː/
bridge n C **	/brɪdʒ/
bus station n C	/'bʌs steɪʃn/
castle n C **	/'kɑːsl/
cathedral n C	/kə'θiːdrəl/
church n C ***	/tʃɜːtʃ/
cinema n C **	/'sɪnəmə/
crime n C/U ***	/kraɪm/
culture n U ***	/'kʌltʃə/
flat n C **	/flæt/
industrial adj ***	/ɪn'dʌstriəl/
library n C ***	/'laɪbrəri/
metro n C	/'metrəʊ/
museum n C ***	/mjuː'ziːəm/
nightclub n C	/'naɪtklʌb/
nightlife n U	/'naɪtlaɪf/
park n C **	/pɑːk/
opera house n C	/'ɒp(ə)rə haʊs/
pollution n U **	/pə'luːʃn/
public transport n U	/pʌblɪk 'trænspɔːt/
restaurant n C ***	/'rest(ə)rɒnt/
shopping centre n C	/'ʃɒpɪŋ sentə/
stadium n C	/'steɪdiəm/
studio n C **	/'stjuːdiəʊ/
theatre n C **	/'θɪətə/
traffic n U ***	/'træfɪk/
tram n C	/'træm/
train station n C ***	/'treɪn steɪʃn/

Other words & phrases

abroad adv **	/ə'brɔːd/
area n C ***	/'eəriə/
banker n C	/'bæŋkə/
cash n U ***	/kæʃ/
century n C ***	/'sentʃəri/
chat v *	/tʃæt/
cheap adj ***	/tʃiːp/
clan n C	/klæn/
coal n U *	/kəʊl/
community n C ***	/kə'mjuːnəti/
conference n C **	/'kɒnf(ə)rəns/
countryside n U **	/'kʌntrisaɪd/
dirty adj ***	/'dɜːti/
discourage v	/dɪs'kʌrɪdʒ/
drive (sb) mad v	/draɪv 'mæd/
encourage v ***	/ɪn'kʌrɪdʒ/
flatmate n C	/'flætmeɪt/
flag n C	/flæg/
grim adj	/grɪm/
guest n C **	/gest/
immigrant n C	/'ɪmɪgrənt/
independence n U **	/ɪndɪ'pendəns/
normal adj ***	/'nɔːml/
online adj/adv	/ɒn'laɪn/
ordinary adj **	/'ɔːdn(ə)ri/
origin n C **	/'ɒrɪdʒɪn/
outdoor adj	/aʊt'dɔː/
owner n C ***	/'əʊnə/
passenger n C **	/'pæsɪndʒə/
peace n U ***	/piːs/
picnic n C	/'pɪknɪk/
producer n C *	/prə'djuːsə/
programme n C ***	/'prəʊgræm/
put (sb) off v	/pʊt 'ɒf/
reunion n C	/riː'juːniən/
rollerblading n U	/'rəʊləbleɪdɪŋ/
scarf n C	/skɑːf/
settle down v	/'setl daʊn/
skating n U	/'skeɪtɪŋ/
sofa n C	/'səʊfə/
space n U ***	/speɪs/
strange adj ***	/streɪndʒ/
tartan adj/n	/'tɑːtn/
tourist n C **	/'tʊərɪst/
twin n C *	/twɪn/
whisky n U	/'wɪski/

4A | Online dating

Speaking

1 Work in pairs. Discuss these questions.

6 MILLION DATES
America's biggest internet dating agency now has more than 6 million people who visit its website every month.

- Do you know anyone who uses the internet to make friends?
- Do you think that the internet is a good way to meet other people?
- What are the advantages and disadvantages of internet dating?

Reading

1 Look at the advertisement from an internet dating agency and answer the questions.

1 How old is Lynn?
2 Does she have any children?
3 What is her job?
4 What does she do in her free time?
5 What adjectives does she use to describe her personality?
6 What adjectives does she use to describe her perfect partner?
7 What does her perfect partner enjoy doing?

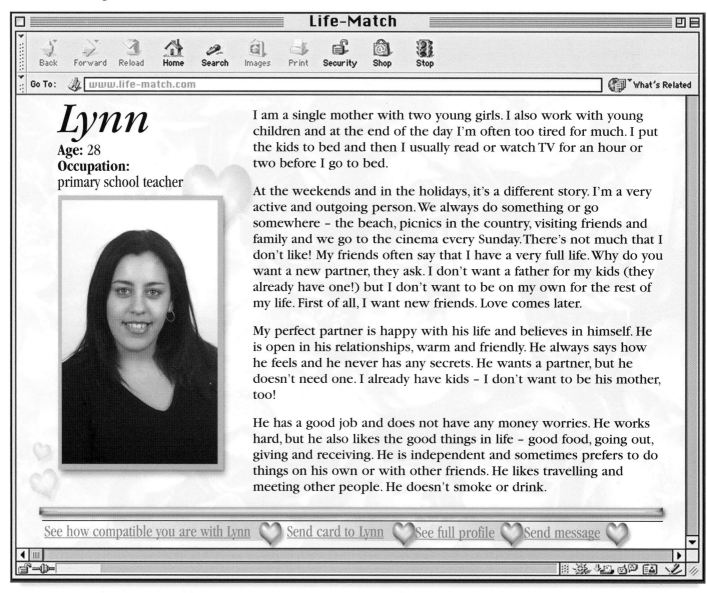

Life-Match

Back Forward Reload Home Search Images Print Security Shop Stop

Go To: www.life-match.com   What's Related

Lynn

Age: 28
Occupation: primary school teacher

I am a single mother with two young girls. I also work with young children and at the end of the day I'm often too tired for much. I put the kids to bed and then I usually read or watch TV for an hour or two before I go to bed.

At the weekends and in the holidays, it's a different story. I'm a very active and outgoing person. We always do something or go somewhere – the beach, picnics in the country, visiting friends and family and we go to the cinema every Sunday. There's not much that I don't like! My friends often say that I have a very full life. Why do you want a new partner, they ask. I don't want a father for my kids (they already have one!) but I don't want to be on my own for the rest of my life. First of all, I want new friends. Love comes later.

My perfect partner is happy with his life and believes in himself. He is open in his relationships, warm and friendly. He always says how he feels and he never has any secrets. He wants a partner, but he doesn't need one. I already have kids – I don't want to be his mother, too!

He has a good job and does not have any money worries. He works hard, but he also likes the good things in life – good food, going out, giving and receiving. He is independent and sometimes prefers to do things on his own or with other friends. He likes travelling and meeting other people. He doesn't smoke or drink.

See how compatible you are with Lynn   Send card to Lynn   See full profile   Send message

2 Work in groups of three, A–C. You are going to read internet advertisements for three different men. Read the advertisement and tick (✔) the sentences that are about your man.

A: Turn to page 128.
B: Turn to page 130.
C: Turn to page 132.

1 He does not have a job.
2 He does not like cities.
3 He enjoys going to restaurants.
4 He has a daughter.
5 He is a very active person.
6 He is not very rich.
7 He is often not at home.
8 He is quiet and friendly.
9 He likes being on his own.
10 He likes being with other people.
11 He loves music.
12 He wants a romantic partner.
13 He wants an intelligent partner.
14 He wants to have a family.
15 His perfect partner doesn't work too much.

3 Who is the best partner for Lynn? Read the information about your man again. Underline all his good and bad points.

In your group, compare the information about the different men and decide who is the best partner.

GRAMMAR: present simple

We use the present simple to talk about habits and things that are generally/always true.
*I usually **watch** TV before I go to bed.*
*I already **have** kids.*

Remember to add -s to the third person singular.
*He **works** hard and he **likes** the good things in life.*

Frequency adverbs and phrases
We usually put words like *often, sometimes, never* before the main verb, or after the verb *to be*.
*He **never** has any secrets.*
*I'm **often** too tired to do much.*

We can put phrases like *every day, once a week* at the beginning or end of the sentence.
*We go to the cinema **every Sunday**.*

> SEE LANGUAGE REFERENCE PAGE 44

1 Before choosing a partner, Lynn asked the men some questions. Rearrange the words to make her questions.

1 do   do   friends   with   what   you   your ?
2 being   like   do   other   people   with   you ?
3 cities   do   friends   have   in   other   you ?
4 away   do   from   how   much   home   spend   time   you ?
5 daytime   do   in   the   do   what   you ?

2 Look at the men's answers to Lynn's questions. Change *I* to *he* and make any other necessary changes.

1 I often invite friends for dinner or I go to their houses.
2 I like my friends but I don't enjoy big groups of people.
3 Every year, I spend about two months away for work, so I don't travel in the holidays.
4 I get up late and then I sometimes see a friend for lunch.

3 Work in pairs. Ask and answer the questions in exercise 1.

4 Make the sentences true for you using words and phrases from the boxes.

| always usually often sometimes never | once twice three times | a | day week month |
| | every | | year |

1 I get up late in the morning.
2 I go for a walk in the afternoon.
3 I am tired in the evenings.
4 I have dinner in a restaurant.
5 I read before I go to bed.
6 I visit friends at the weekend.

5 Make questions from the sentences in exercise 4. Begin: *How often do you ... ?*

Work in pairs. Ask and answer the questions.

PRONUNCIATION: final -s

1 🌐 1.34 Listen to the pronunciation of the final -s in these words. There are two ways of pronouncing the letter -s at the end of singular verbs and plural nouns.

/z/   goes   lives   days   friends
/s/   likes   wants   books   streets

2 🌐 1.34 Listen and repeat.

3 How do you pronounce the final -s in these words?

knows   learns   maps   spends   talks   writes
facts   parties   problems   questions   states   things

4 🌐 1.35 Listen to the recording to check.

VOCABULARY & SPEAKING: weddings

1 Find these things in the pictures.

> bouquet   bride   church   groom
> priest   ring   wedding cake

2 Complete the description of English weddings with words from the box.

> ceremony   guests   honeymoon
> reception   registry office   speech

The (1) ____ usually takes place in a church or (2) ____. After the ceremony, the couple and their (3) ____ go to the (4) ____, where they drink champagne and eat the wedding cake. Later on, at the wedding meal, the best friend of the groom makes a (5) ____. The married couple often leave the party early to go on their (6) ____.

3 🔘 **1.36** Listen to the recording to check your answers.

4 Describe a wedding that you have been to. Use these questions to prepare what you are going to say.

- Who got married?
- Where and when were the ceremony and the reception?
- What did the bride and groom wear?
- Who did you go with?
- How many guests were there? Who were they?
- Was there any music at the wedding?
- What did you eat and drink?
- Did anyone make a speech? What did they say?
- Did anything interesting or unusual happen?

READING

1 *Marriage is a thing of the past.* Do you agree? Work in pairs. Explain why or why not.

2 Read the magazine article and find out if the writer agrees that marriage is a thing of the past.

COMMENT

IF YOU ASK ME ...

Sue Carey disagrees with her university professor

(1) ____ More and more people are living together and having children without getting married, she told us. The number of divorces is increasing all the time. It doesn't matter if you are single or married, she said with a smile of victory. 'The prison of marriage belongs to an older generation!'

(2) ____ But now, twenty years later – is marriage dead? You do not need to think about it for long: go to any newsagent and look at the magazines on sale. On the cover of every popular magazine like *Hello!* someone is getting married. Or maybe someone is getting divorced. The stories sell the magazines and in thousands of offices around the world, people are sitting around and looking at the wedding photos of the rich and famous.

(3) ____ In the UK, people are waiting until they are older to get married, but the number of weddings is actually increasing. True, divorces are also going up, but people are getting married again, for a second, third or fourth time.

(4) ____ In the year after university, I went to the weddings of four of my friends. My own (first) marriage was two years later. We want to read about marriage, look at films and photos, and do it ourselves. It appears that we can't get enough of it. Sorry professor, but the conclusion seems clear: marriage is very much alive and well.

3 Read the article again and put the sentences a–d in the gaps 1–4.

a Marriage is certainly changing.

b Marriage, said one of my professors at university, belongs to the past.

c She sounded sure of herself and we all agreed – or, at least, nobody disagreed.

d The simple fact is that most of us believe that marriage is good for us.

4 Work in pairs. Discuss these questions.

- Is marriage changing in your country? How?
- At what age do people usually get married?
- What are the advantages and disadvantages of getting married?

GRAMMAR: present continuous

We use the present continuous to talk about things that are happening now or around now.

What **are** you **doing**? **I'm preparing** my speech.
More and more people **are getting** married.
Why **is** the number of weddings **increasing**?

We cannot normally use some verbs (stative verbs) in the continuous form.

| agree | belong | cost | know | like | love |
| matter | mean | need | seem | understand | want |

> SEE LANGUAGE REFERENCE PAGE 44

1 Complete the sentences. Put the verbs in brackets into the present continuous.

1 Hi. Yes. I'm on the train. We _____ (come) into Central Station.
2 Excuse me! I _____ (try) to work!
3 I _____ (tell) you the truth. I promise.
4 Let's stay here. It _____ (rain) outside.
5 And three players _____ (speak) to the referee who _____ (hold) up a red card.

Imagine a situation for each sentence. Who is speaking? Where are they?

2 Choose the correct verb form to complete the sentences.

1 The average UK wedding usually *costs / is costing* about £13,000.
2 We can see the Princess now – she *wears / 's wearing* a beautiful white dress.
3 Every time I *get / am getting* divorced, I keep the house.
4 Look! She *doesn't wear / isn't wearing* her wedding ring.

5 More and more women in England *keep / are keeping* their own name when they get married.
6 *Do you ever talk / Are you ever talking* to your husband?
7 My girlfriend *doesn't love / isn't loving* me.
8 It *doesn't matter / is not mattering* if you're married or not.

3 Look at the picture of a wedding reception on page ooo. Prepare five questions with the present continuous about the picture.

How many people are dancing?
What is the man with the white jacket doing?

4 Work in pairs. Close your books and ask your partner the questions you have prepared.

DID YOU KNOW?

1 Work in groups. Read about some wedding traditions in Britain and America and discuss these questions.

- Are they the same in your country?
- What wedding traditions do you have in your country?

The groom arrives at the wedding before his bride.

The bride wears a long white dress and a group of young girls (bridesmaids) follow her into the church.

The bride throws a bouquet of flowers in the air and other single women try to catch it. The woman who catches it will be the next to get married.

The bride and groom cut the wedding cake together.

After a wedding, the groom carries the bride into their new home.

A woman wears her wedding ring on the third finger of the left hand.

4c | At the movies

SPEAKING

1 Look at the photos from three films.
What do you think is happening in each photo?

2 Work in pairs. Choose one of the pictures and prepare a short dialogue (three or four lines long) to go with it.

3 Perform your dialogue in front of the class. The other students must decide which photo you have chosen.

LISTENING

1 🌐 1.37 Listen to a woman talking about the film in the poster below. What kind of film is it?

2 🌐 1.37 Listen to the recording again. Put the events in the correct order.

☐ Joe and Kathleen have an argument about business.
☐ Joe and Kathleen kiss.
☐ Joe finds out that Kathleen is his internet friend.
☐ Joe opens a huge bookstore near Kathleen's shop.
☐ Joe visits Kathleen.
☐ Kathleen meets a man in an internet chatroom.
☐ Kathleen's bookshop closes.
☐ Kathleen splits up with her boyfriend.

Look at tapescript 1.37 on page 136 to check your answers.

3 Explain the connection between the words in the box and the story of Joe and Kathleen.

> café   cold   children   flowers
> journalist   park

Kathleen's going out with a journalist.

4 If you have seen this film, did you like it?
If you have not seen this film, would you like to see it? Why or why not?

VOCABULARY: relationship verbs

1 Complete the phrases in columns A and B with a word from the box.

> about (x2)   in (x3)   on   out (x2)   to   up

A
1 He asked her ____ and
2 He was crazy ____ her and
3 They had a big argument ____ something and
4 They had a lot ____ common and
5 They went ____ together for a long time but

B
a she didn't want to get married ____ him.
b she was ____ love with him, too.
c then they split ____.
d they went ____ a date to the cinema.
e they fell ____ love very quickly.

2 Now complete the sentences in column A with a phrase from column B. Sometimes there is more than one possible answer.

3 Work in pairs. Use the expressions in exercise 1 to talk about people you know.

My brother, Lewis, asked my best friend, Stephanie, out.

FUNCTIONAL LANGUAGE: telling stories

> When we tell a story informally (for example, personal stories, or the story of a film), we often use the present simple.
>
> *She **doesn't know** his real name, but they **seem** to have a lot in common and they **get on** really well.*

1 Work in groups of four: pair A and pair B.

Pair A: Turn to page 126.
Pair B: Turn to page 131.

Read the story of the film twice and then close your books.

2 Now practise telling your story together.

3 Swap partners and work with a student who read about a different film. Tell each other your stories.

PRONUNCIATION: /ɪ/ & /iː/

1 🔘 1.38 Listen to the recording and repeat the words in the table.

/ɪ/	/iː/
live	leave
think	teeth
still	street
rich	feel
hit	meet

2 Underline the sounds /ɪ/ and /iː/ in the film titles below.

> Beauty and the Beast   The Big Sleep   Mission Impossible   Pretty Woman
> E.T.   Robin Hood: Prince of Thieves   The Prince of Egypt

3 🔘 1.39 Listen to the recording to check your answers.

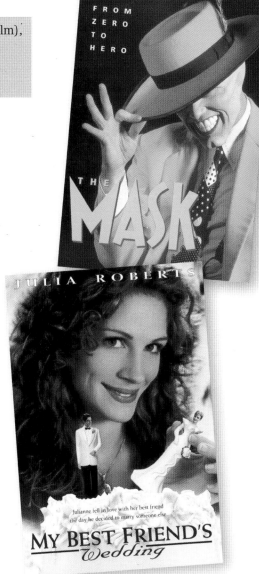

4D | Going out

SPEAKING

1 Work in pairs. Discuss these questions.

- Which famous person would you like to have a date with? Why?
- Where would you like to go?
- What would you like to do on the date?

LISTENING

1 🔘 1.40–1.41 Listen to two conversations. Who is speaking to who? What are they talking about?

Ruby   Davina

Patrick   Stuart

2 🔘 1.40–1.41 Listen to the conversations again and complete the sentences with Davina (D), Patrick (P), Stuart (S) or Ruby (R).

1 __D__ had dinner with Patrick at a restaurant.
2 _____ is having a dinner party on Saturday.
3 _____ has a business dinner with an important client.
4 _____ knows a nice restaurant near the river.
5 _____ is busy in the morning.
6 _____ wants to go to the pub.
7 _____ would like to go out for a meal.
8 _____ doesn't want to get a taxi.
9 _____ needs to get home early.

FUNCTIONAL LANGUAGE: invitations & suggestions

1 In Listening exercise 1, which conversation was about:

- someone inviting another person?
- someone making suggestions?

2 Choose the correct verb form to complete the invitations and suggestions.

Invitations and suggestions

1 Would you like *go / to go / going*	
2 Shall we *go / to go / going*	
3 Why don't we *go / to go / going*	to the cinema?
4 How about *go / to go / going*	
5 What about *go / to go / going*	
6 Let's *go / to go / going*	to the cinema.

Responses

OK,	*that's a good idea.*
Yes,	*why not?*

I'd rather … (+ infinitive)
I'd rather not.
I'd love to, but I'm afraid I'm busy.
That's very kind of you, but …

Look at tapescripts 1.40–1.41 on page 136 to check your answers.

3 Complete the sentences. Put the verbs in brackets into the correct form.

Marilyn: Hi, Wolfgang, would you like (1) _____ (*go*) out somewhere on Monday?
Mozart: _____
Marilyn: What a pity! Why don't we (2)_____ (*do*) something on Tuesday, then?
Mozart: All right. Let's (3) _____ (*do*) that. Where shall we (4) _____ (*go*)?
Marilyn: How about (5) _____ (*go*) to a club?
Mozart: _____
Marilyn: Well, why don't we (6) _____ (*have*) a meal at the Hard Rock Café?
Mozart: _____
Marilyn: OK. That's a good idea. Where shall we (7) _____ (*meet*)?

4 Complete the dialogue in exercise 3 with the sentences a–c.

a I'd rather not. I'm not too keen on clubbing.
b I'd rather go for a pizza, if that's OK with you.
c That's very kind of you, Marilyn. I'd love to, but I'm afraid I'm busy on Monday.

5 Work in pairs. Practise the dialogue.

Roleplay

6 Imagine you are a famous person (alive or dead). Decide what you like doing when you go out for the evening.

Work in pairs. Try to make a date.

GRAMMAR: prepositions of time

in +	month (*in* January) year (*in* 2004) season (*in* the summer) *the morning, the afternoon, the evening*
on +	day(s) (*on* Monday, *on* Mondays) dates (*on* 7ᵗʰ June) *Monday morning, Tuesday evening*
at +	time (*at* 3 o'clock, *at* dinner time) *night* *the weekend*

SEE LANGUAGE REFERENCE PAGE 44

1 Look at tapescripts 1.40–1.41 on page 136. Find more examples of prepositions of time: *in, on* and *at.*

2 Complete the sentences with *in, on* or *at.*

1 We met ____ Friday February 14ᵗʰ.
2 I went to a party ____ the evening and Michael was there.
3 We spoke for ages and, ____ midnight, he finally asked for my phone number.
4 He called me ____ Saturday morning.
5 We had our first date ____ the evening.
6 I saw him again ____ Monday and Wednesday.
7 I met his parents ____ the weekend.
8 I asked him to marry me ____ Sunday evening.
9 Our wedding is ___ March – on the 14ᵗʰ!

3 Complete the sentences with *in, on* or *at* and a time expression.

In my country/town …

1 the most popular time to get married is …
2 people usually have dinner …
3 most people go on holiday …
4 the best time to go shopping is …
5 the best programmes on TV are …
6 the roads are really busy …

4 Work in pairs. Compare your sentences.

SPEAKING

1 Work in groups. In the listening, Davina asks Patrick out on a date. What are the dating 'rules' for men and women in your country?

• Who usually asks who out – the man or the woman?
• Who usually pays for the date?
• Where do people go on a first date?
• How long do people date before they get married?
• Are the 'rules' for dating changing in your country? How?

Useful language

It varies (= it's not always the same)
It depends (on …)
On the whole, … (= usually/generally)

2 What about you? Are you the same as most people in your country?

GRAMMAR

Present simple

We use the present simple to talk about habits and things that are generally/always true.

> I **buy** a newspaper every day.
> Mark **comes** from Australia.

We can also use the present simple to tell a story informally, for example, personal stories, or the story of a film.

> She **doesn't know** his real name, but they **seem** to have a lot in common and they **get** on really well.

Affirmative & Negative		
I	work don't work	
He/She/It	works doesn't work	in a bank.
You/We/They	work don't work	

Question			
Where	do	I	work?
	does	he/she/it	
	do	you/we/they	

Short answer	
Do you work in a bank?	Yes, I do. / No, I don't.
Does she live at home?	Yes, she does. / No, she doesn't.

The present simple with *I/you/we/they* has the same form as the infinitive. We usually add *-s* to the verb with the third person singular, (*he*, *she* and *it*). There are two groups of exceptions.

1 We add *-es* to verbs that end in *-o, -s, -sh, -ch, -x.*
   she watch**es**   he go**es**   it finish**es**
2 We change *-y* to *-ies* in verbs that end in *-y.*
   she stud**ies**   he car**ries**   it fl**ies**

Frequency adverbs & phrases

We can use frequency expressions with the present simple to talk about how often something happens.

We usually put single words (*never, rarely, sometimes, often, usually, generally, always*) before the main verb.

> He **always** wakes up late.
> Do you **usually** get up early?

If the verb is *to be*, we put these words after the verb.

> She is **always** tired.
> They were **never** late.

We can put phrases (*once a week, twice a month, every year*) at the beginning or the end of the sentence.

> He studies **twice a week**.
> **Twice a week**, he goes to English classes.

Present continuous

We use the present continuous to talk about things that are happening now or around now.

> What **are** you **doing**? I'**m cooking** a meal.
> My husband'**s working** very hard at the moment.

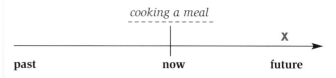

Affirmative & Negative		
I	'm 'm not	
He/She/It	's isn't	eating.
You/We/They	're aren't	

Question			
What	am	I	eating?
	is	he/she/it	
	are	you/we/they	

Short answer	
Are you going to the party?	Yes, I am. / No, I'm not.
Are they going to the party?	Yes, they are. / No, they aren't.

We make the present continuous with *is/are* + infinitive + *-ing*. There are some spelling exceptions. See the notes on past continuous on page 24.

See page 54 for more information about the present continuous.

Stative verbs

We cannot normally use stative verbs in the continuous form. Here are some common stative verbs.

> *agree   appear   believe   belong   cost   dislike   fit   forget   hate   know   like   love   matter   mean   need   own   prefer   remember   seem   understand   want*

> Yes, I **agree** with you. Not ~~I'm agreeing with you~~.
> I **understand** Italian. Not ~~I'm understanding Italian~~.

Prepositions of time

in +
- month (**in** *January*)
- year (**in** *2004*)
- season (**in** *the summer*)
- periods of time (**in** *the 1990s*, **in** *the 20th century*, **in** *the holidays*)
- the morning, the afternoon, the evening

on +
- day(s) (**on** *Monday*, **on** *Mondays*, **on** *my birthday*, **on** *Christmas Day*)
- dates (**on** *7th June*, **on** *Friday 13th*)
- Monday morning, Tuesday evening

We use *on Mondays* (plural) to talk about Mondays in general – something we do every Monday. We use *on Monday* (singular) to talk about either Mondays in general, or one particular Monday.

> **On Mondays/Monday,** *I usually go out with my best friend.*
> **On Monday,** *I'm seeing the doctor.*

at +
- time (**at** *3 o'clock*, **at** *dinner time*)
- night
- the weekend
- holiday periods (**at** *Easter*, **at** *Christmas*)

We can make the time more approximate by putting an adverb between *at* and the time.

| at | ***about, almost, around, just after, just before nearly*** | *two o'clock* |

FUNCTIONAL LANGUAGE

Invitations & suggestions

Would you like to + infinitive … ?
Shall we + infinitive … ?
Let's + infinitive … .
Why don't we + infinitive … ?
How about + verb + *-ing* … ?
What about + verb + *-ing* … ?

Responses

OK.
Yes, that's a good idea.
Yes, why not?

I'd rather + infinitive …
I'd rather not.
I'd love to, but I'm afraid I'm busy.
That's very kind of you, but …

When we say *no* to an invitation or suggestion, it is polite to give a reason.

WORD LIST

Weddings

bouquet *n C*	/buːˈkeɪ/
bride *n C*	/braɪd/
bridesmaid *n C*	/ˈbraɪdzmeɪd/
ceremony *n C* *	/ˈserəməni/
champagne *n U*	/ʃæmˈpeɪn/
church *n C* ***	/tʃɜːtʃ/
groom *n C*	/gruːm/
guest *n C* **	/gest/
honeymoon *n C*	/ˈhʌnimuːn/
marriage *n C/U* ***	/ˈmærɪdʒ/
priest *n C* *	/priːst/
reception *n C* *	/rɪˈsepʃn/
registry office *n C*	/ˈredʒɪstriɒfɪs/
ring *n C* ***	/rɪŋ/
speech *n C* ***	/spiːtʃ/
wedding cake *n C/U*	/ˈwedɪŋ keɪk/

Relationships

ask (sb) out	/ɑːsk aʊt/
be crazy about (sb)	/biː ˈkreɪzi əbaʊt/
have an argument about (sth)	/hæv ən ˈɑːgjʊmənt əbaʊt sʌmθɪŋ/
have (sth) in common	/hæv ɪn ˈkɒmən/
go out with (sb)	/gəʊ aʊt wɪð/
get married to (sb)	/get ˈmærɪd tuː/
be in love with (sb)	/biː ɪn ˈlʌv wɪð/
split up	/splɪt ˈʌp/
go (out) on a date	/gəʊ ɒn ə ˈdeɪt/
fall in love with (sb)	/fɔːl ɪn ˈlʌv wɪð/
partner *n C* ***	/ˈpɑːtnə/
divorce *n C* *	/dɪˈvɔːs/
divorced *adj* *	/dɪˈvɔːst/

Other words & phrases

active *adj* ***	/ˈæktɪv/
agency *n C* **	/ˈeɪdʒ(ə)nsi/
arrange *v* ***	/əˈreɪndʒ/
average *adj* **	/ˈævrɪdʒ/
believe in sth *v* ***	/bəˈliːv ɪn sʌmθɪŋ/
bookstore *n C*	/ˈbʊkstɔː/
boss *n C* **	/bɒs/
business *n C/U* ***	/ˈbɪznəs/
carry on *v*	/kæri ˈɒn/
cigar *n C*	/sɪˈgɑː/
cold *n C* **	/kəʊld/
conclusion *n C* ***	/kənˈkluːʒn/
cover *n C* ***	/ˈkʌvə/
dead *adj* ***	/ded/
disadvantage *n C* *	/dɪsədˈvɑːntɪdʒ/
friendly *adj* **	/ˈfrendli/
generation *n C* ***	/dʒenəˈreɪʃn/
intelligent *adj* **	/ɪnˈtelɪdʒ(ə)nt/
jacket *n C* **	/ˈdʒækɪt/
journalist *n C* **	/ˈdʒɜːnəlɪst/
kid *n C* **	/kɪd/
kiss *v* *	/kɪs/
magazine *n C* **	/mægəˈziːn/
matter *v* ***	/ˈmætə/
newsagent *n C*	/ˈnjuːzeɪdʒ(ə)nt/
on my/her own	/ɒn maɪ/hɜː əʊn/
outgoing *adj*	/aʊtˈgəʊɪŋ/
perfect *adj* **	/ˈpɜːfɪkt/
personality *n C* **	/pɜːsəˈnæləti/
prefer *v* ***	/prɪˈfɜː/
princess *n C*	/prɪnˈses/
prison *n C* ***	/ˈprɪzn/
professor *n C* *	/prəˈfesə/
promise *v* ***	/ˈprɒmɪs/
referee *n C*	/refəˈriː/
romantic *adj*	/rəʊˈmæntɪk/
secret *adj/n C* **	/ˈsiːkrət/
share *v* **	/ʃeə/
single mother *n C*	/sɪŋgl ˈmʌðə/
smile *n C/v* ***	/smaɪl/
unusual *adj* **	/ʌnˈjuːʒʊəl/
vegetarian *adj/n C*	/vedʒəˈteəriən/
vice versa *adv*	/vaɪs ˈvɜːsə/
victory *n C* **	/ˈvɪkt(ə)ri/
yoga *n U*	/ˈjəʊgə/

SPEAKING

1 Work in pairs. Discuss these questions.

- What time of year do tourists come to your country?
- Which parts of your country do the tourists go to?
- What do they do there?

READING

1 You are going to read an article about the place in the photograph. Which of these words do you think you will find in the article? Explain why or why not.

> city   fast food   jungle   path   ruins
> tea bag   train   valley   views

2 Read the article and say if the sentences are true (T) or false (F).

1 Machu Picchu was built in 1911. F
2 It is extremely popular with tourists. T
3 The only way to Machu Picchu is on foot. T
4 Ana Redondo thinks there are too many tourists. T
5 Tourists leave their rubbish on the Inca Trail. T
6 She thinks the cable car is good for Machu Picchu. F
7 Ana's organization is trying to stop the cable car. T

3 <u>Underline</u> the arguments for and against the cable car. Who do you agree with?

The Ruins of Machu Picchu

For centuries, the Inca city of Machu Picchu was lost in the jungle. Then, in 1911, the American explorer, Hiram Bingham, discovered the ruins of the city. It is one of the most extraordinary places in the world. The city ruins, the Inca bridge, the
5 mountain views and the beautiful river valley below are all absolutely breathtaking.

Today it is also one of the most popular tourist destinations in the world. Many people choose to follow the Inca Trail, a centuries-old path of 43 km that takes three or four days on foot. Others take the train and then
10 a bus for the last part of the journey.

Now a hotel company is going to build a cable car to the top of Machu Picchu. 'The cable car is good news for Machu Picchu,' says a company spokesman. 'There are going to be a lot more tourists and that means more jobs for the local people. Looking after the ruins is
15 expensive. With the extra money, we can spend more on looking after them.'

However, the plan is not popular in Peru. Ana Redondo, a tour guide, explains the problem. 'There are already more than 300,000 tourists that go to Machu Picchu every year. The Inca Trail is crowded and
20 dirty with old tea bags and water bottles everywhere. The new cable car is going to bring 400 tourists every hour! The company is also going to build a large hotel and tourist centre with souvenir shops, fast food restaurants and so on. It is the end of Machu Picchu.'

Ana is an activist who belongs to an organization that wants to save
25 Machu Picchu. She says that the organization is going to stop the company's plans. 'Tomorrow we are meeting government ministers. Next week some people from UNESCO[1] are coming here to look at the plans. Next month we are organizing an international conference. We are not going to stop until the cable car idea is dead.'

[1] United Nations Educational, Scientific and Cultural Organization

VOCABULARY: compound nouns

1   We can often put a noun together with another word to make a compound noun. Compounds nouns are sometimes written as one word, sometimes as two words and sometimes with a hyphen in the middle. There are no rules, so use a dictionary if you are not sure.

boyfriend   dinner party   T-shirt

Read the article again. How many compound nouns can you find?

2   Can you name the objects in the picture below?

3   Match words from column A with words from column B to check your answers.

A	B
back	bag
camping-gas	book
credit	camera
first-aid	card
flash	glasses
guide	kit
insect	knife
mobile	light
pen	pack
sleeping	phone
sun	spray
video	stove

Use a dictionary to find out if the compound nouns are written as one or two words.

4   Work in pairs. You are going to walk the Inca Trail to Macchu Picchu. You can take six objects from the picture with you. Decide together which ones you are going to take.

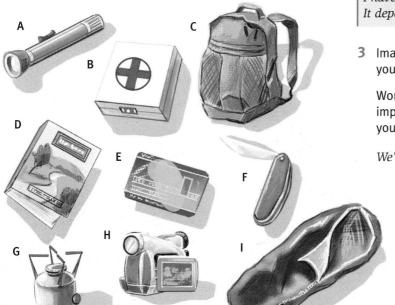

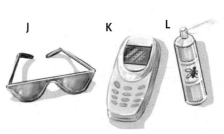

GRAMMAR: future 1 (future plans)

We can use both *am/is/are going to* + infinitive and the present continuous to talk about plans in the future.
The new cable car is going to bring 400 tourists every hour.
Some people from UNESCO are coming here.

Often we can use either form, but when we want to show that the plan is more arranged/fixed, we use the present continuous.
The company is going to build a large hotel.
(This is their plan.)
Tomorrow, we are meeting government ministers.
(The plan is fixed in our diaries.)

> SEE LANGUAGE REFERENCE PAGE 54

1   Rearrange the words to make questions.

1   after are do going lesson the to what you ?
2   are get going home how to today you ?
3   cooking dinner evening is this who your ?
4   anything are at doing the weekend you ?
5   are birthday doing for next what you your ?
6   are going have holiday next to when you your ?

2   Work in pairs. Ask and answer the questions in exercise 1. Use the expressions in the Useful language box to help you.

Useful language

I'm not sure.
I haven't decided yet.
It depends …

3   Imagine that you are the mayor of your town. How can you make your town a better place for tourists?

Work in pairs. Think of six things that you can do to improve your town for tourists. Tell the rest of your class your ideas.

We're going to build a new airport.

5B | Planes

A

B

SPEAKING

1 Work in pairs. Think of a long/interesting/boring/ frightening journey you have been on. Describe your journey.

VOCABULARY: air travel

1 Find these things in the pictures.

> boarding card   check-in   hand luggage
> overhead locker   seat belt   security guard

2 Put the phrases in the correct order.

☐ **Fasten** your **seat belt** and wait for **take-off**.
☑ **Book** your **flight** and get your **ticket**.
☐ Get on the plane and find your **seat**.
☐ Go to the airport **terminal**.
☐ Show your ticket and **passport** at **passport control**.
☐ Go to the **departure gate** and show your **boarding card**.
☐ Go to the **departure hall** and into the **duty-free shop**.
☐ **Pack** your bag(s).
☐ Put your **hand luggage** in the **overhead locker**.
☐ Go through **security**.
☐ Go to the **check-in** and **check in** your **luggage**.

LISTENING

1 Describe what is happening in the pictures above. Use the vocabulary to help you.

2 🔘 1.42–1.44 Listen and match the conversations 1–3 to the pictures A–C.

3 🔘 1.42–1.44 Listen to the conversations again and choose the correct answer.

1 What is Mike's seat number?
   a) 21A   b) 23A   c) 23F
2 When does his plane board?
   a) 12.00   b) 12.15   c) 12.30
3 What is his departure gate?
   a) 21   b) 31   c) 41
4 What can't Mike take on the plane?
   a) his comb   b) his jacket   c) his mobile phone
5 Where is Mike going?
   a) Dublin   b) Glasgow   c) London
6 What does Mike order to drink?
   a) coffee   b) hot chocolate   c) tea

C

FUNCTIONAL LANGUAGE: requests
PRONUNCIATION: intonation

1 There are many ways of asking for something and asking another person to do something. Look at tapescripts 1.42–1.44 on page 137. <u>Underline</u> all the requests. Then find different ways of responding to the requests and complete the table below.

2 Find five more mistakes in the dialogue and correct them.

                 I'd

Passenger: Excuse me, ~~I~~ like a cup of coffee, please.

Attendant: I'm afraid but we're not serving drinks any more, sir. The plane is going to land in about twenty minutes.

Passenger: Oh, please, could I just have a cup of coffee? Please!

Attendant: I afraid that's not possible, sir. Could you to fasten your seat belt and close the table in front of you, please?

Passenger: Well, OK. Er, I wonder if could I go to the toilet before we land.

Attendant: Yes, of course. But can you being quick, please?

Requests			
(Excuse me,)	*I'd like*	*a glass of water* *a coffee* *(+noun)*	
	I'd like to *Can I* *Could I* *I wonder if I could*	*have a receipt* *see your passport* *(+infinitive)*	*please.*
	Can you *Could you*	*stand over here* *(+infinitive)*	

Responses	
☺	☹
Yes, s _ _ _	*I'm a _ _ _ _ _ that …*
o _ c _ _ _ _ _	
c _ _ _ _ _ _ _	*I'm s _ _ _ _, but …*

3 🔘 **1.45** To make polite requests, we always say *please*. Friendly intonation is also important. Listen to these two sentences said in different ways.

Excuse me, could I have a coffee, please?
Can you stand over here, please?

4 🔘 **1.45** Listen and repeat.

5 🔘 **1.46** Listen to the requests. Put a tick (✓) if they are polite and a cross (✗) if they are not.

1 Excuse me, can I have a window seat, please? ✓
2 Could I get past?
3 I wonder if I could have another glass of water, please.
4 Can you sit down?
5 I'd like a black coffee.
6 Could you put your bag up there, please?
7 Can I see your passport, please?

6 Work in pairs. Practise the dialogue in exercise 2. Remember to use friendly intonation.

Roleplay

7 Work in pairs, A and B. You are going to do two roleplays.

Roleplay 1

A: You are a passenger on a long-distance flight. You want to request some things from the flight attendant. Decide what to ask for. Use the ideas on page 129 to help you.

B: You are a flight attendant. Help the passenger.

Roleplay 2

A: You are a flight attendant. One of your passengers is very difficult. Look at the ideas on page 131 and choose some of the problems.

B: You are a passenger. Listen to what the flight attendant asks you to do.

5c | A weekend break

Vocabulary & speaking: hotels

1 Complete the form below with words and phrases from the box.

> air conditioning   central heating   countryside
> gym   lift   minibar   single   twin

Location	town centre ☐
	near the sea ☐
	(1) _____ ☐

Room	double ☐
	(2) _____ ☐
	(3) _____ ☐
	family ☐

Hotel facilities	restaurant ☐
	bar ☐
	swimming pool ☐
	sauna ☐
	(4) _____ ☐
	free parking ☐
	(5) _____ ☐

Room facilities	shower ☐
	bath ☐
	(6) _____ ☐
	(7) _____ ☐
	satellite TV ☐
	(8) _____ ☐
	internet connection ☐
	room service ☐

2 Look at the list of room and hotel facilities again. Choose the four most important facilities from the list for the following people:

1 A family with two children staying at the hotel for two weeks for their summer holiday.
2 A business person staying for three nights at the hotel for a conference.
3 A couple staying one night at the hotel. They are going to arrive late and leave early the next day.

3 What are the most important room or hotel facilities for you? Explain your reasons.

For me, an internet connection is the most important because …

4 What is the best (or worst) hotel you have ever stayed in? Work in pairs. Ask and answer these questions.

- How long ago was it?
- Where was it?
- How long did you stay?
- Why did you go there?
- Who did you go with?
- What was the hotel like?
- Was there anything special about the hotel?

Listening

1 Look at the photo of a hotel in Brighton (in the south of England). Would you like to stay there? Why or why not?

2 🔘 1.47 Two people went to the hotel for the weekend. Listen to the recording and tick (✓) the problems that they had.

1 broken lift
2 cold shower
3 dirty bathroom
4 no central heating
5 room too small
6 unfriendly hotel manager

3 🔘 1.47 Listen again and put the events in order.

☐ They found another hotel.
☐ 1 They arrived at the hotel.
☐ They gave their key to the woman at reception.
☐ They had a cold shower.
☐ They paid for the room.
☐ They went to get their bags.
☐ They went to the cinema.

4 How much can you remember of Nicki and Gavin's experiences? Tell their story.

COLEG LLANDRILLO COLLEGE
LIBRARY RESOURCE CENTRE
CANOLFAN ADNODDAU LLYFRGELL

123584

GRAMMAR: future 2 (will)

We use *will* (*'ll*) + infinitive when we decide something at the moment of speaking.

I forgot about the shower. **I'll ask** *my husband to fix it.* (She is deciding now.)

We use *am/is/are/going to* + infinitive when we have already made the decision. (See page 000.)

We've got tickets for the cinema. We're going to see *the new film.* (She decided some time ago.)

> SEE LANGUAGE REFERENCE PAGE 54

1 Complete the sentences with *'ll* and a verb from the box.

give   see   tell   think

1 So, outside the cinema at eight o'clock?   Yes, OK. I ____ you later.
2 Dad, can I borrow the car for the weekend?   I ____ about it.
3 Tell me when you arrive, OK?   OK, I ____ you a call.
4 What does this word mean?   I ____ you later.

2 You are a friendly hotel manager. Some guests have some problems. What do you say?

1 I'm sorry, sir. I'll send someone to look at it.

1 The TV is making a strange noise.
2 We need to get up very early in the morning, but we don't have an alarm clock.
3 There's no water in the minibar.
4 Our room smells of cigarettes. It's horrible.
5 I'm very hungry, but the restaurant is closed.
6 The door to the gym is locked.
7 There's a spider in the bath!

3 Complete the dialogue between a guest and a hotel manager with *'ll* or the correct form of *going to*.

Guest: Excuse me, I (1) _____ visit the old part of town this afternoon. Can you tell me the way?
Manager: Yes, no problem. I (2) _____ give you a map.
Guest: Is it far?
Manager: No, not far. Do you want to walk or take a bus? It's a nice walk.
Guest: Oh, well, I (3) _____ walk, I think.
Manager: Or, if you like, I (4) _____ take you in my car. I (5) _____ do some shopping this afternoon.
Guest: That's kind of you. Thanks. When (6) _____ (you) leave?
Manager: About four o'clock.
Guest: Great. I (7) _____ see you here at four o'clock.
Manager: OK. I (8) _____ see you later.

4 🔘 **1.48** Listen to the recording to check your answers. Then work in pairs and practise the dialogue.

DID YOU KNOW?

1 What do you think the connection is between Las Vegas, the Eiffel Tower and a waterfall? Read the text to find out.

It is the hotel capital of the world. It has fourteen of the biggest hotels in the world and more than 125,000 hotel rooms. Many of the 37 million tourists who come here every year come to see the hotels. The Rio Hotel, for example, has an Ipanema beach, waterfalls, four swimming pools and sixteen restaurants. At the Venetian Hotel, you can take a gondola, and you can climb the Eiffel Tower or visit the Arc de Triomphe at the Paris Hotel.

Many tourists never go outside their hotels, which have everything you could possibly want: bars, restaurants, sports centres and pools, concerts, cinemas, theatres, casinos – even theme parks. In fact, there is little reason to leave your hotel. The only thing to visit is .... more hotels!

2 Work in pairs. Ask and answer these questions.

- What else do you know about Las Vegas?
- Do you know anybody who has been there? Would you like to go?
- What famous hotels are there in your country? Why are they famous?

READING

1 Read the webpage and match the pictures A–H to the different holidays.

Heaven Holidays

Looking for something different? We have the holiday for you.

Sea holidays

Scuba Safari
Experience the beauty of the seas of Borneo

Titanic Times
An unforgettable dive to the wreck of the Titanic

Dolphin Days
Swim with the dolphins of the Bahamas

Adventure holidays

Route 66
An incredible journey from Chicago to Los Angeles by Harley-Davidson

Mountain Memories
Cycling through the volcanic valleys of Reunion Island

Mach 3
Fly a Russian MiG-25 jet and see the world from above the clouds

Haunted holidays

Monster Party
Looking for the Loch Ness monster (includes visits to whisky distilleries)

Feast of Lanterns
Experience the magic of the Hungry Ghost Festival in Malaysia.

Yeti Hunt
Two weeks in the high Himalayas on the trail of the yeti

History trails

Great Wall
Explore the villages and temples of Mongolia and northern China

Mayan Treasures
See the lost Mayan pyramids in the rain forest of Mexico.

Alexander the Great
Follow the path of Alexander the Great through the historic cities of Turkey

2 Read about some more holidays. What type of holiday are they?

1
Meet the Shojo
Explore the Pacific islands of southern Japan in the company of Shojo ghosts

2
Siberian White Water
Kayak down the Katun River

3
Inca Gold
Follow the trail of the conquistadors and discover the ancient Peruvian cities

4
Grand Canyon
Paragliding and sky diving in America's Wild West

5
Arctic Ice
A visit by submarine to a wreck under the Arctic ice

6
1492
Discover the Jamaica and Puerto Rico of Christoper Colombus

E   F   G   H

3 Match the paragraphs 1–4 to the holidays in the webpage advertisement.

1   I'm really looking forward to riding the motorbike. I hope to go with a friend, but if he hasn't got enough money, I intend to go alone. I've got a brother in Los Angeles and I plan to stay with him when I get there.

2   We would like to learn some Chinese before we go, because we want to meet lots of people when we're there. My wife is looking forward to seeing the wall, but I'm more interested in finding out about the people who live in that part of the world.

3   I know it's going to be difficult so I plan to do a lot of practice on my bike before I go. I intend to take a lot of photos of the volcanoes and the animals and everything. I hope to get some pictures of the monkeys. I want to have an exhibition of the photos when I get back.

4   I would really like to see the monster, but it doesn't matter too much. I'm also interested in seeing Scotland and I plan to visit the village where my father was born. My husband is looking forward to tasting all the different whiskies.

4 Which of these holidays do **not** interest you? Why?

VOCABULARY: verb patterns

1 Choose the correct form of the verb to complete the sentences.

1   **I hope to** *find / finding* the yeti.
2   **I intend to** *take / taking* some Turkish lessons.
3   **I'm very interested in** *learn / learning* more about the yeti.
4   **I'm looking forward to** *swim / swimming* with the dolphins.
5   **I plan to** *spend / spending* two weeks in the jungle.
6   **I want to** *visit / visiting* the old temples.
7   **I would like to** *read / reading* more about Alexander.

Find the phrases in **bold** in Reading exercise 3 to check your answers.

2 Choose one of the holidays from the advertisement. Prepare answers to these questions.

- Which holiday do you want to go on?
- Would you like to go with another person or alone?
- Why are you interested in that holiday?
- Do you intend to prepare for the holiday in any way?
- What do you plan to take with you?
- What are you looking forward to most in the holiday?
- What do you hope to do when you are there?

3 Now work in pairs. Ask and answer the questions.

PRONUNCIATION: silent letters

1 Circle the silent letters in the words below.

1   cas**t**le   6   receipt
2   climb   7   ghost
3   foreign   8   Wednesday
4   hour   9   whole
5   knife   10   wreck

2   🔊 **1.49** Listen to the recording to check your answers.

3 How many more words can you think of with silent letters?

SPEAKING

1 Two friends from Australia are coming to visit you for a week. It is their first visit to your country. You are going to be their guide.

First of all, decide what you intend to do with them. Look at the list and use ideas of your own.

- visit different parts of the country
- things to do and see
- means of transport
- places to stay
- places and things to eat
- people to introduce them to
- things to do on the last night?

2 Work in pairs and discuss your plans. Then tell the rest of the class.

GRAMMAR

Going to

Going to

We can use *going to* + infinitive to talk about plans in the future. The action has been decided before the person speaks.

> *We're going to save money to buy a flat.*
> *I'm going to buy a present for Amanda. It's her birthday.*

Affirmative & Negative				
I	'm 'm not			
He/She/It	's isn't	going to	phone him tonight.	
You/We/They	're aren't			
Question				
When	am is are	I he/she/it you/we/they	going to	phone him tonight?
Short answer				
Are you going to phone?		Yes, I am. / No, I'm not.		
Is she going to phone?		Yes, she is. / No, she isn't.		

When we talk about future plans with the verb *go*, it is normal to 'drop' the infinitive, *to go*.

> *I'm going to the cinema this evening.*
> Not ~~I'm going to go to the cinema this evening~~.

Present continuous for future

We can also use the present continuous to talk about future plans. We can often use either the present continuous or *going to* without changing the meaning, but when we want to show that the plan is more arranged or more fixed, we use the present continuous.

> *The teachers **are going to ask** for more money.*
> (This is their plan.)
> *We're **meeting** the managers at ten on Monday.*
> (The plan is fixed in our diaries.)

See page 44 for more information about the present continuous.

Will + infinitive

We use *will* + infinitive when we decide something at the moment of speaking.

> *Don't worry. I'll ask my husband to fix the window this afternoon.* (She is deciding now.)

We sometimes use *will* to make offers.

> *If you like, I'll take you in my car.*

Affirmative & Negative			
I He/She/It You/We/They	'll won't	phone.	
Question			
When	will	I he/she/it you/we/they	phone?
Short answer			
Will you phone?	Yes, I will. / No, I won't.		

FUNCTIONAL LANGUAGE

Requests

I'd like + noun.
I'd like to + infinitive …
Can I + infinitive … ?
Could I + infinitive … (*please*)?
I wonder if I could + infinitive …
Can you + infinitive … ?
Could you + infinitive … ?

Responses

Yes, sure.
Yes, of course.
Yes, certainly.

I'm afraid that …
I'm sorry, but …

When we say *no* to a request, it is polite to give a reason.

Word list

Compound nouns

backpack *n C*	/ˈbækpæk/
boyfriend *n C* *	/ˈbɔɪfrend/
cable car *n C*	/ˈkeɪbl kɑː/
camping-gas stove *n C*	/ˈkæmpɪŋ ˈgæs stəʊv/
credit card *n C*	/ˈkredɪt kɑːd/
dinner party *n C*	/ˈdɪnə pɑːti/
first-aid kit *n C*	/ˈfɜːst ˈeɪd kɪt/
flashlight *n C*	/ˈflæʃlaɪt/
guide book *n C*	/ˈgaɪd bʊk/
insect spray *n U*	/ˈɪnsekt spreɪ/
mobile phone *n C*	/ˈməʊbaɪl ˈfəʊn/
penknife *n C*	/ˈpen naɪf/
sleeping bag *n C*	/ˈsliːpɪŋ bæg/
sunglasses *n plur*	/ˈsʌŋglɑːsɪz/
tea bag *n C*	/ˈtiː bæg/
tour guide *n C*	/ˈtʊə gaɪd/
T-shirt *n C*	/ˈtiː ʃɜːt/
video camera *n C*	/ˈvɪdiəʊ kæmrə/
water bottle *n C*	/ˈwɔːtə bɒtl/

Air travel

board *v*	/bɔːd/
boarding card *n C*	/ˈbɔːdɪŋ kɑːd/
book *v* *	/bʊk/
check in *v*	/tʃek ˈɪn/
check-in *n U*	/ˈtʃekɪn/
departure *n C*	/dɪˈpɑːtʃə/
duty-free *adj*	/ˈdjuːti ˈfriː/
fasten *v* ***	/ˈfɑːsən/
flight *n C* ***	/flaɪt/
gate *n C* **	/geɪt/
hall *n C* ***	/hɔːl/
hand luggage *n U*	/ˈhænd lʌgɪdʒ/
land *v* **	/lænd/
locker n *C*	/ˈlɒkə/
luggage *n U*	/ˈlʌgɪdʒ/
overhead *adj*	/əʊvəˈhed/
pack *v* *	/pæk/
passport *n C* *	/ˈpɑːspɔːt/
passport control *n U*	/ˈpɑːspɔːt kəntrəʊl/
seat *n C* ***	/siːt/
seat belt *n C*	/ˈsiːt belt/
security *n U* ***	/sɪˈkjʊərəti/
security guard *n C*	/sɪˈkjʊərəti gɑːd/
take-off *n C/U*	/ˈteɪk ɒf/
terminal *n C*	/ˈtɜːmɪn(ə)l/
ticket *n C* ***	/ˈtɪkɪt/

Hotels

air conditioning *n U*	/ˈeə kəndɪʃnɪŋ/
central heating *n U*	/ˈsentrəl ˈhiːtɪŋ/
connection *n C* ***	/kəˈnekʃn/
countryside *n U* **	/ˈkʌntrisaɪd/
facility *n C* ***	/fəˈsɪləti/
gym *n C*	/dʒɪm/
lift *n C* *	/lɪft/
location *n C* **	/ləʊˈkeɪʃn/
minibar *n C*	/ˈmɪnibɑː/
room service *n U*	/ˈruːm sɜːvɪs/
satellite *n C* *	/ˈsætəlaɪt/
sauna *n C*	/ˈsɔːnə/
shower *n C* *	/ˈʃaʊə/
single *adj* ***	/ˈsɪŋgl/
twin *adj*	/twɪn/

Verb patterns

be interested in + verb + *-ing* ***
hope to + *infinitive* ***
intend to + *infinitive* ***
look forward to + verb + *-ing*
plan to + *infinitive* ***
want to + *infinitive* ***
would like to + *infinitive*

Other words & phrases

activist *n C*	/ˈæktɪvɪst/
afterwards *adv* **	/ˈɑːftəwədz/
ancient *adj* **	/ˈeɪnʃ(ə)nt/
attendant *n C*	/əˈtendənt/
beach *n C* **	/biːtʃ/
beauty *n U* **	/ˈbjuːti/
bell *n C* **	/bel/
breathtaking *adj*	/ˈbreθteɪkɪŋ/
build *v* ***	/bɪld/
calm *adj* **	/kɑːm/
capital *n C* ***	/ˈkæpɪtl/
casino *n C*	/kəˈsiːnəʊ/
cleanliness *n U*	/ˈklenlinəs/
climb *v* ***	/klaɪm/
cloud *n C* ***	/klaʊd/
comb *n C/v*	/kəʊm/
comfortable *adj* **	/ˈkʌmftəbl/
crowded *adj* *	/ˈkraʊdɪd/
depend *v* ***	/dɪˈpend/
destination *n C* *	/destɪˈneɪʃn/
discover *v* ***	/dɪˈskʌvə/
distillery *n C*	/dɪsˈtɪləri/
dive *n C/v* *	/daɪv/
dolphin *n C*	/ˈdɒlfɪn/
exhibition *n C* **	/eksɪˈbɪʃn/
explore *v* ***	/ɪkˈsplɔː/
extraordinary *adj* *	/ɪkˈstrɔːdnri/
extremely *adv* ***	/ɪkˈstriːmli/

fast food *n U*	/ˈfɑːst ˈfuːd/
festival *n C*	/ˈfestɪvl/
fix *v* **	/fɪks/
ghost *n C*	/gəʊst/
give up *v*	/gɪv ˈʌp/
hang on *v*	/hæŋ ˈɒn/
historic *adj*	/hɪˈstɒrɪk/
horrible *adj* *	/ˈhɒrəbl/
hunt *n C/v* *	/hʌnt/
ice *n U* **	/aɪs/
incredible *adj*	/ɪnˈkredəbl/
journey *n C* ***	/ˈdʒɜːni/
jungle *n C/U*	/ˈdʒʌŋgl/
kayak *n C*	/ˈkaɪæk/
key *n C* ***	/kiː/
local *adj* *	/ˈləʊkl/
lock *v* **	/lɒk/
luxury *n U*	/ˈlʌkʃəri/
magic *n U* *	/ˈmædʒɪk/
map *n C* **	/mæp/
metal *n C/U* ***	/ˈmetl/
mind *v* ***	/maɪnd/
minister *n C* **	/ˈmɪnɪstə/
monster *n C*	/ˈmɒnstə/
motorbike *n C*	/ˈməʊtəbaɪk/
nervous *adj* **	/ˈnɜːvəs/
object *n C* ***	/ˈɒbdʒɪkt/
organization *n C* ***	/ɔːgənaɪˈzeɪʃn/
path *n C* ***	/pɑːθ/
receipt *n C* *	/rɪˈsiːt/
rubbish *n U* *	/ˈrʌbɪʃ/
ruins *n pl*	/ˈruːɪnz/
save *v* ***	/seɪv/
search *v* **	/sɜːtʃ/
shout *v* ***	/ʃaʊt/
sign *n C* ***	/saɪn/
sky diving *n U*	/ˈskaɪ daɪvɪŋ/
smell *n C/v* **	/smel/
souvenir *n C*	/suːvəˈnɪə/
spider *n C*	/ˈspaɪdə/
spokesman *n C* ***	/ˈspəʊksmən/
stairs *n pl* **	/steəz/
submarine *n C*	/ˈsʌbməriːn/
temple *n C*	/ˈtempl/
throw *v* ***	/θrəʊ/
trail *n C* *	/treɪl/
treasure *n C/U*	/ˈtreʒə/
vacancy *n C* *	/ˈveɪkənsi/
valley *n C* *	/ˈvæli/
view *n C* ***	/vjuː/
volcano *n C*	/vɒlˈkeɪnə/
wall *n C* ***	/wɔːl/
waterfall *n C*	/ˈwɔːtəfɔːl/
welcome *v* **	/ˈwelkəm/
wreck *n C*	/rek/
yacht *n C*	/jɒt/

6A Junk food

VOCABULARY: food

1 Look at these items of food from America. Tick (✓) the items on the shopping list that you can see.

2 How often do you eat the food on the list? Which of them do you think are 'junk food'?

READING

1 Look at the picture of Elvis Presley. What sort of food do you think he liked?

2 Now read the book review. While you read, put a ! next to the facts you find most surprising.

eggs
sausages
peanut butter
pizza
French fries
hamburgers
ice cream
chocolate
donuts
strawberry yoghurt
cookies
potato chips
noodles
hot dogs

Eating the Elvis Presley Way

David Adler Blake Publishing

There are more than 400 books about Elvis Presley. There are books about his music, his films, his life, his death, his religion – and his food. There is the *Presley Family Cookbook, The Elvis Presley Cookbook, Elvis' Favorite Recipes,* and now *Eating the Elvis Presley Way.* What makes this book different? To begin with, this is not a cookbook. You can find recipes here, but this book is the story of Elvis' life. It is the story of the food that he ate and the people who cooked it for him. And an extremely interesting life it was, too.

The food in the first two or three chapters is quite normal – baby food, boring school dinners, army meals when he was doing his military service, that sort of thing. But later, when Elvis was rich and famous, it is a very different story. With all the money in the world, Elvis chose to eat like a child. Elvis got up late and his first meal of the day was breakfast at five o'clock in the afternoon: bacon and eggs, or sausage and eggs. After that, it was snacks: pizza and hot dogs, hamburgers and fries, chocolate and cakes – all day and every day. Elvis even had a fridge in his bedroom for his favorite snacks.

As the years passed, Elvis' eating problems became really serious. One day, when Elvis was going to the White House to meet the President, he was feeling a bit hungry and ate 250g of chocolate and then 12 donuts in his taxi. Another time, he ordered a large ice cream for breakfast. He ate it quickly, ordered a second, a third, a fourth and a fifth before falling asleep again. Elvis' last meal before he died was four scoops of ice cream with six chocolate cookies.

Elvis was an extremely unhappy man. His food and the drugs that he took made him feel good, but killed him in the end. It's a fairly sad story, but a fascinating one, too.

Recommended ★★★★★

3 Read the review again and say if the sentences are true (T) or false (F).

1 This is the first book about Elvis Presley and food.
2 It is different from the other books about Elvis and food.
3 His eating problems started when he was a child.
4 He had breakfast early in the morning.
5 He ate a lot of junk food.
6 He had food in his bedroom.
7 The President gave him a large box of chocolates.
8 Elvis didn't like ice cream very much.

4 Complete the definitions with an adjective from the review.

1 When someone is f____, a lot of people know their name.
2 A f____ story, place or person is very interesting.
3 Your f____ thing or person is the one that you like best.
4 You feel h____ when you want to eat.
5 When you are unhappy, you feel s____.
6 When you have a s____ problem, you are very worried about it.

5 What else do you know about Elvis Presley? Why do you think that Elvis had eating problems?

GRAMMAR: modifiers

We can make an adjective stronger or weaker with a modifier. We put this before the adjective.

Weak
a bit hungry

Medium
quite _____
fairly _____

Strong
very _____
really _____
extremely _____

> SEE LANGUAGE REFERENCE PAGE 64

1 <u>Underline</u> examples of modifiers before adjectives in the book review. Use them to complete the examples in the language box.

2 Put the modifiers in the correct place in the sentences.

1 Burger Paradise is always busy. (*very*)
2 I like The New York Donut Shop but the service is slow. (*a bit*)
3 I think that the chicken burgers at The Alabama Chicken are good. (*really*)
4 The fast food shops on Main Square are expensive. (*fairly*)
5 The hot dogs at The Happy Sandwich are nice. (*quite*)
6 The Magic Hamburger in my town is popular. (*extremely*)

3 Make six sentences about places where you can eat out in your town. Use modifiers and adjectives. Here are some more adjectives that you can use.

cheap	dirty	fashionable	friendly	healthy
lively	small	unhealthy		

SPEAKING

1 Do you know any 'theme' restaurants like the Hard Rock Café or Planet Hollywood? What is special about them?

Have you ever been to a 'theme' restaurant? What was it like?

2 Work in pairs. Plan your own 'theme' restaurant. Use these questions to help you.

• What is the theme of your restaurant? (sport, music, cinema, a famous person, a country, a historical period, etc)
• What is the name of your restaurant?
• What kind of food and drink do you serve?
• What does the restaurant look like?
• Do the waiters and waitresses wear uniforms? What kind?
• What kind of music do you want?
• How much does a meal cost in your restaurant?

3 Describe your restaurant to other students in the class. Decide which restaurant is the best.

6B | Slow food

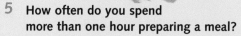

Are You A Foodie?

Answer our questionnaire to find out if you are a foodie.

1 How long is a typical meal in your home?
a) less than 30 minutes
b) 30–90 minutes
c) more than 90 minutes

2 How often do you eat in front of the TV?
a) less than once a week
b) once a week
c) more than once a week

3 How many of the following do you eat at least once a week?
a) crisps   b) chips
c) chocolate biscuits
d) microwave dinner

4 How many recipe books do you have?
a) 0   b) 1–5   c) more than 5

5 How often do you spend more than one hour preparing a meal?
a) less than once a week
b) once a week
c) more than once a week

6 How often do you go to a restaurant (not fast food or pizza!)?
a) less than twice a month
b) 2–4 times a month
c) more than 4 times a month

Answers on page 128.

SPEAKING

1 Work in pairs and do the quiz. Take it in turns to ask the questions. (A foodie is someone who enjoys eating or cooking different types of food.)

2 Now turn to page 128. Add up your points and read the description for your score. Does it describe you well?

Who is the biggest 'foodie' in the class?

LISTENING

1 🔘 1.50 Listen to part of a radio interview about food in Italy. Choose the best title for the programme.

1 How to make Bolognese sauce
2 Fast food in Italy
3 Slow food in Bologna
4 Tagliatelle or spaghetti?

Spaghetti Bolognese
(spaghetti with a sauce made with tomatoes, meat, onions and herbs)

2 🔘 1.50 Read the passage below and then listen again. <u>Underline</u> the incorrect information and explain what is wrong.

The radio presenter is in Bologna, not Rome.

The radio presenter is in <u>Rome</u>, an Italian city where people eat Spaghetti Bolognese. Spaghetti is a speciality of Bologna. Bolognese sauce from supermarkets is made from many different ingredients. It is very similar to Ragu sauce. Ragu is quicker to prepare.
'Slow food' is a movement that started in France in 1997. It has members in about twenty countries and they are interested in making food more enjoyable and more traditional.

3 Do you agree with Maura that *good food is slow food*? Why or why not?

What traditional foods are there in your country? What parts of the country do they come from?

VOCABULARY: adjectives (opposites)

1 Complete the words by putting vowels (*a, e, i, o, u*) in the spaces. Then match the adjectives in column A to their opposites in column B.

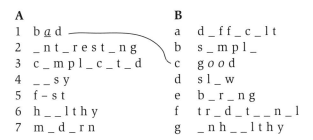

A
1 b _a_ d
2 _ n t _ r e s t _ n g
3 c _ m p l _ c _ t _ d
4 _ _ s y
5 f - s t
6 h _ _ l t h y
7 m _ d _ r n

B
a d _ f f _ c _ l t
b s _ m p l _
c g *o* *o* d
d s l _ w
e b _ r _ n g
f t r _ d _ t _ _ n _ l
g _ n h _ _ l t h y

2 Find an adjective in exercise 1 that you can use with the words below.

1 costume   dancing   marriage   song   teacher

   traditional

2 face   film   person   picture   place

   _____

3 answer   explanation   story   problem   question

   _____

4 baby   diet   eating   food   lifestyle

   _____

3 Choose an adjective from exercise 1 and think of five things you can describe with that adjective.

Work in pairs. Tell your partner the five things.
Your partner must guess the adjective that you chose.

PRONUNCIATION: word stress 1

1 🔘 1.51 Listen to these words and count the syllables.

1   2

heal / thy

1 h e a l t h y   6 c o m p l i c a t e d
2 d i f f i c u l t   7 s i m p l e
3 e n j o y a b l e   8 a r t i f i c i a l
4 m o d e r n   9 t r a d i t i o n a l
5 i m p o r t a n t

2 Mark the stress in each word and say the words.

   ☐
   heal / thy

3 🔘 1.51 Listen to the recording again to check your answers.

GRAMMAR: comparatives

> We use the comparative form to compare two things or people.
>
> We make the comparative of short adjectives with the adjective + -*er* (+ *than*).
>
> > slow → slower   The service in the restaurant
> > was **slower than** usual.
>
> 1 When the adjective ends in -*e*, add –*r*.
> > nice → nicer   The sauce is **nicer** with spaghetti.
>
> 2 When the adjective ends in -*y*, remove the -*y* and add –*ier*.
> > easy → easier   It's **easier than** you think.
>
> 3 With some adjectives you need to double the last consonant.
> > big → bigger   Can we have a **bigger** table, please?
>
> We make the comparative of longer adjectives with *more* + adjective (+ *than*).
> > It's a **more traditional** recipe.
> > Food is **more interesting than** that.
>
> There are two very common irregular comparatives.
> > good → better (than)   bad → worse (than)

➤ SEE LANGUAGE REFERENCE PAGE 64

1 Correct the mistakes in the sentences.

   more traditional
1 I like ~~traditionaler~~ ∧ cooking recipes.
2 Juice is healthyer for you than beer.
3 Chinese food is more interesting English.
4 Bologna is hoter than London.
5 A real sauce is gooder than sauce in a bottle.
6 The Spanish often eat later than the Dutch.
7 Pizzas are more cheap than steak and chips.

2 Use comparatives to complete the sentences below about your country.

1 The food in my country is _____ than American food.
2 The food that we eat is _____ than 20 years ago.
3 Fast food is becoming _____.
4 These days, people want to eat _____ food.
5 It's _____ to eat in a restaurant than at home.
6 Restaurants are _____ than they used to be.

Work in pairs. Compare your sentences.

3 Work in pairs. Turn to page 130 and look at the pictures. How many differences can you find?

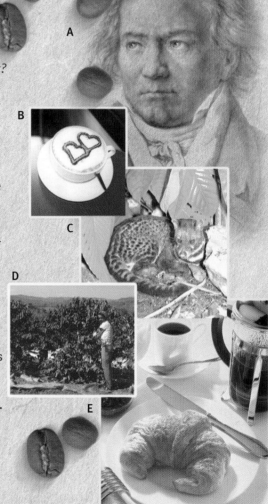

Coffee Break

1 *Can you imagine getting up in the morning without a coffee for breakfast? What is a good meal without a coffee at the end of it? Coffee is probably the world's favourite drink, but most of us never give it a second thought. How much do you know about coffee?*

2 The Turks gave us the word *coffee* and the Italians gave us *espresso* and *cappuccino*, but Finland is the biggest coffee-drinking country in the world. Coffee originally came from Ethiopia, but Colombia and Brazil are now the most important coffee-producing countries.

3 There are more than 100 different varieties of coffee bean and Jamaican Blue Mountain is said to have the best taste. However, the most expensive coffee in the world (at $660/kilo) is Kopi Luwak. An Indonesian cat called Paradoxurus is especially fond of coffee beans and Kopi Luwak is made from its droppings!

4 We all know coffee addicts – people who can do nothing in the morning until their second or third cup of coffee. The most famous coffee addicts in the world were probably the French writers Balzac (40 cups a day) and Voltaire (more than 50 cups a day). Beethoven was also a coffee lover – he always counted 60 beans for each cup of coffee that he made.

5 The most fashionable coffee bars in the US now serve 'coffee art'. Artists in California draw leaves, hearts and other designs in your coffee.

SPEAKING

1 Work in pairs. Discuss these questions.

- What is your favourite drink?
- Where and when do you drink it?
- Do you prefer tea or coffee? How do you take it? (white/black, strong/weak, with/without sugar)
- What drinks are traditional in your country?

READING

1 Read the magazine article about coffee.
Match the pictures A–E to the paragraphs 1–5.

2 Read the article again. Explain the connection between coffee and the countries below.

1 *Brazil is an important coffee-producing country.*

1	Brazil	5	Jamaica
2	Finland	6	The United States
3	France	7	Turkey
4	Indonesia		

3 Find words in the article that match the definitions.

1 at the beginning = o_____
2 kinds, sorts = v_____
3 the fruit of the coffee plant = b_____
4 people who cannot stop taking a drug = a_____

GRAMMAR: superlatives

> We use the superlative form to compare more than two things or people.
>
> We make the superlative of short adjectives with *the* + adjective + *-est*.
> cheap → the cheap**est**
> large → the larg**est**
> hot → the hot**test**
> happy → the happi**est**
> Finland is **the biggest** coffee-drinking country in the world.
>
> We make the superlative of longer adjectives with *the* + *most* + adjective.
> the most interesting   the most traditional
> The **most expensive** coffee in the world is Kowi Luwak.
>
> There are two very common irregular superlatives.
> good → the best   bad → the worst
> Jamaican Blue Mountain has **the best** taste.

> SEE LANGUAGE REFERENCE PAGE 64

1 Find six examples of superlatives in the article about coffee.

2 Complete the sentences in the quiz. Put the adjectives in brackets into the superlative form.

Amazing Food Facts

1 _____ (*expensive*) meal in the world was in London in 2001 and cost
a) £24,000   b) £44,000   c) £84,000 for six people.

2 _____ (*good*) caviar in the world comes from
a) the Caspian Sea   b) Lake Titicaca in Bolivia
c) the Eastern Mediterranean.

3 _____ (*large*) pub in the world is the Mathäser in Munich, Germany.
It seats
a) 5,500   b) 7,500   c) 9,500 people.

4 _____ (*big*) doughnut in the world was made in New York in 1993.
It was almost
a) 3m   b) 5m   c) 10m in diameter.

5 _____ (*long*) hot dog in the world was made in Chicago. It measured
a) 2m   b) 3m   c) 8m.

6 _____ (*popular*) fast food in Britain is
a) hamburgers   b) pizzas   c) sandwiches.

7 _____ (*heavy*) tomato in the world weighed
a) 15kg   b) 30kg   c) 50kg.

8 Samuel Adams Triple Bock is _____ (*strong*) beer in the world. It contains
a) 12%   b) 15%   c) 18% alcohol.

3 Work in pairs. Choose the correct answers in the quiz.

4 🔊 1.52 Listen to the recording to check your answers.

5 Work in pairs. Think of places you know where you can drink (cafés, bars, hotels etc). Make sentences about these places, using superlatives. You can use adjectives from the box or think of your own.

> bad   big   cheap   expensive
> fashionable   friendly   good
> near to the school   traditional

Central Café is the nearest café to the school.

DID YOU KNOW?

1 Read the text and answer the questions.

> Starbucks started as a small coffee shop in Seattle. In the 1990s, the company grew and it now serves coffee to more than 11 million customers around the world every week. With more than 6,000 stores in the US, Japan, the UK, China, Spain, Austria and other countries, Starbucks is becoming the McDonalds of coffee.

• How many of the following can you find near where you live?

> Burger King   Dominos Pizza
> Häagen Dazs   Kentucky Fried Chicken
> McDonalds   Starbucks

• What other big food chains do you know?
• What do you like eating or drinking in these places?

SPEAKING

1 Work in pairs. Look at the types of restaurant in the box and discuss these questions.

- Which type of food have you tried?
- Which do you like best?
- Which ones can you find in your city/town?

| Italian | French | Chinese | Indian | Mexican |

2 What restaurants do you know in your town? Which is:

- the best?
- the most fashionable?
- the most popular?
- the cheapest?

3 Which restaurant in your town would you choose for a class meal. Why?

VOCABULARY: eating out

1 Look at the restaurant bill and find words that match the definitions.

1 waiter

1 the person who takes your order = _ _ _ _ _ _
2 the last course = _ _ _ _ _ _ _
3 the first course = _ _ _ _ _ _ _
4 tax = _ _ _
5 a fixed choice of two or three courses = _ _ _ _ _ _ _
6 the money you pay for your waiter/waitress =

_ _ _ _ _ _ _ _ _ _ _ _ _
7 the most important part of the meal = _ _ _ _ _ _ _ _ _ _

2 How much do you pay for the items on the bill in restaurants in your town? Is *La Vie en Rose* more or less expensive?

LISTENING

1 🔘 **1.53** Listen to a man booking a restaurant and complete the booking form.

2 🔘 **1.53** Listen to the conversation again. Underline the words that you hear.

1 I'm afraid our *first / next / last* booking is at 9.30, sir.
2 We all make *bookings / mistakes / progress*, don't we?
3 There's a very *nice / pretty / romantic* table for two next to the window.
4 That sounds *excellent / marvellous / perfect*.
5 It's our French class' *annual / monthly / weekly* meal.

LA VIE EN ROSE

5✮✮✮✮✮ *French cooking in a romantic restaurant near the river.*
Join Manu and Gérard, our French chefs, for a true French experience.
For that special occasion …

27 Bridge Street
Tel: 727 4848

11/12/05   22.13
LA VIE EN ROSE

Your waiter today is 03 Jean-Paul

	£	€
1 x set menu @	19.00	26.22
1 x starter (mixed salad) @	4.50	6.21
1 x main course (cassoulet) @	11.50	15.87
1 x dessert (lemon sorbet) @	4.20	5.80
1 x house red @	15.00	20.70
1 x 1 litre mineral water @	3.50	4.83
12% Service charge	6.92	9.56
Sub total	64.62	89.19
VAT (12.5%)	8.08	11.15
Total	**72.70**	**100.34**

Thank you for choosing La Vie en Rose.
Tel: 0800 724 3004 Fax: 0800 724 3005

LA VIE EN ROSE
BOOKING FORM

Customer name _____
Number of people _____

DAY: *Mon / Tue / Wed / Thu / Fri / Sat*
TIME: *Lunchtime: 12.00 / 12.30 / 1.00 / 1.30 / 2.00*
        Evening: 7.00 / 7.30 / 8.00 / 8.30 / 9.00 / 9.30

Smoking / Non-smoking

FUNCTIONAL LANGUAGE 1: making a reservation

1 Who says the sentences below: the customer (C) or the waiter (W)?

1 I'd like to book a table for Friday, please.
2 Certainly, madam. For how many people?
3 What time would you like, madam?
4 That's fine.
5 Could I take your name, please, madam?
6 We look forward to seeing you.

2 🔘 **1.54** Listen to the recording to check your answers.

Roleplay

3 Work in pairs. Practise making a restaurant reservation. Take it in turns to be the customer. Choose the day, the time and the number of people. Begin like this:

Good afternoon. This is … . Can I help you?

PRONUNCIATION: emphatic stress

1 🔘 **1.55** Listen to these phrases from one of the conversations.

☐   ☐
*Not 10 o'**clock**. 10 **people**.*

2 Practise saying these phrases in the same way.

1 House red. Not house white.
2 Good? It was excellent!
3 We said half-past seven, not half-past nine.
4 Tuesday evening. Not Tuesday afternoon.

3 🔘 **1.56** Listen to the recording to check your answers.

FUNCTIONAL LANGUAGE 2: in a restaurant

1 🔘 **1.57** Look at the picture and listen to a conversation. Which comes first: the picture or the conversation?

2 🔘 **1.57** Listen to the conversation again. Put the sentences in the correct order.

☐ Can I take your coats?
☐ Could we have a bottle of house red, please?
☐ Excuse me, have you got an ashtray?
☐ I have a reservation for ten people.
[1] Let me show you to your tables.
☐ That was delicious.
☐ Would you like something to drink?

Roleplay

3 Work in groups. You are going to act out a short sketch in a restaurant. Decide what kind of restaurant it is and who is the waiter.

Useful language	
Would you like …? *I'd like …*	*to have the bill/to see the menu*
Have you got …? *Could we have …?* *I'll have …*	*a drink/an ashtray/something to drink/ the bill/the house white*

GRAMMAR

Modifiers

We can make an adjective stronger or weaker with a modifier, for example, *quite, very*.

Weak
a bit

Medium
quite
fairly

Strong
very
really
extremely

*I feel **a bit sad**.*
*We usually eat **quite healthy** food.*
*It's an **extremely** expensive restaurant.*

Comparatives & superlatives

We use comparatives to compare two things or people. We use *than* to join the two things we are comparing.

*Fresh sauce is **healthier than** sauce in bottles.*
*This computer is **faster than** the old one.*

We use superlatives to compare more than two things or people. We often use *in* after a superlative.

*He is **the richest** man **in** England.*
*They serve **the best** hamburgers **in** our town.*

With short adjectives, we usually add *-er/-est*.

| strong | stronger | the strongest |
| weak | weaker | the weakest |

When an adjective ends in *-e*, we add *-r/-st*.

| large | larger | the largest |
| nice | nicer | the nicest |

When an adjective ends with *-y* after a consonant, we change the *-y* to *-ier/-iest*.

| busy | busier | the busiest |
| easy | easier | the easiest |

When an adjective with one syllable ends with a consonant after a vowel, we double the consonant.

| big | bigger | the biggest |
| hot | hotter | the hottest |

With longer adjectives, we add *more/the most*.

| modern | **more** modern | **the most** modern |
| traditional | **more** traditional | **the most** traditional |

Some adjectives have irregular comparative and superlative forms.

good	better	the best
bad	worse	the worst
far	further	the furthest

We can make negative comparisons with *less/the least*.

strong	less strong	the least strong
busy	less busy	the least busy
modern	less modern	the least modern

FUNCTIONAL LANGUAGE

Making a reservation

I'd like to book a table for …

Certainly, Madam/Sir.
What time would you like?
For how many people?
Could I take your name, please?
We look forward to seeing you.
I'm afraid we're fully booked.

In the restaurant

Can I take your coats?
Let me show you your table.
Would you like to + infinitive … ?

I'd like to + infinitive …
Have you got + noun?
Could we have + noun?
I'll have + noun.

WORD LIST

Food

bacon *n U*	/ˈbeɪkən/
beer *n C/U* *	/bɪə/
breakfast *n C* **	/ˈbrekfəst/
cake *n C/U* **	/keɪk/
caviar *n U*	/ˈkæviɑː/
chicken *n C/U* **	/ˈtʃɪkɪn/
chip *n C* **	/tʃɪp/
chocolate *n C/U* **	/ˈtʃɒklət/
coffee *n C/U* ***	/ˈkɒfi/
cookbook *n C*	/ˈkʊkbʊk/
cookie *n C*	/ˈkʊki/
crisp *n C*	/krɪsp/
diet *n C* **	/ˈdaɪət/
donut/doughnut *n C*	/ˈdəʊnʌt/
egg *n C* ***	/eg/
(French) fries *n pl*	/fraɪz/
fruit *n U* ***	/fruːt/
ham *n U*	/hæm/
hamburger *n C*	/ˈhæmbɜːgə/
hot dog *n C*	/ˈhɒt dɒg/
ice cream *n C*	/aɪs ˈkriːm/
junk food *n C*	/ˈdʒʌŋk fuːd/
lemon *n C/U*	/ˈlemən/
meal *n C* ***	/miːl/
mineral water *n U*	/ˈmɪn(ə)rəl wɔːtə/
noodles *n plur*	/ˈnuːdlz/
pasta *n U*	/ˈpæstə/
peanut butter *n U*	/ˈpiːnʌt ˈbʌtə/
pizza *n C/U*	/ˈpiːtsə/
potato *n C* **	/pəˈteɪtəʊ/
recipe *n C* *	/ˈresəpi/
rice *n U* *	/raɪs/
salad *n C/U* *	/ˈsæləd/
salt *n U* *	/sɔːlt/
sauce *n C/U* *	/sɔːs/
sausage *n C*	/ˈsɒsɪdʒ/
snack *n C*	/snæk/
sorbet *n U*	/ˈsɔːbeɪ/
steak *n C/U*	/steɪk/
strawberry *n C*	/ˈstrɔːb(ə)ri/
sugar *n U* **	/ˈʃʊgə/
tomato *n C*	/təˈmɑːtəʊ/
yoghurt/yogurt *n C/U*	/ˈjɒgət/

Eating out

bill *n C* ***	/bɪl/
course *n C* ***	/kɔːs/
dessert *n C/U* *	/dɪˈzɜːt/
main course *n C*	/meɪn kɔːs/
service charge *n C*	/ˈsɜːvɪs tʃɑːdʒ/
set menu *n C*	/set ˈmenjuː/
starter *n C*	/ˈstɑːtə/
VAT *n U*	/viː eɪ tiː/; /væt/
waiter *n C*	/ˈweɪtə/
waitress *n C*	/ˈweɪtrəs/

Other words & phrases

addict *n C*	/ˈædɪkt/
alcohol *n U* *	/ˈælkəhɒl/
annual *adj* **	/ˈænjuəl/
army *n C* ***	/ˈɑːmi/
artificial *adj* *	/ɑːtɪˈfɪʃl/
ashtray *n C*	/ˈæʃtreɪ/
authentic *adj*	/ɔːˈθentɪk/
bean *n C*	/biːn/
bedroom *n C* **	/ˈbedruːm/
boring *adj* **	/ˈbɔːrɪŋ/
box *n C* ***	/bɒks/
busy *adj* ***	/ˈbɪzi/
chapter *n C* ***	/ˈtʃæptə/
chemical *n C* ***	/ˈkemɪkl/
costume *n C*	/ˈkɒstjuːm/
count *v* ***	/kaʊnt/
customer *n C* ***	/ˈkʌstəmə/
delicious *adj* *	/dɪˈlɪʃəs/
dish *n C* **	/dɪʃ/
draw *v* ***	/drɔː/
droppings *n pl*	/ˈdrɒpɪŋz/
drug *n C* ***	/drʌg/
face *n C* ***	/feɪs/
fascinating *adj* *	/ˈfæsɪneɪtɪŋ/
flavour *n C* *	/ˈfleɪvə/
fresh *adj* ***	/freʃ/
fridge *n C* *	/frɪdʒ/
healthy *adj* **	/ˈhelθi/
heart *n C* ***	/hɑːt/
ingredient *n C*	/ɪnˈgriːdiənt/
kill *v* ***	/kɪl/
laboratory *n C* *	/ləˈbɒr(ə)tri/
leaf *n C* ***	/liːf/
lifestyle *n C*	/ˈlaɪfstaɪl/
lively *adj*	/ˈlaɪvli/
market *n C* **	/ˈmɑːkɪt/
marvellous *adj*	/ˈmɑːvələs/
measure *v* ***	/ˈmeʒə/
microwave *n C/v*	/ˈmaɪkrəweɪv/
military service *n U*	/ˈmɪlɪt(ə)ri ˈsɜːvɪs/
movement *n C* ***	/ˈmuːvmənt/
occasion *n C* ***	/əˈkeɪʒn/

order *v* ***	/ˈɔːdə/
plant *n C* ***	/plɑːnt/
presenter *n C*	/prɪˈzentə/
preservative *n C*	/prɪˈzɜːvətɪv/
progress *n U* ***	/ˈprəʊgres/
scoop *n C*	/skuːp/
serve *v* ***	/sɜːv/
service *n U* ***	/ˈsɜːvɪs/
shopping list *n C*	/ˈʃɒpɪŋ lɪst/
silly *adj* *	/ˈsɪli/
sparkling *adj*	/ˈspɑːklɪŋ/
special *adj* ***	/ˈspeʃl/
speciality *n C*	/speʃiˈæləti/
supermarket *n C* *	/ˈsuːpəmɑːkɪt/
taste *n/v* ***	/teɪst/
taxi *n C* ***	/ˈtæksi/
weak *adj* **	/wiːk/
weigh *v* **	/weɪ/

7A | Rising stars

SPEAKING

1 Read this description of a job. What is the job?

I work for the government and I deal with – everything! I work in a beautiful office in Washington. I work with lots of different people. It's very well-paid. It's also temporary. What do I do?

2 Think of another job and make three sentences about it.
Work in pairs. Read your sentences to your partner. Your partner must guess the job.

VOCABULARY: work

1 Choose the correct words to complete the sentences.

1 Many film stars had very different *jobs / works* before they started their acting *careers / jobs*.
2 Madonna hated her *career / work* at a donut shop, but she needed a *job / work*.
3 Brad Pitt had a *career / job* as a dancing chicken outside a restaurant before he began his *career / job* as an actor.
4 Tom Cruise was thinking of a *career / work* in the church before finding *job / work* in the movies.

2 Complete the sentences in column A with a phrase from column B.

A		B	
1	At the donut shop, Madonna was **in charge**	a	**of work**.
2	She was **fired**	b	**as** a model.
3	Brad Pitt used to **work**	c	**for** cleaning the tables.
4	When he was young, he was often **out**	d	**from** the job.
5	For a time, Tom Cruise **earned**	e	**of** the coffee machine.
6	He was **responsible**	f	**a living** in a New York restaurant.

3 Work in pairs. Talk about someone you know who:

- is out of work.
- does not need to earn a living.
- has an interesting career.
- has had lots of different jobs.
- has a very responsible job.
- loves/hates her/his work.

My sister is out of work.
She lost her job when her company closed.
She's finding it very difficult to get another job.

LISTENING

1 🔊 1.58 Listen to three people on a radio talk show. They are speaking about famous people they have met in their jobs. Match the speakers to the stars.

1	Valerio	a	Brad Pitt
2	Michelle	b	Tom Cruise
3	Tony	c	Leonardo Di Caprio
		d	Tom Hanks
		e	Madonna
		f	Jennifer Aniston

2 🔊 1.58 Listen to the talk show again. Complete the sentences with Valerio (V), Michelle (M) or Tony (T).

1 ___ can't remember a star's name.
2 ___ comes from New Jersey.
3 ___ is Australian.
4 ___ lives in Santa Monica.
5 ___ saw a star recently.
6 ___ thought the stars were cute.
7 ___ was interested in the star's girlfriend.
8 ___ works as a customer service assistant.

3 Have you ever met anyone famous?

GRAMMAR: present perfect simple

We can use the present perfect simple to talk about our experiences. We often use it with *ever* and *never*.
Have you ever **met** anyone famous?
Yes, I've **met** Tiger Woods.
I've never **visited** England.

We use the present perfect simple to focus on the experience, not when or where it happened. If we want to give more details, we use the past simple.
I've **met** Tiger Woods.
I **met** him in New York in 2001.

> SEE LANGUAGE REFERENCE PAGE 74

1 What are the infinitives of the past participles in the box?

| done | drunk | driven | earned | eaten | found |
| hated | helped | met | served | spoken | worked |

Put the verbs into two groups: regular and irregular.

regular   *earned*
irregular   *done*

2 Complete the dialogue. Put the verbs in brackets into the past simple or the present perfect simple.

A: _____ you ever _____ (*hear*) of Thomas Mapother IV?
B: No, I _____ (*never / hear*) of him. Who is he?
A: He's an actor. He _____ (*make*) loads of famous films.
B: Well, I _____ (*never / see*) a film with him in it.
A: What about *Mission Impossible*? It was on TV last night. _____ you _____ (*see*) it?
B: Yes, but that _____ (*be*) with Tom Cruise.
A: Ah, but Thomas Mapother IV is Tom Cruise's real name. He _____ (*change*) it before he got famous.

3 Work in pairs. Practise the dialogue.

4 Work in groups. Take it in turns to make questions using the prompts below. If the answer is *yes*, ask more questions to find out the details.

Have you ever driven a sports car?
What kind of car was it?

* drive / a sports car
* eat / in an expensive restaurant
* find / anything interesting in the street
* have / a temporary summer job
* live / in a different town
* lose / your job
* stay / in a five star hotel
* work / in an office
* win / a prize or a competition

5 Now tell the class about the people you spoke to.

Helen and John have both had a summer job, but Helen worked in a restaurant and John worked for his father.

PRONUNCIATION: /æ/ & /ʌ/

1 Underline any six words in the table below.

past simple /æ/	past participle /ʌ/
began	begun
drank	drunk
ran	run
sang	sung
swam	swum

🔘 1.59 Now listen to the recording and tick (✓) the words you hear. When you hear the six words that you have underlined, say *Bingo*.

2 Work in pairs. Say a word from the table in exercise 1. Your partner must say if they hear a verb in the past simple or a past participle.

7B Hard work

VOCABULARY & SPEAKING: verb collocations (work)

1 Put the sentences in the correct place in the diagram.

a You apply for a job.
b ~~You finish your studies~~.
c You get promoted.
d You get the job.
e You go for an interview.
f You go on a training course.

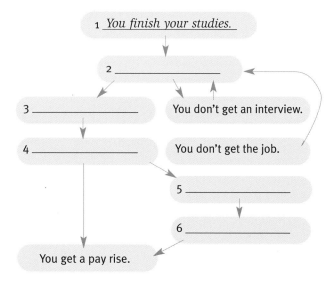

1 *You finish your studies.*

2 _____

3 _____

You don't get an interview.

4 _____

You don't get the job.

5 _____

6 _____

You get a pay rise.

2 Complete the text about Pat Side's experience of work with the verbs in the box.

applied	~~finished~~	got (x2)	had	left
lost	was (x2)	went (x2)		

3 🔘 **2.1** Listen to the recording to check your answers.

4 What kind of work have you done? Describe your own experiences, using the expressions in exercise 1.

READING

1 Read the first paragraph of the magazine article opposite. What do the two women have in common?

2 Read the rest of the article and decide if the sentences are true (T) or false (F).

1 She describes her experience of looking for work.
2 It was difficult to find a job.
3 She had some money problems.
4 She enjoyed her experience.

3 Put the diary extracts a–d into the gaps 1–4 in the article.

a Finally, finally, my unemployment benefit cheque arrived and I went to the post office to cash it. At the same time, I paid the gas and electricity. I've never felt so happy!
b I went for an interview at the Jobcentre today. Mr Mills, my interviewer, gave me application forms for six jobs.
c Tomorrow I return to my old life. My job, my home, my car and no more interviews. This is the hardest four weeks I've ever had and I realize how lucky I am.
I really hope Pat finds a job soon.
d I've done half of the month. I wanted to go out with some friends, but I haven't got enough money.

4 Work in pairs. Discuss these questions.

• What is unemployment benefit (line 17)?
• How much is unemployment benefit in your country?
• Is there an unemployment problem in your country?

Back to Work

When Pat Side's children (1) *finished* their studies and
(2) _____ home, Pat wanted to find a job. She
(3) _____ no qualifications, so she (4) _____ on a training course to become an assistant in a home for retired people. After the course, she (5) _____ for many different jobs. She (6) _____ for a few interviews, but it was six months before she (7) _____ a job. She (8) _____ good at her work and, two years later, she (9) _____ promoted to 'senior assistant'. She also (10) _____ a small pay rise. Unfortunately, the home closed a year after that and Pat (11) _____ her job.

Life on the Other Side

E arlier this year, successful journalist Pat Side was preparing an article about the problems
5 of mothers who want to return to work. By chance, she met another woman who had the same name as her and was the same
10 age. The other Pat Side was unemployed and looking for a job. The two women agreed to exchange lives for four weeks and to write about their experiences.

Day 2 (1) _____

15 **Day 4** Tomorrow, I've got interviews for four different jobs. The salaries are low – more or less the same as my unemployment benefit. But if I don't apply for the jobs, I lose my benefit! It's crazy!

Day 5 I didn't get the jobs. They said I was too old. It's
20 the first time in my new life that I've wanted to cry.

Day 8 Back to the Jobcentre. I waited for three hours to speak to Mr Mills. They said he was in a meeting, but I think he was having a long lunch. He gave me two more application forms …

25 **Day 12** I've never worried about money too much, but today I got two bills in the post. Gas and electricity. I haven't got the money. What am I going to do?

Day 14 (2) _____

Day 15 Another interview today. I didn't have the money
30 for the bus so I walked. Five miles in the cold and rain and I didn't get the job. Chips again for dinner.

Day 16 (3) _____

Day 18 I went for another interview today and took the bus. Surprise, surprise – I didn't get the job. They said I
35 was too qualified.

Day 29 I've filled in seventeen application forms and been to seven interviews, but no success. I begin to think this is all a waste of time.

Day 30 (4) _____

40 *Two weeks after this article was written, Pat Side found a job in a telephone call centre. She enjoys her new work and says that the money is good.*

SPEAKING

1 Imagine that you can exchange your life with the life of someone else for four weeks. Make notes about a typical day in your new life.

2 Work in pairs. Ask and answer questions about your new life.

DID YOU KNOW?

1 Work in pairs. Look at the bar chart comparing different salaries in the United Kingdom and discuss these questions.

- Do you think the differences in salary are fair?
- How would you change the order?
- What is a good salary in your country?
- What are the best and worst paid jobs in your country?

doctor

lawyer

dentist

engineer

accountant

police officer

train driver

Who has the best-paid job?

computer programmer

teacher

social worker

nurse

waiter / waitress

sales assistant

7c | Job selection

READING

1 How often do you read your horoscope? Do you believe what it says?

2 Read the magazine article and choose the best title.

1 Horoscopes are a waste of time
2 Why you should read your horoscope
3 Astrology and the secret police

It's 9 o'clock in the morning and you have already arrived at work. There are a million things to do: check your email, finish something you started yesterday, get ready for that meeting, tidy up your desk … stop, hold it! Have you read your horoscope yet?

or many people, a horoscope is a good way to waste five inutes, but if you haven't looked at your star sign yet, it's ime that you did. Somebody, somewhere has already tudied **your** horoscope and made decisions about **your** uture.

ike it or not, astrology is important. Millions and millions of eople around the world actually believe in it. American residents, the secret police, national football managers and uccessful business people have all used horoscopes in their ork. The great American banker, J P Morgan, once said, illionaires don't use astrology. Billionaires do.'

Every time you write your date of birth on a form (to apply for a job or promotion, for example), somebody, somewhere will probably look at the astrological information it contains. Does this person have the right personality for the job? Will they work well with the other people? How important is work in their life? Is this person a good traveller? How ambitious are they?

So even if you think that horoscopes are a waste of time, it's often interesting to know what other people are thinking about you. Oh, by the way, have you read your boss's star sign yet?

3 The article was badly torn out of the magazine. What is the first word in each line of paragraphs 2 and 3?

4 Read the article again. Complete the sentences with words from the text.

1 Some people think that horoscopes are a _ _ _ _ _ of time.
2 Many different kinds of people _ _ _ _ _ _ _ in astrology.
3 People sometimes make _ _ _ _ _ _ _ _ _ about your future after studying your horoscope.
4 People can get your astrological information when you fill in an _ _ _ _ _ _ _ _ _ _ _ form for a job.
5 They are interested in finding out about your _ _ _ _ _ _ _ _ _ _ _ .

GRAMMAR: present perfect simple with *already* & *yet*

We usually use *already* in positive sentences. We use it to emphasize that something has happened before now (perhaps earlier than expected).
*It is early in the morning, but she has **already** arrived at work.*

We use *yet* in negative sentences and questions. We use it to talk or ask about something that has not happened, but will probably happen soon.
*Have you checked your email **yet**?*
*No, I haven't done it **yet**.*

> SEE LANGUAGE REFERENCE PAGE 74

1 Complete the dialogue with *already* or *yet*.

A: Have you finished _____?
B: No, not _____. Another few minutes, OK?
A: But you've _____ taken two hours!
B: I know, but I haven't really understood the problem _____.
A: I've _____ explained it to you twice!
B: Just give me a few more minutes, OK?

2 Work in pairs. Practice the dialogue.

3 Work in pairs, A and B.

A: Turn to page 131. Look at the *Things to do* list. Ask your partner questions.
Have you … yet?
B: Turn to page 132. Look at the *Things to do* list. Answer your partner's questions.
Yes, I have.   No, I haven't.   No, not yet.

4 Make sentences that are true for you using the prompts. For each sentence, give some extra information.

1 *I haven't finished my studies yet. I'm going to take my final exams next year.*

1 finish my studies
2 find the perfect job
3 meet the love of my life
4 buy my own home
5 travel to lots of different countries

VOCABULARY: adjectives & nouns (personality)

1 What star sign are you? Think of three people you know. What are their star signs?

Now read the star signs for you and for them. Do you agree with the information?

2 Complete the table with words from the horoscope.

definition	adjective	noun
wants to be successful	(1) _____	ambition
shows strong feelings	(2) _____	emotion(s)
can create new ideas	imaginative	(3) _____
does not need other people	(4) _____	independence
can understand things quickly	intelligent	(5) _____
does not mind waiting	patient	(6) _____
has special abilities	skilled	(7) _____
can understand what other people are feeling	(8) _____	sensitivity

SPEAKING

1 Work in groups. Discuss the jobs in the box. Decide which are the most important qualities people need to do these jobs and explain why. Use the words and phrases in the horoscope to help you.

> lawyer   police officer   sales person   teacher

Good police officers are calm people because they often have to deal with dangerous situations.

Now choose the best star sign for each job.

2 Imagine the perfect boss. Describe her/him in eight sentences.

The perfect boss …
… has a lot of patience.
… gives you a bonus every year.

ARIES 21/03 – 20/04
When they stop thinking about themselves, they are excellent managers. Well-organized and with very good people skills, they need to learn a bit more patience.

TAURUS 21/04 – 21/05
Not the most imaginative people in the world, but they are the best people to have near you if you are looking for action. When they do things, they do them well.

GEMINI 22/05 – 21/06
Their independence is important to them and they work better on their own than in a team. Lots of imagination and ideas, but they get bored quickly.

CANCER 22/06 – 23/07
They seem calm and organized, but Cancers have a secret sensitivity. Look after them well, and they will look after you.

LEO 24/07 – 23/08
Strong, patient and skilled, Leos want to be boss – and they often are. They have great ambition, but be careful of them if they do not get what they want.

VIRGO 24/08 – 23/09
They often live for their work and they are not very emotional people. They learn quickly and do not need a lot of help. Calm, but sometimes too calm.

LIBRA 24/09 – 23/10
Librans are a happy balance of many opposites: imagination and hard work, patience and speed. They are liked by other people.

SCORPIO 24/10 – 22/11
Their main strength is their ability to change. With their natural intelligence, they understand situations quickly and know what to do next.

SAGITTARIUS 23/11 – 21/12
Honest and straightforward in the way they work, but when things don't go well, they can get worried. Patient and kind with other people.

CAPRICORN 22/12 – 20/01
Naturally skilled managers, they are independent and strong. They are more sensitive than they seem and they are good listeners.

AQUARIUS 21/01 – 19/02
They like their work and they enjoy working with other people. They do not usually show their emotions. Quite ambitious, but they make good friends.

PISCES 20/02 – 20/03
Intelligent and imaginative, they have good people skills, but they find it difficult to make important decisions.

7D | The recruitment agency

SPEAKING

1 Work in pairs. Discuss these questions.

- What's the best way to find a job? Make a list.
  (For example, go to a recruitment agency)
- Is it easy or difficult to find work in your town?

VOCABULARY: curriculum vitae

1 Look at extracts 1–6 from a CV (curriculum vitae). Match them to the highlighted words or phrases in the recruitment agency advertisement.

(1) ____
1. Mr R. Dailly (college tutor),
   Doncaster University, Box 478B, Doncaster

2. Mrs Mary Whitehead (General Manager),
   Socks Are Us, High Street, Halifax

(2) ____
2002 – 2004 Socks Are Us,
Halifax (Manager)

2000 – 2001 CD Heaven,
Halifax (Assistant Manager)

(3) ____
Alison Peabody
Date of birth: 4th March 1978
Address: 39d, Victoria Road, Halbridge
Tel: 0719 376488
Email: ali.peabody@quickmail.com

(4) ____
2000 DMS (Diploma of Marketing and Sales)
1999 BA Business Studies
1996 Three A levels: English, Business Studies, History

(5) ____
1999–2000 University of Doncaster
1989–1996 Brunel School for Girls, Halifax

(6) ____
Cinema, travel, tennis, eating out

2 Work in pairs. Ask and answer questions using the words and phrases in the advertisement.

Could you tell me about your education?
What qualifications have you got?

Can't find a job?
Want to find a new job?
Looking for a better job?
Not sure what to do?

Sayers Recruitment & Training can help!

Send us a short letter/CV with your personal details and information about your education, qualifications, professional experience and personal interests.
Include the names of two referees.
We can find the right job for you! Speak to one of our experienced career advisers.

For more information, visit our website
www.sayers-rt.com or send your CV to
davinasayers@srt.net

LISTENING

1 🔘 2.2 Listen to a conversation in the SRT recruitment agency. Underline the correct information in the notes below.

Name:	Miss / Ms Ruby Tuesday
Qualifications:	none / MA Philosophy
Interests:	computers / cooking
Ideal job:	selling hamburgers / she doesn't know!

72

2 🔘 **2.2** Listen to the conversation again. Tick (✓) the advice that Davina gives to Ruby.

1 Write a longer CV.
2 Study philosophy.
3 Get a qualification.
4 Improve your appearance.
5 Buy a smart suit.
6 Buy some fashionable earrings.
7 Have a haircut.
8 Arrive for interviews on time.

3 Do you agree with Davina's advice? What would you say to Ruby?

FUNCTIONAL LANGUAGE: advice

Asking for advice
What should I do?
Should I + infinitive ?

Giving advice
You should/shouldn't + infinitive
I (don't) think you should + infinitive
(If I were you,) I'd + infinitive
Why don't you + infinitive … ?
What about + verb + *-ing* … ?

1 Rearrange the words to make questions and sentences that give/ask for advice.

1 go   I   I   or   should   should   stay ?
2 decide   quickly   shouldn't   too   you
3 about   don't   it   think   why   you ?
4 ask   friends   I   should   think   you   your
5 a   get   if   I   I'd   job   new   were   you
6 a   about   agency   going   recruitment   to   what ?

2 Work in pairs. A friend of yours has some problems at work. Give your friend some advice.

1 *Why don't you write him a letter?*
  I think you should speak to his boss!

1 My boss never listens to my ideas.
2 I've got a new job and no one talks to me in the office.
3 I want to take a day off next Friday and I don't want to tell my boss.
4 My boss was angry with me because I was late for the third time this week.
5 I've got too much work to do and I'm feeling really stressed.

Roleplay

3 You are going to ask for some careers advice. Think about your answers to these questions. Make notes if necessary.

- What do you do now?
- What other jobs have you had?
- What qualifications do you have?
- What are you good at? (organizing, working with people, etc)
- What are you interested in? (music, sport, etc)
- What is important for you in a job? (money, travel, working regular hours, etc)
- What kind of job would you most like to do?

4 Work in pairs. Take it in turns to interview each other, using the questions in exercise 4. Give your partner some careers advice.

PRONUNCIATION: email & website addresses

1 🔘 **2.3** Listen to the email and website addresses.

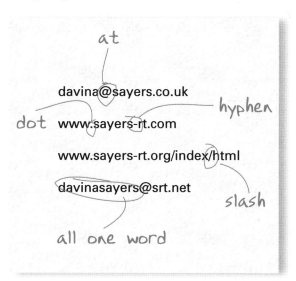

2 Work in pairs, A and B.

A: Turn to page 129.
B: Turn to page 131.

Dictate the addresses to your partner.

3 Write four more email or website addresses and dictate them to your partner.

GRAMMAR

Present perfect simple 1

We use the present perfect simple to talk about general or personal experiences.

> I **have had** many different jobs.

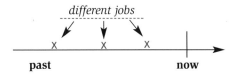

We do not usually refer to a specific time when we use the present perfect simple. We only know that the action (or actions) happened before now.

> I **have visited** many countries. (= in my life)

We use the past simple when we refer to a specific time.

> I **worked** as a waitress **last summer**.

We make the past perfect simple with *have/has* + past participle.

Affirmative & Negative		
I	've haven't	
He/She/It	's hasn't	worked abroad.
You/We/They	've haven't	

Question			
Where	have has have	I he/she/it you/we/they	worked abroad?

Short answer	
Have you worked abroad?	Yes, I have. / No, I haven't.
Has he worked abroad?	Yes, he has. / No, he hasn't.

We use *ever* in questions when we want to ask about a person's life up to the present time.

> **Have** you **ever worked** in a restaurant?
> (= at any time in your life?)

Already & yet

We can use the present perfect simple with *already* and *yet*.

We use *already* in positive sentences and we usually put it before the past participle. We use *already* with completed actions that happen before now or sooner than expected.

> I've **already** found a job.
> She's **already** finished her studies.

We use *yet* in questions and negative sentences and we put it at the end of the sentence. We use *yet* to ask if an action is complete or to say that it is not complete. We use it when we think the action will happen soon.

> Have you read your horoscope **yet**?
> I haven't checked the mailbox **yet**.

See page 104 for more information about the present perfect simple.

FUNCTIONAL LANGUAGE

Asking for advice

What should I do?
Should I + infinitive?

Giving advice

You should + infinitive …
You shouldn't + infinitive …
I (don't) think you should + infinitive …
(If I were you,) I'd (wouldn't) + infinitive …
Why don't you + infinitive?
What about + verb + *-ing*?

WORD LIST

Work

boss *n C* ***	/bɒs/
application form *n C*	/æplɪˈkeɪʃn fɔːm/
apply for *v* ***	/əˈplaɪ fɔː/
be fired (from a job)	/biː ˈfaɪəd/
career *n C* **	/kəˈrɪə/
CV (curriculum vitae) *n C*	/siː viː/
diploma *n C*	/dɪˈpləʊmə/
do (sth) for a living	/duː fɔː ə ˈlɪvɪŋ/
earn *v* **	/ɜːn/
education *n U* ***	/edjʊˈkeɪʃn/
in charge (of sth/sb)	/ɪn tʃɑːdʒ/
interview *n C* **	/ˈɪntəvjuː/
job *n C* ***	/dʒɒb/
office *n C* ***	/ˈɒfɪs/
pay rise *n C*	/ˈpeɪ raɪz/
professional *adj* ***	/prəˈfeʃnəl/
(be/get) promoted	/prəˈməʊtɪd/
promotion *n C/U* *	/prəˈməʊʃn/
qualification *n C* *	/kwɒlɪfɪˈkeɪʃn/
recruitment *n U*	/rɪˈkruːtmənt/
referee *n C*	/refəˈriː/
responsible (for sth) *adj* ***	/rɪˈspɒnsəbl/
retired *adj*	/rɪˈtaɪəd/
salary *n C* *	/ˈsæləri/
temporary *adj* ***	/ˈtemp(ə)rəri/
training *n U* ***	/ˈtreɪnɪŋ/
well-paid *adj*	/wel ˈpeɪd/

Jobs

accountant *n C*	/əˈkaʊntənt/
chauffeur *n C*	/ˈʃəʊfɜː/
computer programmer *n C*	/kəmˈpjuːtə prəʊˈɡræmə/
dentist *n C*	/ˈdentɪst/
doctor *n C* ***	/ˈdɒktə/
engineer *n C* *	/endʒɪˈnɪə/
journalist *n C* **	/ˈdʒɜːnəlɪst/
lawyer *n C* **	/ˈlɔːjə/
manager *n C* **	/ˈmænɪdʒə/
nurse *n C* **	/nɜːs/
police officer *n C*	/pəˈliːs ˈɒfɪsə/
sales assistant *n C*	/ˈseɪlz əˈsɪstənt/
social worker *n C*	/ˈsəʊʃl wɜːkə/
teacher *n C* ***	/ˈtiːtʃə/
train driver *n C*	/ˈtreɪn draɪvə/
waiter *n C*	/ˈweɪtə/
waitress *n C*	/ˈweɪtrəs/

Personality

ambition *n C/U* *	/æmˈbɪʃn/
ambitious *adj*	/æmˈbɪʃəs/
emotion *n C/U* **	/ɪˈməʊʃn/
emotional *adj* **	/ɪˈməʊʃn(ə)l/
honest *adj* **	/ˈɒnɪst/
imagination *n U* *	/ɪmædʒɪˈneɪʃn/
imaginative *adj*	/ɪˈmædʒɪnətɪv/
independence *n U* **	/ɪndɪˈpendəns/
independent *adj* ***	/ɪndɪˈpendənt/
(well) organized *adj* *	/ˈɔːɡənaɪzd/
patience *n U* *	/ˈpeɪʃns/
patient *adj* **	/ˈpeɪʃnt/
sensitive *adj*	/ˈsensətɪv/
sensitivity *n U*	/sensəˈtɪvəti/
skill *n C/U* ***	/skɪl/
skilled *adj*	/skɪld/

Other words & phrases

ability *n C/U* ***	/əˈbɪləti/
adviser *n C* *	/ədˈvaɪzə/
angry *adj* ***	/ˈæŋɡri/
appearance *n U* ***	/əˈpɪərəns/
assistant *adj/n C* **	/əˈsɪst(ə)nt/
astrology *n U*	/əˈstrɒlədʒi/
balance *n U* **	/ˈbæləns/
basic *adj* ***	/ˈbeɪsɪk/
billionaire *n C*	/bɪljəˈneə/
by chance	/baɪ ˈtʃɑːns/
cash *v*	/kæʃ/
celebrity *n C* *	/səˈlebrəti/
cheque *n C* *	/tʃek/
contain *v* ***	/kənˈteɪn/
crazy *adj* **	/ˈkreɪzi/
cute *adj*	/kjuːt/
dot *n C* *	/dɒt/
downtown *adj/adv*	/ˈdaʊntaʊn/
earring *n C*	/ˈɪərɪŋ/
gas *n C/U* ***	/ɡæs/
haircut *n C*	/ˈheəkʌt/
horoscope *n C*	/ˈhɒrəskəʊp/
hyphen *n C*	/ˈhaɪfn/
loads of	/ˈləʊdʒ ɒv/
marketing *n U*	/ˈmɑːkɪtɪŋ/
mile *n C* ***	/maɪl/
millionaire *n C*	/mɪljəˈneə/
movies *n pl*	/ˈmuːvɪz/
natural *adj* ***	/ˈnætʃ(ə)rəl/
naturally *adv* *	/ˈnætʃ(ə)rəli/
philosophy *n U* *	/fɪˈlɒsəfi/
post office *n C*	/ˈpəʊst ɒfɪs/
recently *adv* ***	/ˈriːsntli/
sales *n pl*	/seɪlz/
situation *n C* ***	/sɪtʃuˈeɪʃn/
slash *n C*	/slæʃ/

smart *adj* *	/smɑːt/
star *n C* ***	/stɑː/
star sign *n C*	/ˈstɑː saɪn/
strength *n U***	/streŋθ/
stressed *adj*	/strest/
successful *adj* ***	/səkˈsesfl/
suit *n C* **	/suːt/
team *n C* ***	/tiːm/
tidy (up) *v*	/ˈtaɪdi/
traveller *n C* *	/ˈtræv(ə)lə/
tutor *n C*	/ˈtʃuːtə/
unemployed *adj* *	/ʌnɪmˈplɔɪd/
unemployment benefit *n U*	/ʌnɪmˈplɔɪmənt benɪfɪt/
waste *v* **	/weɪst/
worried *adj* *	/ˈwʌrid/

SPEAKING

1 Work in pairs. Discuss these questions.

• What are the films in the box called in your language?

| Alien | Independence Day | Star Wars |
| Men in Black | Robocop | The Matrix |

• What science fiction films have you seen?
• What happens in them?

In Independence Day, *aliens come to Earth and the President saves the world.*

READING

1 You are going to read about a futurological conference.
(Futurology is the study of the future.)

Look at the titles for the talks. Three of the titles do **not** come from this conference. Put a cross (✗) by these three titles.

a An exciting new theory of time travel
b Armstrong – the first man on the moon
c The world is growing older
d Life in front of the computer screen
e Salyut and Mir – early space stations
f Prisons in space
g Star wars: fact or fiction?
h The advantages of new energy sources
i The end of English lessons?
j The invention of the laser

4TH INTERNATIONAL FUTUROLOGICAL CONFERENCE

22nd–25th May Des Moines, Iowa

CONFERENCE HIGHLIGHTS

1 _____

Dr Judith Amos (author of *Clean New World*)
It might not be long before the sun, the wind and the sea become our main sources of energy. We will live in a cleaner, healthier world. Will it be a safer one, too?

2 _____

Professor J B Gartenberg (University of London)
Research scientists will find cures for most of the world's diseases in the next 50 years. We will all live longer and, by the year 2020, there will be more than one billion people over 60 years old. How will this change our society and how will we pay for the elderly?

3 _____

Randy Oakes (journalist)
The 21st century is the age of the internet. More and more, people are using the internet for business, education, shopping and even to make friends. This talk will explore how internet use will increase in the next 20 years.

4 _____

Duncan Hague (Institute of Sociology)
In the US and the UK, prisons are almost full and crime is increasing every day. Soon, there won't be enough room for all our prisoners. Where will we put them? Space stations may be the answer.

5 _____

Dr Mikhaïl Radvanyi (Lingua Foundation)
Learning a foreign language may soon be a thing of the past. This talk will look at new developments in automatic translation machines.

6 _____

Xavier M Berman (author of *Light Years Away*)
A hundred years ago many scientists said that space travel was impossible. Now they say that we will never be able to travel in time. 'Super string' theory suggests that they might be wrong.

7 _____

Stella May Roche (War on War)
American military scientists are developing new laser technology that may change the world for ever. Laser guns on military satellites will be unstoppable and the future for the smaller countries of the world is extremely frightening.

2 Now read about the conference talks. Match the titles a–j in exercise 1 to the descriptions 1–7.

3 Complete the sentences with words from the box.

> cures   energy   satellites   source   technology   theory

1 The sun is the most important _____ of light for our planet.
2 At the moment, most of our _____ comes from oil.
3 We will need to find _____ for new diseases.
4 Gödel's _____ of time travel says that we will need to travel faster than the speed of light.
5 American military _____ is becoming more and more advanced.
6 _____ in space carry many different kinds of equipment.

4 Which of the talks at the conference would you like to go to? Why?

I'd like to go to the talk by Judith Amos because I'm interested in green politics.

GRAMMAR: predictions 1 (*may, might & will*)

> We can use *will/won't* + infinitive to talk about things we are sure will happen in the future.
> *There **will be** more than 1 billion people over 60 years old.*
> *We **won't be** able to travel in time.*
>
> We can use *may/might* + infinitive when we are less sure things will happen in the future.
> *The world **may become** more dangerous.*
> *Scientists **might find** life on other planets.*
>
> | sure | not sure | sure |
> |---|---|---|
> | ⟵ | | ⟶ |
> | *will* | *may/might* | *won't* |
>
> ⓘ SEE LANGUAGE REFERENCE PAGE 84

1 Correct the mistakes in the sentences.

1 I think that our teacher wills give us a test next week.
2 I may be go to America soon.
3 I may not to get married.
4 I think my country might wins the next World Cup.
5 I'll always remembering the people in this class.
6 I think that it will rains tomorrow.
7 I'll never living in another country.
8 I won't to become rich or famous.

2 Change the sentences in exercise 1 so that they are true for you.

3 How will life be different for you/your family:

• in one year's time?
• in ten years' time?

Work in pairs. Talk about the topics in the box.

> appearance   home   money   work

PRONUNCIATION: contractions 2

1 🔘 2.4 Listen to these contractions and repeat.

I'll   it'll   there'll   we'll   what'll   you'll

2 Match a phrase in column A with a response in column B.

A		B	
1	Aren't you ready yet? Hurry up!	a	I'll be OK.
2	Be careful – it's very dangerous.	b	I won't be long.
3	I wonder where they are.	c	You'll like it.
4	Let's have a drink before the film starts.	d	We'll be late.
5	What's this? I've never eaten that before.	e	They'll be here soon.

3 🔘 2.5 Listen to the recording to check your answers.

4 Work in pairs. Practise the exchanges in exercise 2.

SPEAKING

1 🔘 2.6–2.9 Listen to four people speaking. Match the speakers 1–4 to the topics a–j below.

The future of:
a computers   f medicine
b crime   g my country
c education   h restaurants
d holidays   i shops
e languages   j space travel

2 Choose a topic from the list. You must talk about the topic for thirty seconds without stopping. Before you speak, spend some time preparing what you are going to say.

8B | Space tourists

LISTENING

1 You are going to listen to a radio programme.
All the words in the box appear in the programme.
What do you think it is about?

blast off	contestant	game show
museum	rocket	tourist

2 🌐 2.10 Now listen to check your answers.

3 🌐 2.10 Listen again and answer the questions.

1 How many space tourists have there been?
2 How much did they pay to go into space?
3 Who is organizing the new game show?
4 What countries will the contestants come from?
5 Where will the game show be filmed?
6 What is the prize?
7 Will the winner visit the International Space
Station?
8 Who thinks that space tourism is too dangerous?

4 Would you like to go into space? Why or why not?

VOCABULARY: compound nouns with numbers

1 Look at tapescript 2.10 on page 141 and find these
phrases. Which phrase is correct?

1 20-million dollar cheque / 20-million dollars
cheque
2 thirteen-part show / thirteen-parts show
3 eight-day trip / eight-days trip

2 Match the words from column A with the words
from column B to complete the sentences.

A	B
eight-hour	break
five-star	course
million-dollar	day
ten-minute	hotel
20-euro	house
two-week	note

1 He went to England for a _____ in business
English.
2 Have you got change for a _____?
3 I've never stayed in a _____.
4 Let's stop for a _____ and a cup of coffee.
5 I usually work an _____ but sometimes I do more.
6 She lives in a _____ in the Hollywood Hills.

GRAMMAR: predictions 2 (*maybe, probably, certainly,* etc)

> We can use words like *possibly* and *perhaps* to make our predictions sound more or less probable.
>
> 100%
>
> ⟶
>
> *maybe*   *probably*   *certainly*
> *perhaps*   *definitely*
> *possibly*
>
> We usually put *maybe* and *perhaps* at the beginning of the sentence.
> **Perhaps** *a pop star will be the next space tourist.*
>
> *Possibly, probably, certainly* and *definitely* come after *will* in positive sentences and before *won't* in negative sentences.
> *The contestants will* **certainly** *need to be very fit.*
> *The winner* **possibly** *won't visit the space station.*
>
> ❯ SEE LANGUAGE REFERENCE PAGE 84

1 Put the words in brackets into the correct place in the sentences.

1 We won't discover life on other planets. (*probably*)
2 China will be the first country to land a person on Mars. (*possibly*)
3 Ordinary people won't be able to travel in space for a very long time. (*definitely*)
4 There will be hotels in space in the next twenty years. (*perhaps*)
5 Engineers will build factories in space. (*certainly*)
6 We will stop spending money on space exploration. (*maybe*)

Do you agree with the sentences above?

2 Choose one of the questions below for a class survey. Ask the other students in the class what they think. Use the words in the box in your answers.

definitely	probably	possibly	definitely not

1 Will you ever speak very good English?
2 Will you ever be in trouble with the police?
3 Will you lose your teeth or your hair?
4 Will you have more than five children?
5 Will you live to be 100?

3 Tell the rest of the class the results of your survey in exercise 2.

SPEAKING

1 Think of someone you know who would be a good contestant for *Star Quest*. Why would they be good? Make notes about the following:

- their personality
- their practical skills
- their appearance and health
- other reasons

2 Work in groups. Take it in turns to describe your person. Then decide as a group who is the best person to go on the game show.

PRONUNCIATION: word stress 2

1 <u>Underline</u> the word in each group that has a different stress pattern.

1	certainly	energy	probably	<u>unhappy</u>
2	businessman	engineer	president	scientist
3	dangerous	internet	invention	satellite
4	advantage	computer	conference	contestant
5	equipment	exciting	possible	remember

2 🔘 **2.11** Listen to the recording to check your answers.

8c | Help!

SPEAKING

1 Work in pairs. Ask and answer these questions.

- Do you have a computer at home?
- What do you use it for?
- Are you connected to the internet?
- How often do you use the internet?
- What do you do online?

VOCABULARY: computer actions

1 Label the computer icons A–L with words from the box.

attach	close	copy	cursor	delete	find
open	paste	print	save	send	undo

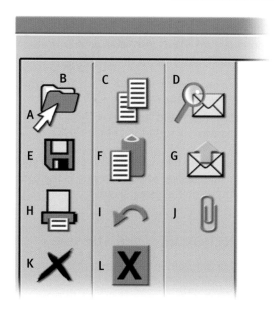

2 Use the words in exercise 1 to complete the sentences.

1 Before you _____ an email, you need to connect to the internet.
2 Do you want to _____ this in colour or black and white?
3 If you make a mistake, you can always _____ it.
4 It's very easy to _____ a picture into a document.
5 Move the _____ to the 'Open document' icon and click on it.
6 Please _____ your CV to your application form.
7 Use a disk or a CD to _____ the work you have done.

LISTENING

1 🔘 **2.12** Listen to a conversation between Mademoiselle Lajolie and Bella. Answer the questions.

- What does Mademoiselle Lajolie want to do?
- Why?

2 🔘 **2.12** Listen to the conversation again and put the instructions for sending an email in the correct order.

☐ Attach your document to the message.
☐ Click on the email icon.
☐ Connect to the internet.
☐ Click on 'Write Mail'.
☐ Log off.
☐ Send the message.
☐ Type the address.
☐ Write your message.

3 Is the order of the instructions the same for your computer? If not, how is it different?

FUNCTIONAL LANGUAGE: giving instructions

We give instructions with:
1 *you* + present simple
   You type *your address there.*

2 the imperative form
   Click *on that button.* **Don't do** *that.*

We can make the order of the instructions easier to understand with sequencing adverbs.

First of all, … Then, …/After that, … Next, …/Afterwards, … Finally, …

1 Look at tapescript 2.12 on page 141. <u>Underline</u> all the instructions and sequencing adverbs.

2 Put the instructions in the correct order.

Checking your English spelling

☐ add it to the languages on the right. You will now
☐ and find 'Tools'. Then, select
☐ be able to use the spell check programme in
☐ English on your computer.
☐ First of all, you click on 'Start' at the bottom of your
☐ 'Language Settings'. Finally, find 'English' and
☐ screen. After that, you click on the 'Programmes' arrow

3 Work in pairs. A friend is writing an essay and wants to find a different word for *world*. Look at the pictures and give her/him instructions.

1 First of all, highlight the word that you want to change.

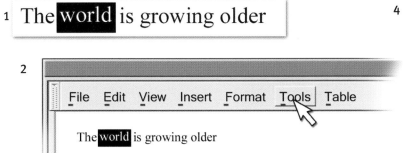

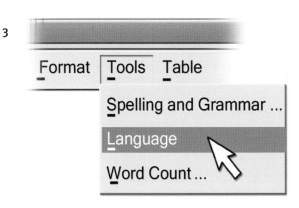

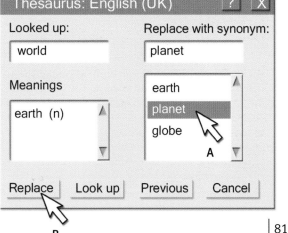

DID YOU KNOW?

1 Read the information about computer games in the US. Do you think the facts are the same or different for your country?

- Half of all Americans over the age of six play computer games.
- More than half of these people are over eighteen. The average age is 29.
- 60% are men and 40% are women.
- Every year, Americans buy more than 200 million computer games.
- Some people play games on their own but more than 60% play with their friends.

2 Work in pairs. Ask and answer these questions.

- What are the most popular computer games in your country?
- Have you ever played any computer games? Which ones? How do the games work?

8D | Great ideas

LISTENING & SPEAKING

1 🔘 2.13–2.17 Listen to the recording and match the descriptions 1–5 to the gadgets A–E opposite.

2 Work in pairs. Discuss these questions.

- Which of these gadgets would you like to buy? For who?
- Which of these will sell the most? Put the gadgets in order (1 = best seller → 5 = worst seller).

strangethings

Go To: http://www.strangethings.com

strangethings.com
strange things for interesting people...

New gadgets

A UV Cipher

B Aurora mood clock

C Walking hand

D Water dispenser

E Glowrings

Click here to see our full catalogue.

A Great Idea?

Ash Sharma, a second–year Business Studies student at Thames Valley University, thinks he has found a good way to make money. He needs £5,000 to get his idea off the ground, but his father has refused to help. What do you think? Read both sides of the story and decide for yourself.

My idea is very simple, really. I already have a small website called businessessays.com (1) _____. Business students at university log on to the site and download essays. They have an essay to write for homework, for example, but they need some help with it. On the site, they find the essay they need, download it (2) _____. At the moment, the site is free but if I can improve it, that will change.

I want to make the site much bigger and my idea is to make it really international. I have found some software that can translate the essays into sixteen different languages. It will be easy to use for people from all round the world. I need about two months to do all the programming (3) _____. When everything is ready, people will pay $2.99 a month to use my service. If it's successful, I will be able to sell advertising, too.

Of course, I can't continue with my university studies and set up the site at the same time. And if I wait, someone else will take my idea (4) _____.

I would like to help my son, but my wife and I agree that it is not a good idea to lend him £5,000 now. There are two main reasons for our decision. My son has an interesting idea (5) _____. Will his idea work? At the moment, it's impossible to say. Are there any other websites that offer a similar service? How successful are these other sites? How many customers will he need before he starts to make money? If the site is successful, will he need to employ other people? How many? How much will he pay his staff (6) _____? And finally – is it legal to help students with their homework? When he has a business plan and when he has the answers to these questions, I will think again.

We also think that it is important for our son to finish his university studies before he starts this website. If he leaves now, it will be too risky. What will happen to him if his idea doesn't work? He will find himself with no job and no qualification, (7) _____, he will find it is difficult to get a good job. There are some things in life that we must wait for (8) _____. After he finishes his studies, we will talk about his idea again.

READING

1 Read the magazine article and answer the questions.

1 How does Ash think that he can make money?
2 Why does Ash want to leave university?
3 Why doesn't Ash's father want to help him?

2 Read the article again and put the phrases a–h into the gaps 1–8.

a and Ash is still very young
b and I need money to buy the software
c and if he does not have a qualification
d and it is very successful
e and it will be too late
f and use it for their work
g and who will look after the finances
h but he does not have a business plan

3 Work in pairs. Discuss these questions.

• Is the website a good idea?
• Is Ash's father right to refuse to lend him the money?
• Is it wrong to download essays from the internet?

VOCABULARY: adjectives with infinitives

1 Complete these sentences with an infinitive from the box.

to finish	to get	to help	to say	to use

1 It will be easy _____ the new website.
2 It is impossible _____ if Ash's idea will work.
3 Is it legal _____ students with their homework?
4 It's important for my son _____ his studies.
5 It's difficult _____ a good job without a qualification.

Look at the article again to check your answers.

2 How many different sentences can you make from the table?

		easy	to be
		possible	to drink
		usual	to find
		legal	to have
It	is	dangerous	to meet
	will be	healthy	to see
	used to be	difficult	to begin
		impossible	to eat
		unusual	to get
		illegal	to make
		safe	to say
		unhealthy	to stop

(… in the rightmost column)

GRAMMAR: present tense in future time clauses

When we are talking about future time in clauses with *if, when, after* and *before*, we use the present tense. We can use *will* in the main clause of the sentence.

subsidiary clause	main clause
If it's successful,	I will be able to sell advertising.
When everything is ready,	people will pay $2.99
After he finishes his studies,	we will talk about his idea again.

The subsidiary clause can also come after the main clause.
*I will be able to sell advertising **if it's successful**.*

 SEE LANGUAGE REFERENCE PAGE 84

1 Complete the text. Put the verbs in brackets into the correct tense. Use *will* or present simple.

A modelling agency has offered a job in Japan to a sixteen-year-old English school student, Emily. She has decided to take the job. 'If I (1) ____ (*not take*) the job, I (2) ____ (*not get*) the chance again,' she said. Before she (3) ____ (*go*), she (4) ____ (*have*) a big party for all her friends. 'I'm so excited,' she said. 'When I (5) ____ (*say*) goodbye to my boyfriend at the airport, I (6) ____ (*be*) very sad. But after I (7) ____ (*arrive*) in Japan, everything (8) ____ (*be*) OK.'
If she (9) ____ (*be*) successful, the agency (10) ____ (*give*) her more work. 'I've never done this before,' she said, 'but I'm sure I (11) ____ (*be*) good at it when I (12) ____ (*have*) a little experience.'

2 Emily's boyfriend does not want her to go. He thinks she will have problems. Make sentences from the prompts.

1 When she arrives, she won't speak the language.

1 When / arrive / not speak the language
2 If / not speak the language / not make friends
3 If / not make friends / feel very lonely
4 If / feel very lonely / want to come home
5 When / come home / not have any qualifications

3 Can you think of any other possible problems that Emily will have? Make sentences with *if, when, before* or *after*.

4 Complete the sentences so that they are true for you.

1 If I don't go out this weekend, I ….
2 I … when I have enough money.
3 After I leave the school today, I …
4 I … before I am 65.

GRAMMAR

Predictions

Modal verbs (*may, might & will*)

We can use *will* + infinitive to talk about things we are sure *will* happen in the future.

> Most people **will live** in cities, not in the country.
> I **will** never **be** famous.
> We **won't win** the match next weekend.

We can also begin the sentence with *I think/don't think/hope/expect*.

> **I think** (that) they **will get** married.

We can use *may/might* + infinitive when we are less sure that things will happen in the future.

> Scientists **may find** a cure for cancer.
> I **might go** to New Zealand for my holidays.

sure	not sure	sure
will	may/might	won't

Adverbs (*maybe, probably, certainly,* etc)

We can use adverbs like *perhaps* and *probably* to make our predictions sound more or less certain.

100%

maybe	probably	certainly
perhaps		definitely
possibly		

We usually put *maybe* and *perhaps* at the beginning of the sentence.

> **Perhaps** you'll pass all your exams and become a doctor.

We put *possibly, probably, certainly* and *definitely* after *will* in positive sentences and before *won't* in negative sentences.

> I **will probably** pass my exams.
> The winner **certainly won't** need to work again.

Present tense in future time clauses

All sentences have a main clause. We can use *will* + infinitive to talk about future time in a main clause.

Sometimes, we also need a subsidiary clause to give information about the time of an action. These clauses can begin with *if, when, after* and *before*. When we want to talk about future time in the subsidiary clause, we use a present tense. We do not use *will* in these subsidiary clauses.

subsidiary clause	main clause
When he has a business plan,	his parents will think again.
After he improves the site,	people will pay for the service.
If his idea doesn't work,	what will happen to him?

We usually separate the two clauses with a comma.

We can also put the subsidiary clause after the main clause. In this case, we do not usually separate the two clauses with a comma.

> What will happen to him if his idea doesn't work?

FUNCTIONAL LANGUAGE

Giving instructions

We can give instructions with *you* + present simple.

> You highlight the word, then **you click** the spell check icon.

We can also use the imperative form.

> **Save** your work before you log off.
> **Don't press** that button!

We can make the order of the instructions easier to understand with sequencing adverbs.

First, …
First of all, …

Then, …
Next, …
After that, …
Afterwards, …

Finally, …

> **First of all**, find the document you want. **Then** attach it to the email. **Finally**, press 'send'.

WORD LIST

Compound nouns with numbers

When we make compound nouns that include numbers, the middle noun is singular.

20-million **dolla**r cheque	/twenti 'mɪljən dɒlə tʃek/
thirteen-**part** show	/θɜːtiːn 'paːt ʃəʊ/
eight-**day** trip	/eɪt 'deɪ trɪp/

Computer actions

arrow n C	/ærəʊ/
attach v *	/ə'tætʃ/
button n C **	/bʌtn/
click n C/v	/klɪk/
connect v ***	/kə'nekt/
copy v **	/kɒpi/
cursor n C	/kɜːsə/
delete v	/dɪ'liːt/
disk n C	/dɪsk/
document n C ***	/dɒkjʊmənt/
download n C/v	/daʊnləʊd/
edit v	/edɪt/
format n U/v *	/fɔːmæt/
highlight v *	/haɪlaɪt/
icon n C	/aɪkɒn/
insert v	/ɪn'sɜːt/
log off v	/lɒg 'ɒf/
log on v	/lɒg 'ɒn/
look up v	/lʊk 'ʌp/
message n C ***	/mesɪdʒ/
paste v	/peɪst/
print n C/v **	/prɪnt/
programme n C/v ***	/prəʊgræm/
replace v ***	/rɪ'pleɪs/
save v ***	/seɪv/
screen n C **	/skriːn/
select v ***	/sɪ'lekt/
site n C ***	/saɪt/
software n U ***	/sɒftweə/
synonym n C	/sɪnənɪm/
table n C	/teɪbl/
thesaurus n C	/θɪ'sɔːrəs/
tool n C **	/tuːl/
type v	/taɪp/
undo v	/ʌn'duː/

Adjectives with infinitives

dangerous ***	/deɪndʒərəs/
difficult ***	/dɪfɪklt/
easy **	/iːzi/
healthy **	/helθi/
illegal **	/ɪ'liːgl/
impossible ***	/ɪm'pɒsəbl/
legal ***	/liːgl/
possible ***	/pɒsəbl/
safe ***	/seɪf/
unhealthy	/ʌn'helθi/
unusual **	/ʌn'juːʒʊəl/
usual ***	/juːʒʊəl/

Other words & phrases

advanced adj *	/əd'vaːnst/
airport n C ***	/eəpɔːt/
alien n C/adj	/eɪliən/
automatic adj *	/ɔːtə'mætɪk/
blast off v	/blaːst 'ɒf/
brilliant adj *	/brɪljənt/
businessman n C	/bɪznəsmæn/
consortium n C	/kən'sɔːtiəm/
contestant n C	/kən'testənt/
crew n C **	/kruː/
cure n C *	/kjʊə/
development n C ***	/dɪ'veləpmənt/
disease n C ***	/dɪ'ziːz/
earth n sing ***	/ɜːθ/
elderly adj **	/eldəli/
energy n U ***	/enədʒi/
equipment n U ***	/ɪ'kwɪpmənt/
essay n C *	/eseɪ/
exploration n U	/eksplə'reɪʃn/
fact n C ***	/fækt/
fiction n U **	/fɪkʃn/
film v	/fɪlm/
finances n pl	/faɪnænsɪz/
foreign adj ***	/fɒrɪn/
freaky adj	/friːki/
frightening adj *	/fraɪtnɪŋ/
game show n C	/geɪm ʃəʊ/
grow v ***	/grəʊ/
hill n C ***	/hɪl/
increase v ***	/ɪn'kriːs/
invention n C *	/ɪn'venʃn/
invisible adj	/ɪn'vɪsəbl/
knowledge n U ***	/nɒlɪdʒ/
laser n C	/leɪzə/
lend v ***	/lend/
litre n C	/liːtə/
luck n U **	/lʌk/
machine n C ***	/mə'ʃiːn/
matrix n C	/meɪtrɪks/
medicine n U **	/medsn/

military adj **	/mɪlɪt(ə)ri/
modelling n U	/mɒdlɪŋ/
moon n C **	/muːn/
museum n C ***	/mjuː'ziːəm/
offer v ***	/ɒfə/
oil n U ***	/ɔɪl/
permission n U **	/pə'mɪʃn/
planet n C *	/plænɪt/
prisoner n C ***	/prɪznə/
product n C ***	/prɒdʌkt/
quest n C	/kwest/
refuse v ***	/rɪ'fjuːz/
risky adj	/rɪski/
rocket n C	/rɒkɪt/
satellite n **	/sætəlaɪt/
science fiction n U	/saɪəns 'fɪkʃn/
scientist n C **	/saɪəntɪst/
similar adj ***	/sɪmɪlə/
society n U ***	/sə'saɪəti/
source n C **	/sɔːs/
space n U ***	/speɪs/
space ship n C	/speɪs ʃɪp/
space station n C	/speɪs steɪʃn/
suggest v ***	/sə'dʒest/
survey n C **	/sɜːveɪ/
talk n C ***	/tɔːk/
text n C ***	/tekst/
theory n C **	/θɪəri/
thirsty adj *	/θɜːsti/
title n C ***	/taɪtl/
translation n C/U *	/trænz'leɪʃn/
trip n C **	/trɪp/
ultraviolet adj	/ʌltrə 'vaɪələt/
unstoppable adj	/ʌn'stɒpəbl/
war n C ***	/wɔː/
wind n U ***	/wɪnd/

9A | What's on

SPEAKING & LISTENING

1 Look at the events below. Think of one person you know who would like to go to each event.

Work in pairs. Tell your partner about the people you have thought of. What other things do these people like doing?

What's on

Ⓐ The Moscow State Circus
Victoria Park
Tues to Sun 7.30pm

Ⓑ Camille Pissarro in London
Paintings of London by the French impressionist
National Gallery, Trafalgar Square
Daily 10am–6pm

Ⓒ Dance Crazy
A exciting afternoon of international dance from Spain, France and Switzerland
Canary Wharf
Saturday 1–5pm

Ⓓ Verdi's Requiem
Verdi's masterpiece conducted by Patrick Davin
Royal Albert Hall
Friday 7.30pm

Ⓔ Mega DJ Battle
Top DJs play house, techno, R & B, hip hop and a special Brazilian tech-funk session
Downstairs at The Sound Barrier, Oxford Street
Saturdays 10pm–2am

Ⓕ Fame – the Musical
Aldwych Theatre
Mon–Sat 7.30pm,
also Sat 3pm

Ⓖ Robbie Williams
Wembley Arena
Thursday, Friday, Saturday
7.30pm

2 🔘 2.18 Listen to part of a radio programme. Put the events in exercise 1 in the order that they are mentioned.

☐ The Moscow State Circus
☐ Camille Pissaro in London
☐ Dance Crazy
☐ Verdi's Requiem
☐ Mega DJ Battle
☐ Fame – the Musical
☐ Robbie Williams

3 🔘 2.18 Listen to the programme again. The reporter makes five mistakes. Underline the information in the events that is different from the information on the programme.

> **Ⓖ Robbie Williams**
> Wembley Arena
> <u>Thursday</u>, Friday, Saturday
> 7.30pm

4 Match the events in column A with the adjectives that the reporter uses in column B.

A		B	
1	The Moscow State Circus	a	cool
2	Camille Pissarro in London	b	depressing
3	Dance Crazy	c	enjoyable
4	Verdi's Requiem	d	exciting
5	Mega DJ Battle	e	fantastic
6	Fame – the Musical	f	fascinating
7	Robbie Williams	g	fun

5 Look at tapescript 2.18 on page 142 to check your answers. Do you agree with the reporter's adjectives?

6 Work in pairs. Imagine you are in London. Ask and answer these questions.

- Which of these events would you like to go to?
- What other things would you like to do in London?
- What kinds of entertainment are available in your town?
- What is on at the moment?

VOCABULARY: *-ing* & *-ed* adjectives

1 In the sentences below, which adjective describes how the speaker feels? Which adjective describes the thing that makes her/him feel this way?

1 I think that kind of music is really *relaxing*.
2 That kind of music makes me really *relaxed*.

2 Complete the dialogues with the correct word.

1 A: I'm so *exciting / excited*. I've got tickets for the Robbie Williams concert.
  B: Robbie Williams? I think his music is old-fashioned and *boring / bored*.
2 A: I'm really *tiring / tired*. I didn't get home until three o'clock this morning.
  B: I know. And it was extremely *annoying / annoyed* that you came home singing!
3 A: I think this music is really *relaxing / relaxed*.
  B: Really? It makes me feel *depressing / depressed*.
4 A: The concert was a bit *disappointing / disappointed*, wasn't it?
  B: Yes, I was *surprising / surprised*. Celine Dion is usually so good.

3 🔘 2.19 Listen to the recording to check your answers. Work in pairs and practise the dialogues.

4 Complete the sentences so that they are true for you.

1 I find … quite frightening.
2 I sometimes feel depressed when …
3 I think that … is/are really fascinating.
4 … is the most boring place in the world.
5 I usually feel relaxed when …
6 I was disappointed when …

PRONUNCIATION: diphthongs

1 Put the words in the box in the correct place in the table.

~~don't~~	down	fame	find	go	home	house	kind
most	out	place	quite	show	sound	Spain	state
stay	time	town	twice				

night /aɪ/	**know** /əʊ/	**now** /aʊ/	**name** /eɪ/
	don't		

2 🔘 2.20 Listen to the recording to check your answers.

3 Think of two other words for each column.

DID YOU KNOW?

1 When people in Britain go out, what do they do? Here is a list, in order, of the most popular activities.

1 going to a pub
2 going for a meal in a restaurant
3 going to a library
4 going to the cinema
5 visiting a historic building
6 going to a disco or nightclub
7 going to a museum or art gallery

2 Work in pairs. Discuss these questions.

• What are the favourite leisure activities of people in your country?
• What about you? What do you like doing?
• Are you typical of the people in your country?

9B | Reality TV

VOCABULARY: TV programmes

1 Match the types of TV programmes in the box to a programme description.

> chat show   current affairs programme
> documentary   game show   sitcom
> soap opera   sports programme

The Wheel of Fortune (1) _____
The winner takes the jackpot prize of $500,000.

Bill Zucker Presents (2) _____
Bill's guests this week are Hollywood legend, Al Pacino and British designer Stella McCartney.

Friends (3) _____
More laughs in tonight's episode as Chandler and Joey look after baby Ben, but leave him on the bus. When they get him back, have they got the right baby? (repeat from second series)

Match of the Day (4) _____
All the goals from today's World Cup games plus news of today's play at Wimbledon.

Eastenders (5) _____
Problems in Walford. Alfie is not welcome at Kat's wedding, but she still loves him. Can he stop the wedding in time?

Horizon (6) _____
Prize-winning film about the life of an urban kangaroo.

Newsbrief (7) _____
An in-depth look at what is happening in the world this week.

2 Describe examples of the different kinds of TV programmes in your country.

3 Work in pairs. Ask and answer these questions.

- Which of these kinds of programmes do you like to watch? Why?
- What are your favourite programmes on TV?
- Are there too many programmes of one kind on TV?

READING

1 Read the article below. Match the paragraphs 1–3 to the descriptions a–e. There are two descriptions that you do **not** need.

a Why people like reality TV
b The beginnings of reality TV
c The end of reality TV
d Making money from reality TV
e Problems with reality TV

Reality TV – love it or leave it

Pop Idol, UK

1 The first reality TV show in the world was called Expedition Robinson and it was shown in Sweden in 1997. Half the population of the country watched the final episode and a new kind of TV programme was born. Two years later in Holland, the first series of Big Brother was filmed. Again, it was a fantastic success and the final programme was watched by 15 million people. There are now more than 20 countries around the world which have Big Brother or Survivor (Expedition Robinson) on their TV screens. The ordinary people who take part in the programmes are known by millions of people in their own countries and reality TV has become big, big business.

2 For the TV producers, reality TV is a dream come true because many of the programmes cost nothing to make. At some point, the television viewers are asked to telephone the programme – to vote or to apply to take part in the show. It is the cost of these telephone calls that pays for the shows. One of the most popular shows is Pop Idol (the programme is called different things in different countries). In the show, a group of attractive young people are made into pop stars. TV viewers vote for their favourite person on the show. The winner makes a record, his or her pictures are published on the covers of magazines, millions of copies of the record are sold and then ... they are quickly forgotten.

3 But not everyone is happy about reality TV. In Portugal, two TV channels got into trouble because they showed too much of the private lives of the people in the shows. In France, reality TV is called 'rubbish TV' and the studios of Loft Story (Big Brother) were attacked three times in one week. In Greece, Big Brother was described as 'an insult to human rights and civilization'. But despite the problems, reality TV continues to do well in most countries and it will be here for some time to come.

2 Read the article again and tick (✓) the things that are mentioned in the text.

1 Reality TV started in Sweden.
2 The prize money for *Survivor* is $1 million.
3 Many countries have reality TV shows.
4 Some people get married after being on a reality TV show.
5 In the UK, *Big Brother* is more popular than *Survivor*.
6 Reality TV makes money when the viewers make phone calls.
7 *Loft Story* and *Pop Idol* are the names of reality TV shows.
8 *Loft Story* has been very successful in France.

3 Which reality TV shows are popular in your country? Do you like reality TV shows? Why or why not?

GRAMMAR: passive

In a normal (active) sentence, we put the agent (the person or thing that does the action) before the verb.

    agent verb
The viewers vote for their favourite programme.

But sometimes:
1 we do not know the agent of the action.
2 the agent is not important.
3 the agent is obvious.
In these cases we can use the passive.

We form the passive with *to be* + past participle.
*The viewers **are asked** to call the programme.* (present simple)
*The studios of Loft Story **were attacked**.* (past simple)

⊙ SEE LANGUAGE REFERENCE PAGE 94

1 Find three examples of the passive form in paragraph 3 of the article.

2 Complete the text with the passive form of the verbs in the box.

| allow | choose | film | give | invite | send | show | teach |

Star Academy
Thousands of young people apply to take part in this programme. They send video tapes to the producers and a group of them (1) *are chosen* to take part. During the series, they live in a castle, where they (2) _____ to sing and dance. They (3) _____ not _____ to speak to their friends or family and every moment of their life in the castle (4) _____. Their lives (5) _____ on TV every evening and, on Saturday, there is a special show. A famous TV star 6) _____ on the show and one of the contestants sings a song with him or her. At the end of the programme, there is a vote and one person (7) _____ home. At the end of the series, the winner is (8) _____ a contract to make an album.

3 🔊 2.21 Listen to the recording to check your answers.

4 Choose the correct verb form to complete the sentences.

For Love or Money
1 This programme *showed / was shown* on American TV for the first time in 2003.
2 In this programme, fifteen women *tried / were tried* to win the heart of a rich young man.
3 In the first episode, the women *learnt / were learnt* that there was also a prize of $1 million.
4 The women *told / were told* to keep the prize a secret from the young man.
5 The man and the women *took / were taken* to different Californian cities to go out on dates.
6 At the end of each week, one woman *left / was left* in the show.
7 In the final show, the last woman *told / was told* she must choose between the man and the money.

5 Think of a reality TV programme that you know. Complete the sentences below to describe the programme.

The contestants are The winner is The programme is	taken given asked shown filmed invited not allowed sent

SPEAKING

1 Work in groups. You are going to plan your own reality TV show. Use these questions to help you.

- What do the people on the show do?
- Where is the show filmed?
- What is the show called?
- How many people take part?
- What sort of people?
- Are there any famous people in the show?
- How is the winner decided?
- What is the prize?

2 You all work for a TV company. Take it in turns to sell your show to the other groups. Then, as a class vote for the best idea.

9c | Oscars and raspberries

SPEAKING

1 Work in pairs. Ask and answer these questions.

- How often do you go to the cinema?
- When was the last time you went?
- Who did you go with?
- What did you see?
- What did you think of the film?

VOCABULARY: films

1 Read the information about *Titanic* below and find words or phrases that match these definitions.

1 clothes that are worn in a film
2 music that is played during a film
3 takes place
4 the main actors are
5 the person in charge of making a film
6 unusual images that are made for a film

TITANIC

Written and directed by James Cameron, *Titanic* is set on the great cruise ship that hit an iceberg and sank in 1912.
It stars Kate Winslet and Leonardo DiCaprio. One of the most successful films of all time.

Titanic won 11 Oscars including:

BEST FILM • BEST DIRECTOR
BEST SOUNDTRACK • BEST SPECIAL EFFECTS
BEST COSTUMES

2 Work in pairs. Discuss these questions.

- Which films can you see at the cinema at the moment in your town?
- What do you know about the stars, the director, the soundtrack, the setting and the story of these films?

READING

1 Read the magazine article and explain the connection between Oscars and raspberries.

Oscars night

Channel 1
22.00 This year's Razzies
22.30 This year's Oscar nominees
23.30 The stars arrive
24.00 The Oscars ceremony – live

1 Tonight is the night that all Hollywood is waiting for. The stars are wearing their best designer clothes and some of them are thinking about the speech they are hoping to make later. The limousines
5 arrive at the red-carpeted entrance to the luxury Kodak Theatre and the stars are photographed by hundreds of hungry paparazzi. There are thousands in the audience, and the ceremony is watched by millions of TV viewers around the world. The winners are instant celebrities and they will earn mega-bucks with
10 more ticket sales and new contracts. Yes, folks, it's Oscars time.

The Academy Awards started back in 1929 and the first ceremony was attended by 250 people, who paid $10 for a dinner ticket. The winners' names were published by the newspapers earlier that evening, so there were no surprises. Two years later, a librarian at the American Academy of Motion
15 Picture Arts and Sciences said that the statue awards looked like her Uncle Oscar. The Academy Awards became Oscars and now, over 75 years later, TV companies pay more than $20 million for the rights to the show. For the advertisers and designers, the record companies and the film studios, for the investors and businessmen, and for the stars themselves, the Oscars is
20 big business.

Meanwhile, on the other side of town in a Santa Monica hotel, the winners of the Golden Raspberry Awards (the Razzies) are announced. The ceremony is shown on cable TV channels and CNN reports the winners. The show costs only $5,000 to produce and the awards are never collected. The Razzies –
25 in their 25th year – are given to actors and film directors for being bad, really bad, and worse than bad. They were started by John Wilson, who says that most Hollywood films are rubbish. There are prizes for Worst Actor and Actress, and Worst Film. Worst Actress of the 20th Century was won by
30 Madonna, with Sylvester Stallone taking the men's prize. 'Some of these people are so bad,' said Wilson, 'they should take up knitting.'

Find out who gets this year's Razzies (22.00), and stay tuned for this year's Oscars ceremony (24.00). Who will get Best Film? Who will make this year's most embarrassing speech? Who will wear the most ridiculous dress? It's all
35 good fun and it's unmissable television.

2 Read the article again and say if the sentences below refer to the Oscars (O) or the Golden Raspberries (R).

1 A ticket for the ceremony cost $10.
2 This ceremony takes place first.
3 Madonna won a top award for acting.
4 They started 25 years ago.
5 The winners make speeches when they get their award.
6 Millions of people watch the ceremony on TV.
7 The ceremony takes place in a Santa Monica hotel.
8 They are named after someone's uncle.

3 What are the best and worst films you have ever seen? Why?

GRAMMAR: passive with agent

In passive sentences, we often don't include the agent of an action (see page 89).
*On the other side of town, the winners of the Golden Raspberries **are announced**.*

Sometimes we want or need to include the agent. We use *by* to include the agent.
*The ceremony is watched **by millions of TV viewers** around the world.*
*The stars are photographed **by hundreds of hungry paparazzi**.*
*The first ceremony was attended **by 250 people**.*

> SEE LANGUAGE REFERENCE PAGE 94

1 Complete the sentences. Put the verbs in brackets into the past simple passive.

1 An early form of cinema ____ (*invent*) by the the Lumière brothers in the 1890s.
2 Their first film ____ (*see*) by 35 people in a Parisian café.
3 The first talking movie, *The Jazz Singer*, ____ (*make*) by Warner Brothers in 1927.
4 In the same year, the world's biggest cinema ____ (*open*) by Samuel Rothapfel with seats for 6,000 people.
5 The first James Bond in the cinema ____ (*play*) by Sean Connery.
6 The James Bond books ____ (*write*) by Ian Fleming, a British spy.
7 The 1981 American presidential election ____ (*win*) by Ronald Reagan, a movie actor.
8 For a short time, Fidel Castro ____ (*employ*) by Hollywood studios as an extra.

2 Rewrite the sentences beginning with the words that are given.

1 An iceberg hits a ship.
A ship _____.
2 Agent J and Agent K follow some aliens.
Some aliens _____.
3 Nicole Kidman plays the role of the cabaret singer.
The role of the cabaret singer _____.
4 A boy and his friends help an alien to return home.
An alien _____.
5 The director used 300,000 extras.
300,000 extras _____.
6 3,682 American cinemas showed this film on its opening day.
On its opening day, this film _____.
7 Ridley Scott directed this story of ancient Rome.
This story of ancient Rome _____.

3 Now match the sentences 1–7 to the films in the box. See page ooo for the answers.

E.T.   Ghandi   Gladiator   Harry Potter and the Chamber of Secrets   Men in Black   Moulin Rouge   Titanic

4 Work in pairs. Use the prompts and your own ideas to make five sentences about films, books or TV programmes you know.

(Film) (Book) (TV programme)	was	made in (a year, a country). written by (name of an author). shown on (name of a TV channel). directed by (name of a director).

5 Work in pairs. Make quiz questions from your sentences in exercise 4.

Spider Man was made in 2002.   When was Spider Man made?

6 Work with another pair of students. Ask and answer the quiz questions.

SPEAKING

1 Work in pairs. Practise the short dialogue from *Titanic*. Remember that this is a very dramatic moment in the film.

ROSE:	I saw the iceberg, Mr Andrews. And I see it in your eyes. Please tell me the truth.
MR ANDREWS:	The ship will sink.
ROSE:	You're certain?
MR ANDREWS:	Yes. In an hour or two or so … all this … will be at the bottom of the Atlantic.
ROSE:	My God. The Titanic? Sinking?
MR ANDREWS:	Please tell only who you must. I don't want to be responsible for a panic. And get to a boat quickly. Don't wait.
ROSE:	Yes, I understand. Thank you.

2 Perform your dialogue in front of the class and listen to the dialogues of other students. Which students will win an Oscar?

9D | Box office

SPEAKING

1 Work in pairs. Look at the programme for a concert hall.

- Who have you heard of?
- Who would you like to see?

PRONUNCIATION: dates

1 Can you say these numbers?

1st	11th	21st
2nd	12th	22nd
3rd	13th	23rd
4th	15th	24th
5th	16th	31st
6th	20th	

🔘 **2.22** Listen to the recording to check your pronunciation.

2 There are many different ways of writing dates.

20th September   20 September
September 20   September 20th
20/9   20/09

🔘 **2.23** Listen to two different ways of saying these dates. Complete the missing words in the spaces below.

1 September _____ twentieth
2 _____ twentieth _____ September

3 🔘 **2.24** Listen to the recording and fill in the missing dates on the concert programme.

4 Work in pairs. Write four dates that are important for you.

Ask your partner what their dates are and why they are important.

20/9 – That's my daughter's birthday.

7 Aug	Los Van Van (Cuban salsa)	8.00
(1) _____	Justin Timberlake	8.00
(2) _____	Craig David	8.00
3–4 Sep	Red Hot Chili Peppers	8.00
(3) _____	An Evening with Cecilia Bartoli	7.30
27–31 Oct	Swan Lake (Tchaikovsky)	1.45 (27–28 Oct) & 7.45 (all dates)
(4) _____	Shakira	8.00
(5) _____	Handel's Messiah	8.15
(6) _____	A Night with Mr Bean	8.30
22 Nov	Wynton Marsalis Septet	7.45
(7) _____	Enrique Iglesias	8.00
4 Dec	A Tribute to The Beatles	8.30
17–24 Dec	Beauty and the Beast	2.00 & 7.00
(8) _____	Johann Strauss New Year Concert	9.30

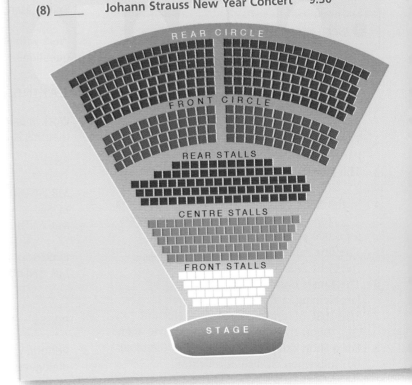

LISTENING

1 Complete the questions with a word or phrase from the box.

| booking fee   box office   circle   credit card   matinee   sold out |

1 When you buy tickets for a show, do you usually go to the _____ or to a ticket agency?
2 When you buy tickets at an agency or on the internet, is there a _____? How much is it?
3 When you buy tickets, do you prefer to pay in cash or by _____?
4 Have you ever wanted to buy tickets for a show that was _____?
5 At the theatre, do you prefer an evening performance or a _____?
6 Do you prefer to sit downstairs in the stalls or upstairs in the _____?

2 Work in pairs. Ask and answer the questions in exercise 1.

3 🔊 2.25–2.28 Listen to four people telephoning the box office of a concert hall. For each person, complete the information in the table.

	speaker 1	speaker 2	speaker 3	speaker 4
concert	Beauty and the Beast	(3)_____	(6)_____	Cecilia Bartoli
date	22 December	(4)_____	3 September	21 September
kind of ticket	stalls	circle	stalls	(9)_____
number of tickets	(1)_____	(5)_____	(7)_____	2 tickets
price	(2)_____	£58.00	(8)_____	(10)_____

4 🔊 2.25–2.28 Listen to the conversations again to check your answers.

FUNCTIONAL LANGUAGE: at the box office

1 Complete column A with a phrase from column B.

A		B	
1	What date would	a	details please?
2	Would you like the matinee	b	do you want?
3	How many tickets	c	fee of two pounds.
4	Where would you like	d	for you.
5	I'll see what seats	e	or the evening performance?
6	I'll just check	f	pounds altogether.
7	I'm sorry, sir,	g	to sit?
8	There's a booking	h	we're sold out.
9	That's fifty-eight	i	we've got available.
10	Could I take your	j	you like?

Look at tapescripts 2.25–2.28 on pages 143–144 to check your answers.

Roleplay

2 Work in pairs, A and B.

A: Choose a show at the Metropolitan Hall that you would like to see. Telephone the box office and book your tickets.
B: You work at the box office of the Metropolitan Hall. Answer the telephone and decide what tickets you have available for the different shows.

SPEAKING

1 Think of a concert you have been to. You are going to talk to a partner about it. Use these questions to prepare what you are going to say.

- What concert was it? When and where?
- Who did you go with?
- How much did you pay for the tickets?
- Why did you go to this concert?
- What kind of music was it?
- How well could you see and hear?
- Did you dance or sing?
- How long was the concert?
- Did you have a good time?

2 Work in pairs. Tell your partner about the concert.

Useful language

The worst/best concert I've been to was …
I've always been a fan of/interested in …
What I liked most about the concert, was …

Metropolitan Hall
Handel's Messiah
Sun 5th Nov 2006 8.15pm
FRONT STALLS B5   £20.00

Metropolitan Hall
Los Van Van
Sat 7th Aug 2006 8.00pm
FRONT CIRCLE M12   £12.00

Metropolitan Hall
A Tribute to the Beatles
Mon 4th Dec 2006 8.30pm
REAR STALLS J10   £15.00

GRAMMAR

Passive

In a normal (active) sentence, we put the agent (the person or thing
that does the action) before the verb.

> **agent verb**
> *The viewers vote for their favourite programme.*

But sometimes:
1   we do not know the agent of the action.
2   the agent is not important.
3   the agent is obvious.
In these cases we often use the passive.

> *The TV studios **were attacked** last night.*
> *A famous TV star **is invited** on the show.*
> *He **was arrested** for driving too fast.*

We make the passive with *to be* + past participle.

Present simple

Affirmative & Negative		
I	'm 'm not	
He/She/It	's isn't	photographed all the time.
You/We/They	're aren't	

Question			
Why	am	I	photographed all the time?
	is	he/she/it	
	are	you/we/they	

Past simple

Affirmative & Negative		
I He/she/it	was wasn't	invited to the party.
You/we/they	were weren't	

Question			
Why	was	I	invited to the party?
		he/she/it	
	were	you/we/they	

We often don't include the agent of an action in passive
sentences.

> *The winners **are announced** at the end of the show.*

Sometimes, we want or need to include the agent. We use *by*
to include the agent.

> *The final episode of Big Brother was watched by **15
> million people**.*
> *The Olympics were started **by the Greeks**.*

FUNCTIONAL LANGUAGE

At the box office

What	date(s)	
	kind of seats	*would you like?*
Which performance		*do you want?*
How many tickets		

Where would you like to sit?
I'll see what seats we've got available.
I'll just check for you.
I'm sorry, sir, we're sold out.
There's a booking fee of …
That's 58 pounds altogether.
Could I take your details, please?

WORD LIST

-ing & -ed adjectives

annoyed **	/ə'nɔɪd/
annoying *	/ə'nɔɪɪŋ/
bored **	/bɔːd/
boring **	/'bɔːrɪŋ/
depressed *	/dɪ'prest/
depressing	/dɪ'presɪŋ/
disappointed *	/dɪsə'pɔɪntɪd/
disappointing	/dɪsə'pɔɪntɪŋ/
excited **	/ɪk'saɪtɪd/
exciting **	/ɪk'saɪtɪŋ/
fascinated	/'fæsɪneɪtɪd/
fascinating *	/'fæsɪneɪtɪŋ/
frightened *	/'fraɪtnd/
frightening *	/'fraɪtnɪŋ/
relaxed *	/rɪ'lækst/
relaxing	/rɪ'læksɪŋ/
surprised **	/sə'praɪzd/
surprising **	/sə'praɪzɪŋ/
tired ***	/'taɪəd/
tiring	/'taɪrɪŋ/

TV programmes

chat show n C	/'tʃæt ʃəʊ/
current affairs programme n C	/kʌrənt ə'feəz prəʊgræm/
documentary n C	/dɒkjʊ'mentri/
game show n C	/'geɪm ʃəʊ/
sitcom n C	/'sɪtkɒm/
soap opera n C	/'səʊp ɒprə/
sports programme n C	/'spɔːts prəʊgræm/

Films

acting n U	/'æktɪŋ/
actor n C ***	/'æktə/
actress n C	/'æktrəs/
direct v **	/'daɪrekt/; /'dɪrekt/
director n C ***	/də'rektə/; /daɪ'rektə/
extra n C	/'ekstrə/
role n C ***	/rəʊl/
setting n C *	/'setɪŋ/
soundtrack n C	/'saʊndtræk/
special effects n pl	/speʃl ɪ'fekts/
star v **	/stɑːl/

Other words & phrases

agent n C *	/'eɪdʒənt/
album n C	/'ælbəm/
announce v *	/ə'naʊns/
arena n C	/ə'riːnə/
attack v ***	/ə'tæk/
attend v **	/ə'tend/
available adj **	/ə'veɪləbl/
award n C **	/ə'wɔːd/
bedtime n U	/'bedtaɪm/
boat n C ***	/bəʊt/
booking fee n C	/'bʊkɪŋ fiː/
building n C ***	/'bɪldɪŋ/
cabaret n C/U	/'kæbəreɪ/
cable TV n U	/'keɪbl tiː 'viː/
circle n C	/'sɜːkl/
civilization n C/U	/sɪvəlaɪ'zeɪʃn/
classical music n U	/klæsɪkl 'mjuːsɪk/
conduct v **	/kən'dʌkt/
contract n C ***	/'kɒntrækt/
cost v ***	/kɒst/
cruise n C	/kruːz/
dance v ***	/dɑːns/
designer n C *	/dɪ'zaɪnə/
detail n C ***	/'diːteɪl/
dream n C/v ***	/driːm/
election n C ***	/ɪ'lekʃn/
entertainment n U **	/entə'teɪnmənt/
entrance n C ***	/'entrəns/
episode n C	/'epɪsəʊd/
event n C ***	/ɪ'vent/
expedition n C	/ekspə'dɪʃn/
fame n U	/feɪm/
fantastic adj	/fæn'tæstɪk/
gorgeous adj	/'gɔːdʒəs/
human rights n pl	/hjuːmən 'raɪts/
iceberg n C	/'aɪsbɜːg/
idol n C	/'aɪdl/
impressionist n C	/ɪm'preʃnɪst/
in-depth adj	/ɪn 'depθ/
insult v *	/ɪn'sʌlt/
invent v **	/ɪn'vent/
investor n C **	/ɪn'vestə/
jackpot n C	/'dʒækpɒt/
kangaroo n C	/kæŋgə'ruː/
knitting n U	/'nɪtɪŋ/
legend n C	/'ledʒ(ə)nd/
limousine n C	/'lɪmə'ziːn/
line-up n C	/'laɪn ʌp/
loft n C	/lɒft/
masterpiece n C	/'mɑːstəpiːs/
matinee n C	/'mætɪneɪ/
musical n C	/'mjuːsɪkl/
old-fashioned adj *	/əʊld 'fæʃənd/

painting n C/U **	/'peɪntɪŋ/
panic n U/v	/'pænɪk/
paparazzi n pl	/pæpə'rætsi/
performance n C ***	/pə'fɔːməns/
pronounce v *	/prə'naʊns/
publish v ***	/'pʌblɪʃ/
raspberry n C	/'rɑːzbəri/
reality n U **	/ri'æləti/
record n C	/'rekɔːd/
report v ***	/rɪ'pɔːt/
requiem n C	/'rekwiəm/
ridiculous adj	/rɪ'dɪkjʊləs/
series n C ***	/'sɪəriːz/
session n C **	/'seʃn/
sold out adj	/səʊld 'aʊt/
spy n C	/spaɪ/
stalls n pl	/stɔːlz/
statue n C	/'stætʃuː/
stay tuned	/steɪ 'tʃuːnd/
survivor n C	/sə'vaɪvə/
talented adj	/'tæləntɪd/
TV channel n C	/tiː 'viː tʃænl/
unmissable adj	/ʌn'mɪsəbl/
urban adj *	/'ɜːbən/
video tape n C	/'vɪdiːəʊ teɪp/
viewer n C **	/'vjuːə/
weekly adj	/'wiːkli/
wharf n C	/wɔːf/

10A | Animal lovers

SPEAKING

1 Work in pairs. Discuss these questions.

● What kinds of animals do people have as pets in your country?

● Choose a pet from the box for the people in the photos. Explain your reasons.

cat	dog	goldfish	hamster	lizard
monkey	parrot	pig	rabbit	rat

● Which is your favourite animal? Why?

A B

C D

READING

1 Do you know any famous Americans who have pets? Make a list.

Now read the article and <u>underline</u> the famous people it mentions. Were they on your list?

2 The writer gives four reasons for why he thinks that Americans are crazy about animals. Tick (✓) the reasons that he mentions.

1 Some hotels have special services for dogs.
2 For some people, pets are more important than children.
3 Some Americans have strange pets (for example, pigs and lizards).
4 There are fashion shows for pets.
5 Some people ask the vet to do strange things.
6 Some people take their pets to psychiatrists.
7 Americans spend a lot of money on their pets.

3 Are people in your country crazy about animals?

THE UNITED STATES OF ANIMALS

For years, I have thought that we Americans are probably crazy. Crazy about animals, that is. But now I am sure. I saw an ad in the paper the other day for the Ritz Hotel in Miami which has been open since September 2002. It has a special dog
5 program, with dog menus, dog movies and dog music in the library. It sounds perfect for Oprah Winfrey who never travels without her dogs. I wonder what the hotel does for other animals of the stars. George Clooney, for example, has had a pig (called Max) for many years and Leonardo DiCaprio has a pet
10 lizard.

In the same newspaper was an article which proves my point. The article, *Hollywood's Super-Vet Tells All*, was about Dr Amy Attas. Dr Attas sounds perfectly normal, unlike some of her customers. Dr Attas has run a veterinary practice, called CityPets,
15 for the last ten years. Her customers are the rich and famous and, since she began the practice, she has looked after the pets of people like Naomi Campbell, Joan Rivers and Uma Thurman.

One of her best stories is about a late-night phone-call that she received from the wife of hockey star, Wayne Gretzky. Their dog
20 was crying and Wayne could not sleep. If Wayne doesn't sleep, he doesn't play good hockey, said the wife. The vet visited the house and examined the dog which had a – cold! Another time,
25 she had a call from Cher, who was in Italy. Cher wanted to bring an Italian dog home with her. It had a skin problem and she wanted Dr Attas to come to the airport to
30 look after it. At midnight.

Crazy stuff, huh? No, the really crazy stuff came from another article, this one in the *Wall Street Journal*. Since this time last
35 year, the US has spent $30 billion on pets. That's about the same as the gross national product of a medium-sized South
40 American country. And that's what I call really crazy.

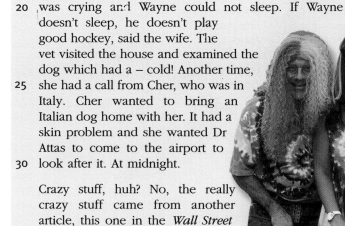

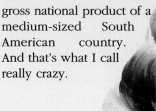

GRAMMAR: present perfect simple with *for* & *since*

We use the present perfect simple for states that began in the past and continue into the present. The states are unfinished.

*How long **have you had** your pet? **I've had** it **for** many years. I've **had** it **since** my sixteenth birthday.*

for *many years*
(a period of time)

past *since my 16ᵗʰ birthday* **now**   **future**
(a point in time)

We use the past simple for actions and states that are finished. Compare these examples.

Present perfect simple
*She's **had** it for many years* (and she still has it).

Past simple
*She **had** it for many years* (but she doesn't have it now).

> SEE LANGUAGE REFERENCE PAGE 104

1 Complete the text. Put the verbs in brackets into the present perfect simple or the past simple.

Oscar Werbeniuk, who is 61, (1) _____ (*live*) all his life in the same New Jersey house. He (2) _____ (*love*) animals, especially cats, since he was a child. He (3) _____ (*find*) his first cat, Tabatha, in the street in 1981, and he (4) _____ (*find*) another 43 cats since then. But Tabatha – who died in 1990 – (5) _____ (*have*) babies and Oscar soon (6) _____ (*have*) more than a hundred cats. For the last fifteen years, there (7) _____ (*be*) more than two hundred cats in his house. Oscar is lucky because his parents (8) _____ (*be*) very rich, so he (9) _____ (*never / worry*) about money. In fact, since 1999, Oscar (10) _____ (*be*) so busy that he (11) _____ (*not / leave*) his house.

2 2.29 Listen to the recording to check your answers.

3 Complete the phrases with *for* or *since*.

1 _____ 2002
2 _____ a day or two
3 _____ Monday
4 _____ yesterday
5 _____ I left school
6 _____ three years
7 _____ a few weeks
8 _____ an hour
9 _____ the lesson started
10 _____ five minutes
11 _____ half past six
12 _____ last week

4 How many different ways can you complete the questions?

1 How long have you been … ?
2 How long have you had … ?
3 How long have you known … ?

5 Work in pairs. Ask and answer the questions in exercise 4.

SPEAKING

1 Work in pairs. Turn to page 132.

Take it in turns to choose one of the animals in the picture. Ask and answer *yes/no* questions to find out which animal it is. Use these questions and your own ideas.

- Has it got four legs?
- Is it a farm animal?
- Is it a kind of bird?
- Do people keep it as a pet?
- Does it eat other animals?
- Can it run very fast?
- Is it dangerous?

10B | Stress

How often have you had a headache in the last twelve months? How many stomach aches have you had? Have you sometimes found it difficult to breathe? Have
5 you had any skin problems? How often have you felt sad or nervous for no good reason? How often have you wanted to cry? How often have you got angry?

If your answer to three or more of these
10 questions is 'too often', you are probably suffering from stress. And if you are suffering from stress, you are not alone. Over half of the adult population has had stress-related symptoms in the last year and many of them
15 have needed help of some kind. Stress is now the major health problem of our times.

Stress, itself, is not an illness, but it can certainly contribute to illnesses, some of them serious. When you feel under stress, your body produces
20 more of the hormones adrenaline and cortisol. As a result, the body needs more oxygen and your heart rate and blood pressure go up. At its most serious, this can lead to heart problems, but stress is also related to weight problems, coughs
25 and colds. Scientists have also discovered that stress can lead to the loss of brain cells.

The most common cause of stress is over-work, but a difficult boss or problems with your colleagues are also common causes. Some jobs
30 are more stressful than others, with teachers and police officers at the top of the scale and beauty therapists at the bottom. From time to time, we hear of celebrities suffering from stress, footballers like Ronaldo or the American actress,
35 Winona Ryder. But stress can affect us all and the figures prove it. 40 million working days are lost in the UK every year because of stress-related illnesses. What is more, people who are suffering from stress do not work as well as usual. The
40 situation is so serious that some companies now offer relaxation and stress management classes.

If you think you, too, are suffering from stress, it's important to know if it is causing you health problems. If it is, see your doctor and talk
45 about it.

SPEAKING & READING

1 Work in pairs. Which of the jobs in the box do you think are especially stressful? Explain why or why not.

accountant	beauty therapist	nurse	doctor
computer	programmer	gardener	police officer
teacher	unemployed person		

Being a doctor is stressful because …

2 Read the article and choose the best title.

1 Adrenaline and cortisol
2 Are you suffering from stress?
3 The most stressful jobs

3 Read the article again and answer the questions.

1 What are three symptoms of stress?
2 How many adults suffer from stress?
3 Which hormones does the body produce when it is under stress?
4 What illnesses are related to stress?
5 Name two stars who have suffered from stress.
6 How many working days are lost in Britain every year because of stress?
7 What are some companies doing about stress?

4 How stressful is your work and day-to-day life?

GRAMMAR: present perfect simple for unfinished time

We use the present perfect simple to talk about finished states that happened in a period of time which is not finished. The time phrases we use (for example *this week, in the last twelve months*) are connected to present time.

> *I've had two days off work **this week**. (This week is not finished.)*
> *How often have you had a headache **in the last twelve months**? (In the last twelve months includes this month.)*

We use the past simple to talk about finished actions and states that happened in a period of time that is also finished. The time phrases we use (for example, *last Friday, two years ago*) are not connected to present time.

> *I was ill **last Friday**.*
> *He went to relaxation classes **two years ago**.*

> ⊙ SEE LANGUAGE REFERENCE PAGE 104

1 Mark the phrases unfinished time (U) or finished time (F).

yesterday	last month	this month
in 1998	last week	this week
in my life	one year ago	today
in the last month	since last year	this morning

2 Complete the sentences with the correct verb form.

1 I *have been / went* for a walk a few days ago.
2 I've *done / did* a lot of sport this month.
3 I've *made / made* some good friends this year.
4 I *have been / was* very busy last month.
5 I've *been / was* quite tired in the last two weeks.
6 I *haven't had / didn't have* much free time this week.
7 I *have had / had* a big party for my last birthday.

3 Now change the sentences so that they are true for you.

4 Complete the sentences. Put the verbs in brackets into the present perfect simple or the past simple.

1 How many cups of coffee _____ (*you / drink*) yesterday?
2 How many films _____ (*you / see*) this month?
3 How many times _____ (*you / take*) a train/bus this week?
4 How much money _____ (*you / spend*) today?
5 How much junk food _____ (*you / eat*) last week?
6 How often _____ (*you / be*) late for school/work this year?
7 How often _____ (*you / be*) ill last year?
8 Which countries _____ (*you / visit*) in the last five years?

5 Work in pairs. Ask and answer the questions in exercise 4.

VOCABULARY & SPEAKING: collocations with *get*

1 Complete column A with a phrase from column B.

A	B
1 They **got into** financial **difficulties**	a and the children stayed with their mother.
2 She **got promoted**	b and they closed their company.
3 They **got into trouble**	c and took two months off work.
4 They **got divorced**	d because he was always late.
5 He **got fired**	e with the police.
6 She **got** very **ill**	f in a beautiful church.
7 They **got married**	g because her work was so good.

2 Many events in our lives can cause stress. Put the events in exercise 1 in order of stressfulness.

3 Work in groups. Compare and discuss your lists. As a group, decide on the four most stressful events.

> *I think that getting divorced is the most stressful because …*

> *I don't think that getting promoted is very stressful.*

4 These suggestions come from books about stress. Which ones work for you?

What else do you do when you are feeling stressed?

DEALING WITH STRESS

Do some breathing exercises.
Go shopping and buy something you like.
Go for a walk.
Eat some fruit or vegetables.
Talk to a friend.
Listen to some music.
Think of something positive.
Ask a friend to brush your hair.
Have a ten minute break from what you are doing.

10c | Marathon men

SPEAKING & VOCABULARY: sport

1 Look at these sentences. Mark each one like this:

✓✓   very true for me
✓   true for me
✗   not true for me

1 I am fit.
2 I enjoyed sport at school.
3 My health is very important to me.
4 I like lots of different sports.
5 I would like to run a marathon.

2 Work in pairs. Compare your answers to exercise 1. For each sentence, give some extra information.

3 Match the sports in the box to the pictures A–I.

> aerobics   cycling   golf   running   squash
> swimming   tennis   weight training   yoga

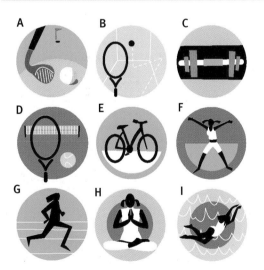

4 Put the sports in exercise 3 into three groups according to the verbs they go with.

do	go	play
aerobics		

5 Which are the best sports to keep fit? Which are the best sports to watch?

LISTENING

1 You are going to listen to part of a sports radio programme. All the things shown in pictures A–F appear in the programme. What do you think it is about?

B   A heart operation

A   Ranulph Fiennes and Mike Stroud

C   The New York Marathon

D   Cairo

E   The Antarctic

F   Millions of pounds

2 2.30 Now listen to the programme to find out if you were right.

3 2.30 Listen again and choose the correct answers.

1 The winner of the men's marathon was *Martin Lel. / Rodgers Rop.*
2 The fastest woman ran the race in *2 hours 10 minutes and 30 seconds. / 2 hours 22 minutes and 31 seconds.*
3 They ran their first marathon in *the North Pole. / Patagonia.*
4 In the last seven days, Fiennes and Stroud have been to *Sydney, Singapore and Cairo. / the Andes, the Amazon and the desert of Oman.*
5 They have raised more than *two / four* million pounds for a multiple sclerosis research centre.
6 Ranulph Fiennes is going *into hospital / to work* soon.

4 Who are the greatest sports heroes in your country? What have they done?

Grammar: present perfect simple with *been* & *gone*

1 Match sentences 1 and 2 to the diagrams A and B.

1 Ranulph has gone to Singapore.
2 Ranulph has been to Singapore.

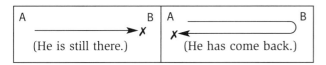

A B	A B
——————→X	X←——————⤸
(He is still there.)	(He has come back.)

2 Complete the dialogue with *been* or *gone*.

Jane: Hello.
Mark: Hi, it's Mark here. Is Rick there please?
Jane: Hi, Mark. No, I'm sorry. He's (1) ____ away for the week.
Mark: Oh? Work? Holiday?
Jane: Both. He's (2) ____ to Patagonia – for a walk.
Mark: Oh, I've (3) ____ there. Twice. It's really nice. Why didn't you go with him?
Jane: Because my boss has (4) ____ to Nepal on business so I'm in charge of the office.
Mark: Nepal? Nice!
Jane: Have you (5) ____ there, too?
Mark: Yes, I've (6) ____ a few times, actually.
Jane: Really? I've only (7) ____ there once. I liked it.
Mark: Yes, it's an excellent place for walking.
Jane: Yes. Well, I'll tell him you called.
Mark: OK. Thanks. Bye, Jane.
Jane: Bye, Mark.

3 2.31 Listen to the recording to check your answers. Then work in pairs and practise the dialogue.

Pronunciation: /ɔː/

1 What are the missing letters in the words below? All the words have the same vowel sound.

1	b e f _ r e	6	c _ l l e d
2	f _ _ r	7	s p _ r t
3	N e w Y _ r k	8	s _ r t
4	n _ r t h	9	t h _ _ g h t
5	r e p _ r t	10	w _ l k i n g

2 Which of these words contain the same sound (/ɔː/)?

1	awful	6	morning
2	caught	7	squash
3	cause	8	thought
4	daughter	9	walk
5	important	10	would

3 2.32 Listen to the recording to check your answers.

Did you know?

1 Read the information about sport in Australia.

Australia is one of the most sporting countries in the world. Although the population is quite small (about 20 million), it has a large number of world champions in many different sports.
About three quarters of all Australians do some kind of sport. The most popular are walking, swimming, aerobics, cycling, tennis and golf. They also enjoy watching sport. The most important events in the sporting calendar are the Grand Final of Australian Rules Football, international cricket matches, the Melbourne Cup (horse racing), international basketball and soccer matches, and the Australian Grand Prix (motor racing).

2 Work in pairs. Discuss these questions.

* What are the most popular sports in your country?
* What are the most important sporting events in your country?
* Describe a sporting event that you have attended.

10D | Doctor, doctor

VOCABULARY & SPEAKING: body & health

1 Label the parts of the body A–J in the picture with the words in the box.

back	chest	ear	eye	head	mouth	neck
nose	stomach	throat				

How many other parts of the body can you name?

2 What do you think is wrong with the people in the doctor's waiting room? Use the language in the boxes to describe them.

He She	's got	a headache. a stomach ache. a cold. a cough. flu. a hangover. a temperature. a pain in his/her back/neck, etc.
His Her	back head stomach throat	hurts.

3 Which person in the picture above needs these things?

1 some **aspirin** or **paracetamol**
2 a **prescription** for **antibiotics**
3 an **appointment** with a **specialist**

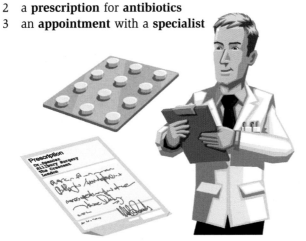

4 Work in pairs. Ask and answer these questions.

- When was the last time you were ill? What was the matter?
- Did you see a doctor? Did the doctor give you a prescription?
- Did you take any time off work/school?

Davina

LISTENING

1 🔘 2.33–2.34 Listen to two men at the doctor's. Why are they quite happy when they leave?

2 🔘 2.33–2.34 Listen to the conversations again. Complete the doctor's notes for both patients.

back	cold	cough	depressed	eyes	flu
paracetamol	specialist	stomach ache		stress	

Name: Stuart Simeon

Symptoms: He's got a headache, a cold and a (1) _____. He's also got pains in his (2) _____, chest and neck. His temperature is 39°.

Other notes: His girlfriend has left him. He seems (3) _____.

Diagnosis: (4) _____

Treatment / Medicine: strong (5) _____

Name: Mike Marks

Symptoms: He is extremely nervous. He's got a (6) _____, but he also says he feels hot and (7) _____. His (8) _____ hurt.

Other notes: He doesn't eat well — he lives on coffee.

Diagnosis: (9) _____

Treatment / Medicine: Appointment with a (10) _____.

3 How often do you go to the doctor's? How do you feel about going to the doctor's?

Mike

Stuart

Mary

FUNCTIONAL LANGUAGE: at the doctor's

1 Look at the phrases. Who is speaking: the doctor (D) or the patient (P)?

a   I feel awful.
b   I think you should take a few days off work.
c   I'll give you a prescription.
d   I'll have a look at you.
e   Is there anything I can take for it?
f   It's nothing to worry about.
g   It's very painful.
h   What's the matter?
i   What's wrong with me?
j   Where does it hurt?

2 Complete the dialogue with phrases a–j from exercise 1.

Doctor: Come in. Take a seat.
Patient: Thank you.
Doctor: Now, (1) _____.
Patient: (2) _____ It's my back.
Doctor: (3) _____
Patient: Here and here.
Doctor: OK. (4) _____ Take off your shirt. Does this hurt?
Patient: Yes, it does. (5) _____ Is it serious?
Doctor: No, (6) _____
Patient: (7) _____ Do you know?
Doctor: I think you've pulled a muscle.
Patient: (8) _____
Doctor: Yes, (9) _____
Patient: Thank you. And what about work? Is it OK to work?
Doctor: No, not at the moment. (10) _____ And come back and see me in ten days.
Patient: OK. I'll make an appointment with the receptionist. Thank you. Bye.

3 🔘 **2.35** Listen to the recording to check your answers. Then work in pairs and practise the dialogue.

Roleplay

4 Work in pairs, A and B.

A: You are the patient. Describe how you feel.
B: You are the doctor. Ask the patient questions about how they are feeling and suggest what she/he should do.

Use the phrases in exercise 1 to help you.

PRONUNCIATION: sentence stress

1 🔘 **2.36** Listen to a joke. Notice how the important words are stressed.

Patient: Doctor, doctor, what did the <u>X</u>-ray of my <u>head</u> show?
Doctor: Absolutely <u>nothing</u>!

2 Work in pairs. Practise reading these jokes. Stress the words that are <u>underlined</u>.

1   Patient: Doctor, doctor, I'm seeing <u>double</u>.
     Doctor: Take a <u>seat</u>, please.
     Patient: Which <u>one</u>?

2   Patient: Doctor, doctor, I've got a <u>memory</u> problem.
     Doctor: How long have you <u>had</u> this problem?
     Patient: <u>What</u> problem?

3   Patient: Doctor, doctor, I feel very <u>nervous</u>. This is the <u>first</u> operation I've ever had.
     Doctor: Don't worry. It's <u>my</u> first time, too.

3 🔘 **2.37–2.39** Listen to the recording to check your pronunciation.

GRAMMAR

Present perfect simple 2

We use the present perfect simple to show the connection between present time and past time.

We use the present perfect simple for states that began in the past and continue into the present. The states are unfinished.

> *How long **have** you **had** your dog?*
> *I've **had** it for many years.*

We use the past simple for finished actions and states. Compare these examples.

Present perfect simple
> *She's **had** a dog for many years* (and she still has it).

Past simple
> *She **had** a dog for many years* (but she doesn't have it now).

We can also use the present perfect simple to talk about finished states that happened in a period of time which is not finished. The time phrases we use (for example, *this week, in the last twelve months*) are connected to present time.

> *I've been ill twice **this year**.*
> *How often have you been ill **this year**?*
> (*this year* is not finished)

We use the past simple to talk about finished actions and states that happened in a period of time that is also finished. The time phrases we use (for example, *last Friday, two years ago*) are **not** connected to present time.

> *I was ill three times **last year**.* (*last year* is finished)

Time phrases
The following time phrases include present time. They are often used with the present perfect simple.

> *today*
> **this** *week/month/year*
> **in** *the last week/the last year/my life*

The following time phrases are not connected to present time. They are not usually used with the present perfect simple.

> *in 1992*
> **last** *week/year*
> *yesterday*
> *one week/two days **ago***

With some time phrases, the connection to the present depends on the time of speaking. *This morning* is connected to present time if it is now before midday. It is not connected to present time if it is now after midday.

> *I've **read** three reports this morning.*
> (spoken at 11.00 am)
> *I **read** three reports this morning.* (spoken at 3.00 pm)

We use *for* to talk about periods of time.
> *I've lived here **for** three years.*
> *He studied **for** ten minutes.*

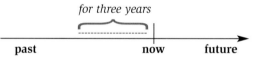

We use *since* to talk about the starting point of an action or state. We never use *since* with the past simple.

> *She's been ill **since** Monday.*
> *I haven't spoken to them **since** we had an argument.*

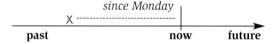

Been & gone
The verb *go* has two past participles: *been* and *gone*.

We use *gone* to show that a person has left a place.

> *He has **gone** to Singapore.*

We use *been* to show that a person has left a place and returned.

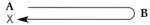

> *He has **been** to Singapore.*

See page 74 for more information about the present perfect simple.

FUNCTIONAL LANGUAGE

At the doctor's

What's the matter?
What's wrong with you?
Where does it hurt?

I feel awful.
It's very painful.
It hurts.

I'll have a look at you.
I'll give you a prescription.
I think you should take a few days off work.
It's nothing to worry about.

WORD LIST

Animals

cat *n C* ***	/kæt/
dog *n C* ***	/dɒg/
goldfish *n C*	/ˈgəʊldfɪʃ/
hamster *n C*	/ˈhæmstə/
lizard *n C*	/ˈlɪzəd/
monkey *n C*	/ˈmʌŋki/
parrot *n C*	/ˈpærət/
pig *n C* *	/pɪg/
rabbit *n C*	/ˈræbɪt/
rat *n C*	/ræt/

Collocations with *get*

get divorced	/get dɪˈvɔːst/
get fired	/get ˈfaɪəd/
get ill	/get ɪl/
get into (financial) difficulties	/get ɪntuː ˈdɪfɪkltɪz/
get into trouble	/get ɪntuː ˈtrʌbl/
get married	/get ˈmærɪd/
get promoted	/get prəˈməʊtɪd/

Sport

aerobics *n U*	/eəˈrəʊbɪks/
champion *n C* *	/ˈtʃæmpiən/
cricket *n U*	/ˈkrɪkɪt/
cycling *n U*	/ˈsaɪklɪŋ/
final *n C*	/ˈfaɪnəl/
golf *n U* *	/gɒlf/
horse racing *n U*	/ˈhɔːs reɪsɪŋ/
marathon *n C*	/ˈmærəθ(ə)n/
motor racing *n U*	/ˈməʊtə reɪsɪŋ/
race *n C* ***	/reɪs/
running *n U*	/ˈrʌnɪŋ/
soccer *n U*	/ˈsɒkə/
squash *n U*	/skwɒf/
swimming *n U*	/ˈswɪmɪŋ/
tennis *n U*	/ˈtenɪs/
weight training *n U*	/ˈweɪt treɪnɪŋ/
yoga *n U*	/ˈjəʊgə/

Body & health

adrenaline *n U*	/əˈdrenəlɪn/
antibiotic *n C*	/ˌæntɪbaɪˈɒtɪk/
appointment *n C* ***	/əˈpɔɪntmənt/
aspirin *n C/U*	/ˈæsprɪn/
back *n C* ***	/bæk/
blood pressure *n U*	/ˈblʌd preʃə/
brain *n C* **	/breɪn/
breast cancer *n U*	/ˈbrest kænsə/
breathe *v* **	/briːð/
cell *n C* **	/sel/
check-up *n C*	/ˈtʃek ʌp/
chest *n* ***	/tʃest/
cold *n C* **	/kəʊld/
cough *n C/v* *	/kɒf/
diagnosis *n C*	/daɪəgˈnəʊsɪs/
ear *n C* ***	/ɪə/
examine *v* ***	/ɪgˈzæmɪn/
exhausted *adj*	/ɪgˈzɔːstɪd/
eye *n C* ***	/aɪ/
flu *n U*	/fluː/
hangover *n C*	/ˈhæŋəʊvə/
headache *n C* *	/ˈhedeɪk/
heart attack *n C*	/ˈhɑːt ətæk/
heart rate *n U*	/ˈhɑːt reɪt/
hormone *n C*	/ˈhɔːməʊn/
hurt *v* ***	/hɜːt/
illness *n C* ***	/ˈɪlnəs/
mouth *n C* ***	/maʊθ/
multiple sclerosis *n U*	/mʌltɪpl skləˈrəʊsɪs/
muscle *n C* **	/ˈmʌsl/
neck *n C* ***	/nek/
nose *n C* ***	/nəʊz/
operation *n C* ***	/ɒpəˈreɪʃn/
oxygen *n U*	/ˈɒksɪdʒ(ə)n/
pain *n C* ***	/peɪn/
painful *adj* *	/ˈpeɪnfl/
paracetamol *n C/U*	/pærəˈsiːtəmɒl/
prescription *n C*	/prɪˈskrɪpʃn/
skin *n U* ***	/skɪn/
specialist *n C* *	/ˈspeʃəlɪst/
stomach ache *n C/U*	/ˈstʌmək eɪk/
suffer (from sth) *v* ***	/ˈsʌfə/
symptom *n C* *	/ˈsɪmptəm/
temperature *n C/U* ***	/ˈtemprɪtʃə/
throat *n C* ***	/θrəʊt/
treatment *n U* ***	/ˈtriːtmənt/
vitamin *n C*	/ˈvɪtəmɪn/
weight *n U* ***	/weɪt/
X-ray *n C*	/ˈeks reɪ/

Other words & phrases

achievement *n C* **	/əˈtʃiːvmənt/
affect *v* ***	/əˈfekt/
arrival *n C/U* **	/əˈraɪvl/
beauty therapist *n C*	/ˈbjuːti θerəpɪst/
bronze *n U*	/brɒnz/
brush *v* *	/brʌʃ/
calendar *n C*	/ˈkælɪndə/
canoe *n C/v*	/kəˈnuː/
cause *v* ***	/kɔːz/
celebrate *v* **	/ˈseləbreɪt/
continent *n C* **	/ˈkɒntɪnənt/
contribute *v* ***	/kənˈtrɪbjuːt/
crazy about (sth) *adj*	/ˈkreɪzi əbaʊt/
cry *v* ***	/kraɪ/
deep *adj* ***	/diːp/
desert *n C/U* **	/ˈdezət/
farm *n C*	/fɑːm/
gardener *n C*	/ˈgɑːdnə/
gross national product (GNP) *n U*	/grəʊs næʃn(ə)l ˈprɒdʌkt/
hockey *n U*	/ˈhɒki/
memory *n C* ***	/ˈmem(ə)ri/
official *adj* ***	/əˈfɪʃl/
over-work *n U*	/əʊvəˈwɜːk/
point *n C* ***	/pɔɪnt/
prove *v* ***	/pruːv/
raise *v* ***	/reɪz/
scale *n C* ***	/skeɪl/
spectator *n C*	/spekˈteɪtə/
stopover *n C*	/ˈstɒpəʊvə/
stress *n U* *	/stres/
stressful *adj*	/ˈstresfl/
stuff *n U* ***	/stʌf/
up to date *adj*	/ʌp tə ˈdeɪt/
vet *n C*	/vet/
veterinary practice *n U*	/ˈvet(ə)nri præktɪs/

11A | Things

VOCABULARY & SPEAKING: personal possessions

1 Labels the pictures A–K with the words.

2 Which of these things are important to you? Why? Which things could you live without?

3 Work in pairs. Describe one of your favourite things.

- What is it?
- How long have you had it?
- Where did you get it?
- Why is it important to you?

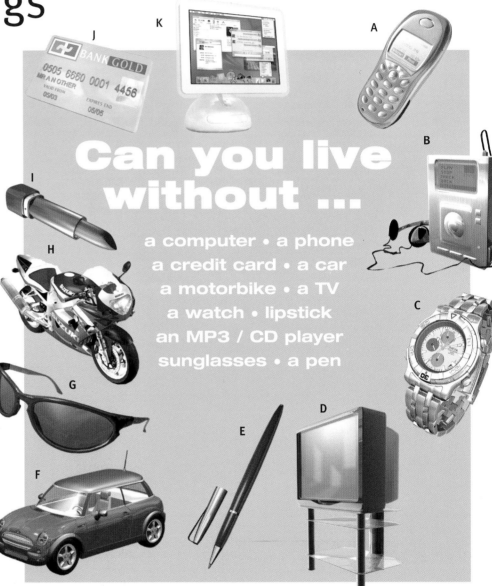

Can you live without ...

a computer • a phone
a credit card • a car
a motorbike • a TV
a watch • lipstick
an MP3 / CD player
sunglasses • a pen

LISTENING

1 Look at the pictures. When were these things fashionable?

2 🔊 2.40–2.41 Listen to Susan and Katy talking about things they really wanted when they were younger. Which of the things do they mention?

3 🔊 **2.40–2.41** Listen again and complete the sentences with Susan (S) or Katy (K).

1 _____ asked her sister for permission.
2 _____ saw someone else with it.
3 _____ still has it.
4 _____ thought it was very sexy.
5 _____ used it in a restaurant.
6 _____ waited two years before buying it.
7 _____ wanted to be independent.
8 _____ wanted to impress her clients.

GRAMMAR: infinitive of purpose

We can use the infinitive (with *to*) to talk about why we do things. It explains the reason or purpose of our actions.

*She wanted a credit card **to pay** for meals in restaurants.*
*She filled out a form **to get** a card.*

> SEE LANGUAGE REFERENCE PAGE 114

1 Underline the infinitives in the following sentences. Which ones are infinitives of purpose?

1 I got a credit card to pay for my clients' meals.
2 I started to spend more money with my new card.
3 I used it to pay for my shopping.
4 I was saving up to buy a Mini.
5 I needed a car to get to work.
6 I used to live a long way from the city centre.

2 Make sentences by joining the phrases in columns A and B with *to*.

*I worked overtime **to** earn more money.*

A	B
1 I worked overtime	a buy a car.
2 I saved £5,000	b earn more money.
3 I wanted a car	c see if I liked it.
4 I went to a garage	d help me choose.
5 I asked a friend to come with me	f pay for it.
6 We went for a drive in one car	e look at the new cars.
7 Then we went back to the garage	g go away at the weekends.

3 Work in pairs. Talk about all the different things you do with the things in the box.

car   mobile phone   computer   credit card

I use my car to go to work.

FUNCTIONAL LANGUAGE: paraphrasing

1 Sometimes you need to paraphrase when you don't know the right word for something.

🔊 **2.42–2.43** Listen to two people talking and fill in the gaps.

1 It's a kind of _____.
  It's a thing you _____.

2 They're a sort of _____.
  You use them to _____.

2 Work in pairs. Turn to page 126. Take it in turns to choose one of the objects and use the phrases in exercise 1 to describe it. Your partner must decide which object you are describing.

PRONUNCIATION: /θ/ & /ð/

1 🔊 **2.44** Listen to the sound at the beginning of these words.

/θ/	/ð/
thanks	than
thing	this
thousand	those

2 Put the words in the box into the correct column in the table in exercise 1.

theatre   their   theory   there   they   think
thirteenth   thought   three   Thursday

3 🔊 **2.45** Listen to the recording and repeat these phrases.

What do you think of their theory?
Do they think the same thing as the others?
Let's meet on Thursday the thirteenth at three o'clock.
They thought the theatre was over there.

11B | Fashion victim

SPEAKING

1 Work in groups. Discuss these statements.

- You can judge a person's personality by their clothes.
- Clothes are more important for women than for men.
- It's important to look smart at work and when you go out.
- Young people are more fashionable than their parents.

VOCABULARY: clothes

1 Match the pictures A–S with the words in the box.

> boots   cardigan   dress   jacket   jeans   jersey
> scarf   shirt   shorts   skirt   socks   suit
> sweatshirt   tie   top   trainers   trousers
> T-shirt   underwear

2 In exercise 1, which word(s):

- is always singular/uncountable? _____
- are always plural? _____ _____

3 Work in pairs. How much can you remember about the other students in your class? What were they wearing in the last lesson?

READING

1 Look at the newspaper headline and photo. Why do you think the man on the right is wearing those clothes?

Read the article to find out if you were right.

Office Worker Flip Flops Out of a Job

'You can't wear those here!' It was a hot summer day, and instead of the usual 'Good morning' from his boss,
5 Philip Dale was told to go home and change out of his casual shorts and flip flops. He refused and, by the end of the morning, he was out of a job.
'I work in an office and we don't have to meet clients. Why can't I wear what I want?' said Mr
10 Dale. 'It's sexual discrimination. Women can wear skirts and shorts. Why do men have to wear hot trousers and ties?'
But the company disagreed. 'This is work, not a holiday on the beach,' said a company spokeswoman.
15 'It is true that Mr Dale does not have to work with customers, but he has to go in and out of the building and we must think about our image. What is more, Mr Dale's contract says very clearly "Employees must wear suitable clothes in the
20 workplace." It's a question of professionalism. Shorts and flip flops are not formal enough.'
However, Mr Dale's lawyer said: 'This is a question of human rights. Companies cannot tell their employees what to wear. Of course, employees
25 should wear clothes that are suitable for their work, but there is nothing wrong with shorts in the summer. We're talking here about a very old-fashioned company. In a modern company, like Adidas, for example, employees can wear what they
30 want. But the really important question here is the question of sexual discrimination. If they must have rules about clothes, they cannot have some rules for men and others for women. It's very simple, really.'
The case continues.

2 Read the article again and say if the sentences are true (T) or false (F).

1 Mr Dale's boss told him to change his clothes.
2 Mr Dale didn't want to change his clothes.
3 He went home to change into different clothes.
4 He often takes his clients out to dinner.
5 There are different rules in the company for men and women.
6 The company thinks that Mr Dale's clothes are too casual.
7 The employees of some companies can choose what they wear.
8 Mr Dale's lawyer thinks that the question of sexual discrimination is very complicated.

3 Work in pairs. Discuss these questions.

- Do you agree with Mr Dale or his company?
- What do you think are the most suitable clothes for work in an office?
- Are there any rules in your country about what you can wear to work?

GRAMMAR: modals of obligation (present time)

We use *must* or *have to* to talk about rules and things that are necessary.
  *Employees **must** wear suitable clothes.*
  *Mr Dale **has to** go in and out of the building.*

We use *don't have to* to say that something is not necessary (but it is possible or allowed).
  *We **don't have to** meet the clients.*

When we ask about rules, we usually use *have to*, not *must*.
  *Why **do** men **have to** wear trousers?*

We use *can* to say that something is possible or allowed.
  *Women **can** wear skirts and shorts.*

We use *can't* to say that something is not possible or not allowed.
  *You **can't** wear those here.*

 SEE LANGUAGE REFERENCE PAGE 114

1 Complete the texts with the correct verb form.

Most men in London's financial offices (1) *can't / have to* wear dark suits to work, but on Fridays everything is different. 23% of companies have a 'dress down' day, when they (2) *do not have to / must* put on their usual suit. Most of them are happy that they (3) *can / can't* wear anything they like at the end of the week.

(4) *Do children in your country have / Have children in your country* to wear a uniform to school? At most private schools in England, children (5) *can't / have to* wear a uniform. In most state schools, children (6) *have to / can't* wear a school sweatshirt, but they (7) *can / don't have to* choose their own trousers or skirt.

Students at the very traditional Oxford University (8) *don't have to / must* wear black gowns when they take their exams. At some colleges, they also (9) *can't / have to* wear the gowns at dinner. At Cambridge, on the other hand, students (10) *can / must* wear normal clothes.

2 Work in pairs. Discuss the rules in the place where you work or study. Talk about the topics in the box.

| clothes | times of work/study | days off |
| responsibilities | other rules | |

3 Think about what you discussed with your partner in exercise 2 and try to complete all of the sentences below. If necessary, speak to your partner from exercise 2 again.

1 I can leave work at 5 o'clock on Fridays and she can, too.

1 I can _____ and she/he can, too.
2 I can't _____, but she/he can.
3 She/He can _____, but I can't.
4 I have to _____ and she/he has to, too.
5 I have to _____, but she/he doesn't.
6 She/He doesn't have to _____, but I do.

READING

1 Look at the two photos above. Are there places like this where you live? Have you ever bought anything in places like this?

2 Read the article and explain the connection between the photos.

3 Read the article again and put the events in the correct order.

☐ Her friends helped her.
☐ Her mother couldn't go to the market.
☐ Kyra and her mother stopped selling food.
☐ She left school.
☐ Her mother started working at the market.
☐ She received a book about candles.
☐ She sold her first candles.
☐ She started making candles.

4 Have you ever worked in a shop or a market? Would you like to? Do you know anyone who has their own business?

Home comforts

With the opening this week of a new branch of *Home Comforts*, Kyra Komac now has 25 stores in her successful international chain of home and furniture shops. But the new store, in London's Camden High Street, takes her back to where it all started. She talks about how the business began.

When I was little, my mother began selling vegetarian food from a stall at Camden Market. She couldn't leave me at home on my own, so I had to go to the market with her.

To begin with, I didn't have to do anything. I just sat there, and my mum told me jokes and stories so I didn't get bored. When I got older, I gave my mum a hand and I really enjoyed it.

Then, one year, my uncle gave me a book for Christmas. It was all about making candles and I loved it. I was fourteen, and I didn't have to go to the market anymore because Mum could leave me at home on my own. I spent my free time making candles of all different shapes and sizes. I made hundreds of them.

One day, my mother was ill so I had to go to the market on my own. I decided to take some candles with me and see if I could sell them. They were sold out in twenty minutes! The next week, my mum gave me some money to buy some wax to make more candles. Again, they sold out really quickly.

Six months later, we decided to stop doing the vegetarian food. My mum and I couldn't make enough candles during the week, so some of my school friends started to help us. I paid them one pound for every candle, and we used to sell them for four or five times that. It was fun and my friends worked with me at the stall.

You could leave school at sixteen and I was in a hurry to leave. My uncle lent us some money and I opened my first shop in Portobello Road. Since then, I've never looked back. In the first store, we only sold incense and candles, but now we sell everything from designer furniture to silver jewellery. Oh, and candles, of course.

GRAMMAR: modals of obligation (past time)

1 Complete the grammar box. Put the phrases a–d in the gaps 1–4.

a This was necessary.   c This was possible.
b This wasn't necessary.   d This wasn't possible.

We use modal verbs to ask and talk about obligation and possibility in the past. We do not usually use *must* or *mustn't* when we are talking about the past.

could + infinitive
You **could leave** school at sixteen.
(1) _____

couldn't + infinitive
She **couldn't leave** me at home.
(2) _____

had to + infinitive
I **had to go** to the market with her.
(3) _____

didn't have to + infinitive
I **didn't have to go** to the market.
(4) _____

> SEE LANGUAGE REFERENCE PAGE 114

2 Complete the text with *had to*, *didn't have to*, *could* or *couldn't*.

My twin brother and I are the oldest in a family of seven. When I was a teenager, I (1) _____ look after my brothers and sisters until my parents came home from work. My brother was really lucky – because he was a boy, he (2) _____ do anything. I (3) _____ see my friends or go out because I (4) _____ do my homework when my parents got home. I wanted to go to college, but I (5) _____ get a place because I did badly in my exams. I got a job where I (6) _____ work in the evenings, so I (7) _____ go to evening school. For ten years I (8) _____ work and study really hard, but I finally got the qualification that I wanted and I became a teacher.

3 🔘 2.46 Listen to the recording to check your answers.

4 Think about when you were a child. Complete each sentence in three different ways.

1 I had to …   3 I could …
2 I didn't have to …   4 I couldn't …

Work in pairs. Compare your sentences.

DID YOU KNOW?

1 Read the text. How many different kinds of shops are mentioned?

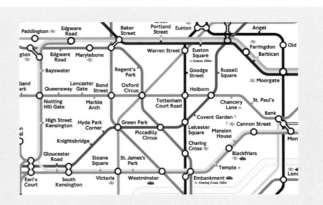

Portobello Road is famous for its street market (weekends), but it also has a lot of interesting antique shops. 🚇 Notting Hill Gate
Oxford Street is London's main shopping street with all the international chains (Gap, H & M, Zara, etc), large department stores and two mega-stores for CDs, DVDs and games. 🚇 Bond Street, Oxford Circus
For books, the best place to go is ***Charing Cross Road***. There are three enormous bookshops and many small specialist bookshops. 🚇 Tottenham Court Road
Go to ***Tottenham Court Road*** for computers, hi-fi, TVs and other electronic equipment. 🚇 Tottenham Court Road
Covent Garden is a lively and popular area with street theatre and music, bars and restaurants. You can find all the usual clothes shops, but also lots of small specialist shops. 🚇 Covent Garden
Bond Street is one of the most expensive streets in London. Chanel, Calvin Klein, DKNY, Versace, Prada – all the big names are here. 🚇 Bond Street, Green Park

2 Work in pairs. Ask and answer these questions.

• Have you ever been to London?
• Which parts of the city did you visit?
• What did you like most and least?
• Would you like to visit any of these areas of London?

SPEAKING

1 Work in pairs. Choose a shopping area of your town. Look at these questions and prepare a short presentation.

• Where is the area that you are going to talk about?
• How can you get there? (bus, underground, etc)
• What kind of shops are there?
• What are your favourite shops?
• Are there any shops that you don't recommend?
• What are the cafés/restaurants in the area like?
• Is there anything else that is good or bad about this area?

11D At the mall

SPEAKING

1 Work in pairs. Discuss these questions.

* Do you like shopping for clothes? What about your friends/family?
* Which are your favourite shops for clothes?
* Where did you buy the clothes that you are wearing?
* Do you prefer to buy clothes with friends or alone? Why?

LISTENING

1 Look at the picture. Why do you think Bella and Mademoiselle Lajolie are unhappy?

2 🔘 **2.47** Listen to the conversation to check your answers.

3 🔘 **2.47** Listen again and choose the correct answer.

1 Why does Bella think that shopping is easy for her friend?
   a) Because she has lots of money.
   b) Because everything looks good on her.
2 Why didn't Bella buy the black dress?
   a) Because she thought she looked like a waitress.
   b) Because she wanted a suit.
3 Why does Bella decide to buy a top?
   a) Because it's cheaper than a dress.
   b) Because she looks fat in dresses.
4 Why doesn't Bella want to buy something green?
   a) Because her boyfriend doesn't like green.
   b) Because she doesn't like green.
5 Why does Mademoiselle Lajolie suggest a gold top?
   a) Because gold is relaxed and casual.
   b) Because Bella wears gold jewellery.
6 Who is the party for?
   a) The students and the staff of the school.
   b) Only the staff of the school.

PRONUNCIATION: word linking

1 🔊 2.48 Listen to these phrases from the conversation. Notice how some of the words are joined together.

What do you think?
That's a thought.
We're in a bit of a hurry.
I'm afraid so.
Shall we go in and have a look?

2 Practise saying the phrases in exercise 1 quickly.

VOCABULARY: *fit*, *go with* & *suit*

1 Match the phrases in column A with phrases that mean the same in column B.

A	B
1 Your tie doesn't **go with** your shirt.	a It's the right size for you.
2 That suit **fits** you.	b You look good in that.
3 That dress really **suits** you.	c It isn't a good idea to wear those things together

2 Work in small groups. Look at the people in the picture opposite.

- Do all their clothes fit?
- Do the clothes of each person go well together?
- Do their clothes suit them?

3 Look at the clothes of the other people in your group. Is anyone in your group wearing something that would:

- fit you?
- go with something you are wearing?
- suit you?

FUNCTIONAL LANGUAGE: in a clothes shop

1 Complete the conversations 1–5 with the phrases in the box.

can I help you	excuse me
have you got it	how would you like
I'll take this	I'm afraid not
I'm just looking	I'm looking for
try this on	what size

1 A: Good morning, sir. _____?
   B: No, thanks. _____.

2 A: _____.
   B: Yes, madam. How can I help you?
   A: _____ a black jacket.
   B: Certainly. _____ are you?
   A: Medium.

3 A: Can I _____, please?
   B: Of course, the changing room is over there.

4 A: How does it fit?
   B: Fine, fine. _____ in green?
   A: _____, sir.

5 A: _____, please.
   B: Certainly, madam. _____ to pay?
   A: Credit card.

2 🔊 2.49–2.53 Listen to the conversations to check your answers.

Roleplay

3 Work in pairs, A and B.

A: You work in an expensive clothes shop. A customer walks in. Help the customer. Remember to be polite and friendly. You want the customer to spend lots of money.

B: You are a customer in a clothes shop. You enjoy shopping and you like trying on lots of different things. You are not planning to buy anything today.

GRAMMAR

Infinitive of purpose

We can use the infinitive with *to* to talk about why we do things. It explains the reason or purpose of our actions. We can also use *in order to* + infinitive.

> He went to the bank **to get** some cash.
> He went to the bank **in order to get** some cash.

Modals of obligation

Modal verbs are followed by an infinitive, without *to*. The form is the same for all persons.

Present time
We use *must, mustn't* and *have to* to talk about rules and things that are necessary.

> Students **must** return books to the library.
> You **mustn't** use your mobile phone in a plane.
> You **have to** park here. That street is closed.

We use *don't have to* to say that something is not necessary (but it is possible or allowed).
> Children at this school **don't have to** wear a uniform.

We use *have to* to ask about rules.
> Do I **have to** wear a suit at the wedding?

We use *can* to say that something is possible or allowed.
> Children over the age of ten **can** use the swimming pool.

We use *can't* to say that something is not possible or not allowed.
> You **can't** park your car outside the school..

Past time
We don't use *must* to talk about past time. Instead we use *had to*. We use *had to* to talk about rules and things that were necessary.
> She **had to** start work at 6.00 am every morning.

We use *didn't have to* to say that something was not necessary (but it was possible or allowed).
> I **didn't have to** wear a uniform at school.

We use *did* + subject + *have to* to ask about rules.
> **Did you have** to do any homework when you were a child?

We use *could* to say that something was possible or allowed.
> I **could** stay out until ten o'clock when I was sixteen.

We use *couldn't* to say that something was not possible or not allowed.
> She **couldn't** go to college because she failed her exams.

FUNCTIONAL LANGUAGE

Paraphrasing

It's a kind of …
It's a thing you …
They're a sort of …
You use them to + infinitive …

In a clothes shop

(How) can I help you?
What size do you take/are you?
How would you like to pay?

I'm just looking.
I'm looking for …
Can I try this on, please?
I'll take this.

WORD LIST

Personal possessions

car n C ***	/kɑː/
CD player n C	/siː ˈdiː pleɪə/
computer n C ***	/kəmˈpjuːtə/
credit card n C	/ˈkredɪt kɑːd/
lipstick n C/U	/ˈlɪpstɪk/
motorbike n C	/ˈməʊtəbaɪk/
MP3 player n C	/em piː ˈθriː pleɪə/
pen n C **	/pen/
phone n C ***	/fəʊn/
sunglasses n plur	/ˈsʌnglɑːsɪz/
TV n C ***	/tiː ˈviː/
watch n C **	/wɒtʃ/

Clothes

boot n C **	/buːt/
cardigan n C	/ˈkɑːdɪgən/
changing room n C	/ˈtʃeɪndʒɪŋ ruːm/
dress n C **	/dres/
fit v ***	/fɪt/
flip flops n pl	/ˈflɪp flɒps/
go with v	/ˈgəʊ wɪð/
gown n C	/gaʊn/
jacket n C **	/ˈdʒækɪt/
jeans n plur **	/dʒiːnz/
jersey n C	/ˈdʒɜːzi/
scarf n C	/skɑːf/
shirt n C ***	/ʃɜːt/
shorts n plur	/ʃɔːts/
skirt n C **	/skɜːt/
sock n C	/sɒk/
suit n C **	/suːt/
suit v ***	/suːt/
sweatshirt n C	/ˈswetʃɜːt/
tie n C *	/taɪ/
top n C ***	/tɒp/
trainers n plur	/ˈtreɪnəz/
trousers n plur **	/ˈtraʊzəz/
try on v	/traɪ ˈɒn/
T-shirt n C	/tiː ʃɜːt/
underwear n U	/ˈʌndəweə/

Other words & phrases

antique n C	/ænˈtiːk/
awful adj **	/ˈɔːfl/
bargain n C	/ˈbɑːgɪn/
bloke n C	/bləʊk/
branch n C **	/brɑːntʃ/
candle n C	/ˈkændl/
case n C ***	/keɪs/
casual adj	/ˈkæʒuəl/
chain n C **	/tʃeɪn/
client n C	/ˈklaɪənt/
department store n C	/dɪˈpɑːtmənt stɔː/
discrimination n U *	/dɪskrɪmɪˈneɪʃn/
electronic adj **	/elekˈtrɒnɪk/
employee n C **	/emplɔːˈiː/
enormous adj **	/ɪˈnɔːməs/
formal adj ***	/ˈfɔːml/
furniture n U **	/ˈfɜːnɪtʃə/
garage n C *	/ˈgærɪdʒ/
gold n U **	/gəʊld/
hurry v *	/ˈhʌri/
image n C ***	/ˈɪmɪdʒ/
impress v **	/ɪmˈpres/
incense n U	/ˈɪnsens/
instead (of) adv ***	/ɪnˈsted/
investment n C ***	/ɪnˈvestmənt/
jewellery n U **	/ˈdʒuːəlri/
joke n C *	/dʒəʊk/
judge v **	/dʒʌdʒ/
medium adj *	/ˈmiːdiəm/
mega-store n C	/ˈmegə stɔː/
mum n C **	/mʌm/
overtime n U	/ˈəʊvətaɪm/
professionalism n U	/prəˈfeʃnəlɪz(ə)m/
recommend v ***	/rekəˈmend/
roof n C ***	/ruːf/
sell out v	/sel ˈaʊt/
seriously adv **	/ˈsɪəriəsli/
sexy adj	/ˈseksi/
shape n C ***	/ʃeɪp/
sign v *	/saɪn/
silver n C *	/ˈsɪlvə/
size n C ***	/saɪz/
spokeswoman n C	/ˈspəʊkswʊmən/
stall n C	/stɔːl/
store n C **	/stɔː/
suitable adj ***	/ˈsuːtəbl/
uniform n C **	/ˈjuːnɪfɔːm/
wax n U	/wæks/
wheel n C ***	/wiːl/

12A | Around the world

SPEAKING

1 Work in groups. Answer these questions.

- What do you know about the people below?
- Where did they come from?
- Why are they famous?
- What else do you know about them?

Christopher Columbus Neil Armstrong
Jacques Cousteau Roald Amundsen
Marco Polo

Compare your answers with another group.

2 Do you know of any explorers or adventurers from your country?

GRAMMAR: prepositions of movement

1 Match the prepositions in the box to the pictures A–H.

| across | along | around | into | out of |
| over | past | through | | |

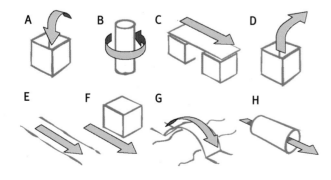

2 Choose the correct preposition to complete these sentences.

1 **1434** The Portuguese explorer, Gil Eannes, was the first European to sail *over / past* Cape Bojador on the coast of Africa.
2 **1492** Columbus first sailed *across / along* the Atlantic Ocean.
3 **1522** Juan Sebastian del Cano became the first man to sail *around / through* the world.
4 **around 1800** The Scottish explorer, Mungo Park, travelled on horse and on foot *along / into* the Niger River in West Africa.
5 **around 1800** The German explorer, Alexander von Humboldt, travelled *out of / through* the Amazon jungle and collected plants.
6 **1928** Amelia Earhart was the first woman to fly *over / past* the Atlantic Ocean.
7 **1961** Yuri Gagarin was the first man to go *across / into* space.
8 **1969** Neil Armstrong climbed *around / out of* his spaceship and became the first man on the Moon.

3 Describe your journey from home to school. Use as many prepositions of movement as possible.

I go out of my house and get into my car. I drive along Green Street …

LISTENING

1  2.54 Listen to a news report about an American adventurer, Steve Fossett. Answer these questions.

1 What is the latest world record that he has broken?
2 Which of these activities has Steve Fossett **not** tried?

balloning   dog racing   flying   space travel
long-distance swimming   speed sailing

2 🔘 2.54 Listen again and complete the sentences with the correct number.

1 Steve Fossett landed at Lake Yamma Yamma, which is _____ miles north of Sydney.
2 He has tried to fly around the world in a balloon _____ times.
3 The journey took him a little less than _____ days.
4 His journey began on June _____ at Northam in Western Australia.
5 His departure was delayed for _____ hours because of high winds.
6 He swam the Channel between France and England in _____.
7 In 2001, he sailed across the Atlantic in four days and _____ hours.
8 He holds the world gliding record for 500 and _____ kilometres.

3 For some people, Steve Fossett is a hero. Other people think that his achievements are a waste of time and money. What do you think?

PRONUNCIATION: /ɜː/

1 🔘 2.55 Listen and repeat these phrases.

first person   third world
journey to work   word search

2 Underline the word in each group that does **not** contain the sound /ɜː/.

1 burn   circle   heart   journey
2 birth   compare   early   nervous
3 earn   girl   heard   record
4 interest learn   nurse   service

3 🔘 2.56 Listen to the recording to check your answers.

VOCABULARY: phrasal verbs

1 Replace the words in *italics* with a phrasal verb from the box.

| called off | carried on | gave up | put off |
| sorted out | took off | | |

1 Steve Fossett's balloon *left the ground* from a town in Western Australia.
2 He almost *cancelled* his attempt to fly round the world.
3 He had to *delay* his departure because of a problem with the wind.
4 He *found a solution to* his difficulties.
5 He *continued* with his journey.
6 He *stopped* ballooning after this journey.

Look at tapescript 2.54 on page 146 to check your answers.

2 In these sentences, one of the words or phrases is **not** possible. Cross out the incorrect words.

1 Unfortunately, the *concert / weather / wedding* was called off.
2 Are you going to carry on *seeing him / the Atlantic Ocean / with your studies*?
3 He has decided to give up *his job / his wife / smoking*.
4 The *decision / meeting / world* was put off until next week.
5 She needs to sort out her *good health / money problems / relationship with her boss*.
6 The *helicopter / plane / ship* took off one hour late.

SPEAKING

1 Imagine that you have a 'round the world' plane ticket that allows you to make five stop-overs. Decide where you want to make the stop-overs.

2 Work in pairs. Compare your lists and decide on five places you both want to visit. Plan your route and decide what you are going to do in each place.

3 Tell the other students in your class what you are going to do.

Our first stop-over is going to be Sydney. We want to go there to see the koalas and kangaroos and also to visit the Opera House.

Who has planned the most interesting journey?

12B | Let's dance

SPEAKING

1 Work in pairs. Discuss these questions.

* Which of these festivals have you heard of? What do you know about them?
  Rio de Janeiro Carnival (Brazil)
  Venice Festival (Italy)
  Las Fallas (Valencia, Spain)
  Notting Hill Carnival (London, England)
  Mardi Gras (New Orleans, USA)
* Which of these festivals would you most like to go to? Why?
* What festivals are there in your country? Which is the best?

VOCABULARY & READING: festivals

1 Match the words in the box to the pictures A–H.

> band   costume   fireworks display   float
> parade/procession   mask   speakers   traditional food

2 Read the email about a carnival in Trinidad. Which of the things in exercise 1 does the writer **not** mention?

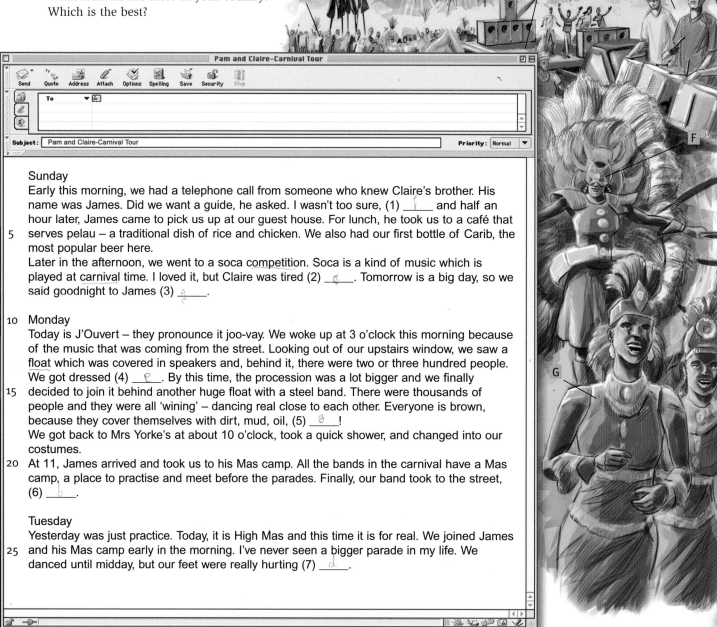

Pam and Claire–Carnival Tour

Send Quote Address Attach Options Spelling Save Security Stop

To

Subject: Pam and Claire–Carnival Tour   Priority: Normal

Sunday
Early this morning, we had a telephone call from someone who knew Claire's brother. His name was James. Did we want a guide, he asked. I wasn't too sure, (1) __f__ and half an hour later, James came to pick us up at our guest house. For lunch, he took us to a café that
5 serves pelau – a traditional dish of rice and chicken. We also had our first bottle of Carib, the most popular beer here.
Later in the afternoon, we went to a soca competition. Soca is a kind of music which is played at carnival time. I loved it, but Claire was tired (2) __c__. Tomorrow is a big day, so we said goodnight to James (3) __g__.

10 Monday
Today is J'Ouvert – they pronounce it joo-vay. We woke up at 3 o'clock this morning because of the music that was coming from the street. Looking out of our upstairs window, we saw a float which was covered in speakers and, behind it, there were two or three hundred people. We got dressed (4) __e__. By this time, the procession was a lot bigger and we finally
15 decided to join it behind another huge float with a steel band. There were thousands of people and they were all 'wining' – dancing real close to each other. Everyone is brown, because they cover themselves with dirt, mud, oil, (5) __d__!
We got back to Mrs Yorke's at about 10 o'clock, took a quick shower, and changed into our costumes.
20 At 11, James arrived and took us to his Mas camp. All the bands in the carnival have a Mas camp, a place to practise and meet before the parades. Finally, our band took to the street, (6) __b__.

Tuesday
Yesterday was just practice. Today, it is High Mas and this time it is for real. We joined James
25 and his Mas camp early in the morning. I've never seen a bigger parade in my life. We danced until midday, but our feet were really hurting (7) __d__.

3 Read the email again and put the phrases a–g into the gaps 1–7.

a   and even chocolate sauce
b   and for the next four hours, we 'wined' and danced with James and his friends
c   and wanted to get an early night
d   so we found a place to watch
e   and went downstairs to join the parade
f   but Claire said yes
g   and went back to the guest house

4 Look at the email again and say what these words refer to.

1   he (line 3)   *James*
2   it (line 8)   _____
3   it (line 11)   _____
4   it (line 13)   _____
5   us (line 20)   _____

GRAMMAR: relative clauses

We can join two sentences with a relative pronoun (*who, that, which*).
> He took us to a café. It serves pelau.
> He took us to a café **that** serves pelau.

We use *who* for people, *which* for things, and *that* for both people and things.

The relative pronoun takes the place of *he, she, it* or *they*.
> We had a phone call from someone **who** ~~he~~ knew Claire's brother.
> Soca is a kind of music **which** ~~it~~ is played at carnival time.

> ◯ SEE LANGUAGE REFERENCE PAGE 124

1 Replace *that* in the following sentences with *who* or *which*.

1   James was a Trinidadian that looked after us.
2   We were woken up by some music that was very loud.
3   They stayed in a guest house that was near the town centre.
4   We joined the people that were 'wining' behind the float.

2 Three of these sentences have a word which should not be there. Cross out the unnecessary words.

1   Pelau is a dish that it is made from rice and chicken.
2   Soca is a kind of music that started in the 1970s.
3   She went to a soca competition which it started in the afternoon.
4   The writer went to Trinidad with a friend who was from college.
5   They bought costumes that cost $250.
6   They stayed with a woman who she was very friendly.

3 Join the pairs of sentences to make one sentence with a relative clause.

1   Venice has a carnival. It is famous for its beautiful masks.
2   Belgium has an important festival. It takes place in Binche.
3   The summer festival in Verona is for music lovers. They like opera.
4   During the Rio carnival, the keys of the city are given to a man. He is called King Momo.
5   At Las Fallas, the people of Valencia make statues of famous people. They are burnt on the last night.
6   At Notting Hill in London, people wear costumes. They cost thousands of pounds.

SPEAKING

1 You are going to talk about a festival that you have been to. Before you speak, prepare your answers to these questions.

- Where and when did the festival take place?
- What does the festival celebrate?
- Does the festival have any special traditions (costumes, food, drink, music, dance, etc)?
- Who did you go to the festival with?
- How long did you stay?
- What did you do there?
- What did you like most and least about the festival?

2 Describe your festival to other students in the class and listen to their descriptions.

12c | Global English

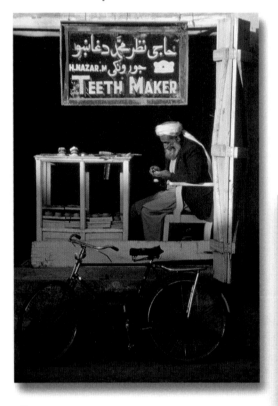

SPEAKING

1 In your town, where can you find signs that are written in English? What do the signs say?

Where can you hear people speaking English? Why is English used?

VOCABULARY: countries & languages

1 Where are these cities?

1 Greece

1	Athens	5	Riyadh	9	Madrid
2	Budapest	6	Tokyo	10	Paris
3	Sao Paolo	7	Beijing	11	Rome
4	Moscow	8	Istanbul	12	Warsaw

Put the countries in order from 1–12 (1= nearest to your country → 12 = furthest from your country).

2 Which languages are spoken in the countries in exercise 1? Write the languages in the correct place in the table.

ending in *-an*	ending in *-ish*	ending in *-ese*	with other endings
Hungarian			

Can you add one more language to each column?

3 In how many different languages can you say *hello*?

4 Which of the languages in exercise 2 are the most widely-spoken in the world? Complete the list with the languages from exercise 2.

The World's Most Widely-Spoken Languages

1   Mandarin Chinese
2   Indian language family
     (Hindi, Bengali, etc)
3   _____
4   _____
5   _____
6   _____
7   _____
8   _____

5 🔊 2.57 Listen to the recording to check your answers.

READING

1 Work in pairs. Discuss these questions.

- How many different countries can you name where English is the first language?
- What kind of English do you find it easiest to understand?
- Is it better to learn American or British English?

2 Read the article. Does the writer think that it is better to learn American or British English?

English as an International Language – no problem, OK?

'You say to-may-to, I say to-mah-to'

The British and the Americans like to talk about the differences between British and American English. There are a few small differences in the grammar and there are a few words that are different on either side of the Atlantic, but the big difference is the
5 accent. Some British films have subtitles in America because people can't understand what the actors are saying, and some American TV series (*The Sopranos*, for example) are difficult for the British to understand.

However, if you listen to Standard English (the language that TV newsreaders use, for example) in Britain or the US, there are no
10 problems of understanding at all. The problems are with the different kinds of American and British English. These different dialects and accents depend on people's social class and the geographical area where they live. It is possible, for example, that a middle-class speaker from the south of England will find it difficult to understand a working-class
15 speaker from the north. In the same way, a wealthy Californian may not understand a working-class New Yorker. All of these people have accents, but the middle-class accents are usually closer to Standard English.

With so many different Englishes, it is difficult for learners of the language. What sort of English should they learn? Is American English
20 better than British English, or the other way round? The answer depends on their reasons for learning English. If they are learning English for their work, the choice will probably be easy. But for many students, it doesn't matter. What matters is that they understand and are understood.

The world is changing and English is no longer the property of the
25 British, Americans or Australians. Most English that you hear and see around the world is spoken or written by non-native speakers – between, for example, a Greek and a German, or between a Russian and an Italian. English is the main language of business, academic conferences and tourism, of popular music, home computers and video games. English
30 has become the Latin of the modern world.

Because of this, the question of American or British English is becoming less and less important. More and more people now talk about English as an International Language – a language that is not American or British. It has hundreds of different accents, but if people can understand what you
35 are saying, no problem. OK?

3 Read the article again and say if these sentences are true (T) or false (F).

1 There are a lot of important differences between British and American grammar.
2 Some Americans can't understand British films.
3 There is only one British accent.
4 For many students, it doesn't matter if they learn British or American English.
5 Many different nationalities use English to communicate.
6 English as an International Language is a kind of American English.

4 Which accents in your language do you find difficult to understand? What do other people think of your accent?

What is the best accent in your language for a student to learn?

PRONUNCIATION: British & American accents

1 ● 2.58 You will hear these words said twice. Which speaker is American and which is British?

| answer | ask | banana | castle |
| dance | example | France | glass |

2 ● 2.59–2.60 Listen to another group of words. You will hear each word said twice: first by an American speaker, then by a British speaker. Mark the stress on the words.

US	UK
☐ ☐	☐ ☐
address	address
café	café
cigarette	cigarette
magazine	magazine
weekend	weekend

12D | Global issues

health

genetic engineering

global warming

animal and nature conservation

internet

education

genetics

SPEAKING & VOCABULARY: global issues

1 Match the newspaper headlines A–N to the global issue above.

A
LA children who cannot read

B
Police need more money to fight online crime

C
Protesters destroy fields

D
Brazil opens rainforest reserve

E
European Parliament to vote on minimum wage

F
NEW AIDS DRUG

G
Temperatures reach record high

H
Researchers find new flu virus

I
Who will save the Javan rhinoceros?

J
FOREST FIRES IN SOUTHERN FRANCE

K
Computer virus shuts down government websites

L
More teachers needed in Central city schools

M
Scientists clone 12 sheep

N
NEW HOSTELS FOR HOMELESS MEN

2 Work in pairs. Discuss these questions.

* Can you think of any other global issues?
* Which three issues are most important to you? Why?
* Which issues are important in your country at the moment?
* Do you know any stories in the news at the moment that are connected to these issues?

LISTENING

1 🔘 2.61–2.64 Listen to four conversations at a party. Which global issues above are discussed?

2 🔘 2.61–2.64 Listen to the conversations again to check your answers. Complete the sentences with a word from the box.

global warming　homeless　internet　junk
organic　newspapers　poor　virus

Conversation 1
1 Mike has had a problem with a computer _____.
2 Bella thinks that the police should do more to stop _____ criminals.

Conversation 2
3 Mademoiselle Lajolie doesn't want to eat _____ food.
4 Patrick thinks that _____ food is a waste of money.

Conversation 3
5 Ruby thinks life is very hard for the _____.
6 Davina thinks that everyone should give money to the _____.

Conversation 4
7 Stuart doesn't care about _____.
8 Mary doesn't believe everything in the _____.

3 Which of the sentences in exercise 2 are true for you?

FUNCTIONAL LANGUAGE: agreeing & disagreeing

1 Complete the table with these phrases.

a I see what you mean, but …
b I'm not sure about that.
c Oh, absolutely/definitely.
d That's how I feel, too.
e That's not the way I see it.
f That's what I think, too.
g Well, maybe, but …
h You must be joking!

agree	partly agree
I agree with you.	I see your point, but …
(1) _____	(4) _____
(2) _____	(5) _____
(3) _____	

disagree	strongly disagree
I'm afraid I disagree.	You can't be serious!
(6) _____	(8) _____
(7) _____	

2 🌐 **2.65** Listen to the phrases and repeat.

3 Work in pairs. Complete and continue the conversation. Use as many of the phrases in exercise 1 as possible.

A: Have you heard the news about _____? It's terrible, isn't it?
B: Yes, I agree with you. I think we should all do something about it.
A: _____. But what?
B: _____.

4 Look at these sentences and decide if you agree, partly agree, disagree or strongly disagree.

1 We should find solutions to our own problems before we try to help the rest of the world.
2 Women worry about the world's problems more than men do.
3 Politicians will find solutions to the world's problems.
4 There is nothing that I can do about the world's problems.
5 It is the job of the United Nations (not national governments) to solve the world's problems.

Work in small groups and compare your opinions.

DID YOU KNOW?

1 Look at the information about Oxfam.

Work in pairs and discuss these questions.

- What charities are there in your country?
- What do these charities do?
- Do you ever give money to charities? Which ones?

Oxfam International

Oxfam International is one of the world's biggest charities. Oxfam's aim is a simple one: to work with others to find lasting solutions to poverty and suffering.

- Oxfam has programmes in more than 70 countries. It works with local people to improve their lives. Oxfam trains health workers and sets up schools, for example.
- Oxfam responds to emergencies, providing food and shelter for people who have lost their homes in floods, hurricanes and war.
- Oxfam speaks to governments and powerful organizations about the problems of poor people. It encourages people to speak for themselves and change their lives for the better.

Oxfam was started in Oxford in 1942. It now has 3,000 partner organizations in 100 countries, including the US, Australia and many countries in Europe.

GRAMMAR

Prepositions of movement

*How long does it take to sail **across** the lake?*

*They walked **along** the street until they found the restaurant.*

*The tour guide took them **around** the walls of the old city and back to their starting-point.*

*The family got **into** the car.*

*She took her lipstick **out of** her handbag.*

*We are now flying **over** London.*

*He drove **past** my house but he didn't stop.*

*It took a long time to go **through** passport control.*

Relative clauses

We can join two sentences with a relative pronoun (*who, that, which*).

> *We often go to a restaurant. It serves Chinese food.*
> *We often go to a restaurant **that** serves Chinese food.*

We use *who* for people, *which* for things, and *that* for both people and things. The relative pronoun takes the place of *he, she, it* or *they*.

> *Yesterday, I met someone **who** went to my old school.*
> *Cheddar is a kind of cheese **which** is very popular in England.*

The examples above are defining relative clauses. A defining relative clause identifies the thing that we are talking about. We do not use a comma before the relative pronoun in a defining relative clause.

FUNCTIONAL LANGUAGE

Agreeing & disagreeing

agree

I agree with you.
That's how I feel, too.
That's what I think, too.
Absolutely.
Definitely.

I see your point, but …
I see what you mean, but …

Well, maybe, but …
I'm not sure about that.
I disagree, I'm afraid.
That's not the way I see it.

You can't be serious!
You must be joking!

disagree

WORD LIST

Phrasal verbs

call (sth) off	/kɔːl ˈɒf/
carry on (+ verb + -ing)	/ˈkæri ˈɒn/
give (sth) up	/gɪv ˈʌp/
pick (sb) up	/pɪk ˈʌp/
put (sth) off	/pʊt ˈɒf/
sort (sth) out	/sɔːt ˈaʊt/
take off	/teɪk ɒf/

Festivals

band n C ***	/bænd/
carnival n C	/ˈkaːnivl/
costume n C	/ˈkɒstjuːm/
display n C **	/dɪˈspleɪ/
fireworks n plur	/ˈfaɪəwɜːks/
float n C	/fləʊt/
mask n C	/maːsk/
parade n C	/pəˈreɪd/
procession n C	/prəˈseʃn/
(loud) speaker n C	/ˈspiːkə/

Countries & languages

Arabic	/ˈærəbɪk/
Brazil	/brəˈzɪl/
China	/ˈtʃaɪnə/
Chinese	/tʃaɪˈniːz/
France	/fraːns/
French	/frentʃ/
German	/ˈdʒɜːmən/
Greece	/griːs/
Greek	/griːk/
Hungarian	/hʌnˈgeəriən/
Hungary	/ˈhʌngəri/
Italian	/ɪˈtæliən/
Italy	/ˈɪtəli/
Japan	/dʒəˈpæn/
Japanese	/dʒæpəˈniːz/
Latin	/ˈlætɪn/
Poland	/ˈpəʊlənd/
Polish	/ˈpəʊlɪʃ/
Portuguese	/pɔːtʃʊˈgiːz/
Russia	/ˈrʌʃə/
Russian	/ˈrʌʃn/
Saudi Arabia	/saʊdi əˈreɪbiə/
Spain	/speɪn/
Spanish	/ˈspænɪʃ/
Turkey	/ˈtɜːki/
Turkish	/ˈtɜːkɪʃ/

Global issues

clone n C/v	/kləʊn/
crime n C/U ***	/kraɪm/
environment n C/U ***	/ɪnˈvaɪrənmənt/
genetic engineering n U	/dʒənetɪk endʒəˈnɪərɪŋ/
genetically modified adj	/dʒənetɪkli ˈmɒdɪfaɪd/
global warming n U	/gləʊbl ˈwɔːmɪŋ/
health n U ***	/helθ/
homeless adj	/ˈhəʊmləs/
minimum wage n C	/mɪnɪməm ˈweɪdʒ/
nature conservation n C	/ˈneɪtʃə kɒnsɜːˈveɪʃn/
organic food n C	/ɔːˈgænɪk fuːd/
poverty n U	/ˈpɒvəti/
protester n C	/prəˈtestə/
rainforest n C/U	/ˈreɪnfɒrɪst/

Other words & phrases

academic adj *	/ækəˈdemɪk/
adventurer n C	/ədˈventʃ(ə)rə/
aeroplane n C	/ˈeərəpleɪn/
attempt n C **	/əˈtempt/
balloon n C	/bəˈluːn/
ballooning n U	/bəˈluːnɪŋ/
charity n C/U **	/ˈtʃærəti/
climatologist n C	/klaɪməˈtɒlədʒɪst/
coast n C **	/kəʊst/
collect v ***	/kəˈlekt/
compare v ***	/kəmˈpeə/
delay v *	/dɪˈleɪ/
dialect n C	/ˈdaɪəlekt/
dirt n U	/dɜːt/
emergency n C **	/ɪˈmɜːdʒ(ə)nsi/
epic adj	/ˈepɪk/
field n C ***	/fiːld/
flood n C *	/flʌd/
forest n C ***	/ˈfɒrɪst/
fortunate adj	/ˈfɔːtʃənət/
generous adj *	/ˈdʒenərəs/
geographical adj	/dʒiːəˈgræfɪkl/
glider n C	/ˈglaɪdə/
gliding n U	/ˈglaɪdɪŋ/
guest house n C	/ˈgest haʊs/
guide n C **	/gaɪd/
handsome adj **	/ˈhæns(ə)m/
helicopter n C	/ˈhelɪkɒptə/
helium n U	/ˈhiːliəm/
horse n C ***	/hɔːs/
hostel n C	/ˈhɒstl/
hurricane n C	/ˈhʌrɪkeɪn/
middle-class adj	/mɪdl ˈklaːs/

mud n U	/mʌd/
native speaker n C	/neɪtɪv ˈspiːkə/
newsreader n C	/ˈnjuːzriːdə/
ocean n C *	/ˈəʊʃn/
onion n C	/ˈʌnjən/
opera n C/U	/ˈɒp(ə)rə/
politician n C **	/pɒlɪˈtɪʃn/
property n U ***	/ˈprɒpəti/
respond v **	/rɪsˈpɒnd/
rhinoceros n C	/raɪˈnɒs(ə)rəs/
sail v **	/seɪl/
sailing n U	/ˈseɪlɪŋ/
soca n U	/ˈsɒkə/
social class n C	/səʊʃl ˈklaːs/
solo adj/adv	/ˈsəʊləʊ/
solution n C **	/səˈluːʃn/
solve v **	/sɒlv/
speed n C/U ***	/spiːd/
steel n U *	/stiːl/
suffering n C/U	/ˈsʌfərɪŋ/
virus n C *	/ˈvaɪrəs/
wage n C ***	/weɪdʒ/
wealthy adj	/ˈwelθi/
working-class adj	/wɔːkɪŋ ˈklaːs/

Communication activities

4c Functional language exercise 1   page 41

Pair A

Read the story of this film twice and then close your books.

The Mask

Stanley Ipkiss is an ordinary guy who works in a bank. One day, a beautiful woman called Tina comes into his bank and he falls in love with her. But Tina works for a gangster who wants to rob the bank. She is not happy with the gangster and wants to leave him. Later that day, Stanley finds a mask in a river. When he puts the mask on, he has special powers. With these special powers, Stanley stops the gangster from robbing the bank. But the gangster gets Stanley's mask and Stanley must help Tina without it. In the end, the gangster is killed and Stanley is a hero.

1b Speaking exercise 2   page 9

Student A

Read your information and use the questions in exercise 1 page 9 to find out about Christine's other friends.

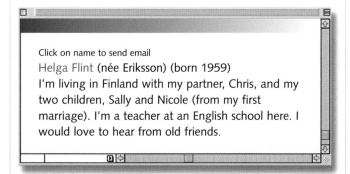

Click on name to send email
Helga Flint (née Eriksson) (born 1959)
I'm living in Finland with my partner, Chris, and my two children, Sally and Nicole (from my first marriage). I'm a teacher at an English school here. I would love to hear from old friends.

3a Speaking exercise 1   page 27

Student A

Read your rolecard and decide what you want to say to your flatmates.

> You share a flat with the other students in your group. There are some problems in the flat and no one is happy.
>
> You are studying for your exams and are very busy. You want to stop smoking but this is not a good time. In the evening, you want to go to bed early, but Student B has always got some friends in his room and they play music all night. You can't sleep.
>
> With your flatmates, make a list of four rules for the flat.
> *No smoking in the flat.*

1d Functional language exercise 3   page 12

Student A

Write two more telephone numbers in column A. Dictate the numbers in column A to your partner. Then listen to your partner and write her/his numbers in column B.

A		B	
a	999	a	_____
b	015 33 30 00	b	_____
c	02 513 23 36	c	_____
d	03273 177 711	d	_____
e	03865 405700	e	_____
f	00 44 207 3641	f	_____
g	_____	g	_____
h	_____	h	_____

Now check your answers with your partner.

11a Functional language exercise 2   Page 107

Take it in turns to choose one of the objects. Describe the object to your partner but do not say what it is. Your partner must guess which object you are describing.

1B Grammar exercise 4 page 9

Student B

Ask and answer questions with your partner to complete the missing information.

Christine Smith left school in 1976. She studied (1 *What?*) _____ at Leeds University and then got a job at (2) *the United Nations in New York*. When she was there, she met (3 *Who?*) _____ at the White House. He worked for (4) *the British Embassy*. They started going out together and they got married (5 *When?*) _____. They now have (6) *seven* children. Christine and her husband now live (7 *Where?*) _____. She works for (8) *the International Red Cross* and he is writing (9) *What?*) _____. Christine wants to get in touch with (10) *old school friends* and promises to reply to all emails.

2C Grammar exercise 2 page 21

Work in pairs. Ask and answer the questions.

Picture A

1 What was the man at the door wearing?
2 What were the other people in the room wearing?
3 What was the man with the red tie holding?
4 What was the woman doing?

Picture B

1 Who was standing at the door?
2 Who was he looking at?
3 What was he wearing?
4 What were the students doing?

Picture C

1 Where was the teacher standing?
2 What was she holding?
3 Where was the boy with bond hair sitting?
4 How many students were taking the exam?

1B Speaking exercise 2 page 9

Student B

Read your information and use the questions in exercise 1 page 9 to find out about Christine's other friends.

Click on name to send email
Nicholas Flint (born 1957)
Working in Orlando, Florida for Disney. I got married for the third time last year, and my wife, Cindy, and I now have a lovely daughter, Verity. We have lots of room and would love to see old friends. Come and stay with us for a holiday.

3C Speaking exercises 1 & 2 page 31

Complete column A with information about a town that you know. Do **not** choose your home town.

	Town A	Town B
Name of town		
Cheap accommodation		
Restaurants		
Nightlife		
Parks and gardens		
Traffic		
Public transport		
Cinemas and theatres		
Crime		
Pollution		

Ask questions about your partner's town. Write the answers in column B.

3A Grammar exercise 3 page 27

Student A

Look at the picture. Then ask and answer questions with your partner to see how many differences you can find.

Charlie's bedroom

9C Grammar exercise 3 page 91

Answers

1 Titanic
2 Men in Black
3 Moulin Rouge
4 E.T.
5 Ghandi
6 Harry Potter and the Chamber of Secrets
7 Gladiator

3A Speaking exercise 1   page 27

Student B

Read your rolecard and decide what you want to say to your flatmates.

> You share a flat with the other students in your group. There are some problems in the flat and no one is happy.
>
> There is never any food in the house. You often buy food, but you think that Student C eats it all. Student C never does any shopping! In fact, you spend more money than everybody else in the flat. It is time for others to pay.
>
> With your flatmates, make a list of four rules for the flat.
> *No smoking in the flat.*

4A Reading exercise 2   page 37

Student A

Read about Jay and tick (✓) the sentences on page 37 that are about him.

Jay

Age: 26
Occupation: primary school teacher

I am a quiet, friendly, guy but I find it difficult to meet other people. My friends say I spend too much time on my own, but I don't like going to clubs and bars. I like being on my own and I often prefer to stay at home and read, do yoga, think about life and listen to music. Music (Bach, Vivaldi, etc) is the big love of my life and I often go to concerts at the weekend. I also enjoy long walks in the country, especially in the mountains. I would like to find someone to share those special moments and, maybe, to find love, too.

My perfect partner has the same interests as me. She is kind and romantic, warm and natural. She is open about everything and wants a man who has a lot of love to give. She's a vegetarian and doesn't smoke. For her money is not important, and she enjoys the simple things in life. She likes children and maybe wants to have a family.

2B Grammar exercise 1   page 19

Answer: Pierce Brosnan

1D Functional language exercise 3   page 12

Student B

Write two more telephone numbers in column A. Listen to your partner and write her/his numbers in column B. Then dictate your numbers (in column A) to your partner.

A		B	
a	911	a	
b	02790 16 16	b	_____
c	02 511 4529	c	_____
d	03223 344323	d	_____
e	0800 60 800	e	_____
f	00 1 245 44 45	f	_____
g	_____	g	_____
h	_____	h	_____

Now check your answers with your partner.

6B Speaking exercise 2   page 58

Calculate your score.

Are You A Foodie?

1	a) 15 points	4	a) 15 points
	b) 10 points		b) 10 points
	c) 5 points		c) 5 points
2	a) 5 points	5	a) 15 points
	b) 10 points		b) 10 points
	c) 15 points		c) 5 points
3	5 points for each food item	6	a) 15 points
			b) 10 points
			c) 5 points

25–45 points Champion foodie
You certainly like your food! You know what food is fashionable, you know the best food shops and you are happy in a kitchen. Your friends sometimes say that you should open a restaurant – and they are probably right.

50–75 points Part-time foodie
You like the idea of cooking, but it's sometimes easier to get something out of the freezer and put it in the microwave. You like going out to restaurants, especially when someone else pays. Food is important for you, but there are more important things in your life.

80–95 points Fast foodie
You probably like traditional food, but your life is too busy for cooking or shopping for food. After all, what's wrong with hot dogs and ice cream? You eat because you need to eat and you don't care too much what it is.

7D Pronunciation exercise 2   page 73

Student A

Dictate the addresses in column A to your partner and write the addresses your partner dictates in column B.

A	B
www.bbc.co.uk	_____
www.google.com	_____
www.geocities.com/index	_____
ruby.tuesday@hotmail.com	_____
marywhitehead@socksareus.net	_____

Now check your answers with your partner.

3A Grammar exercise 3   page 27

Student B

Look at the picture. Then ask and answer questions with your partner to see how many differences you can find.

Charlie's bedroom after a party.

3A Speaking exercise 2   page 9

Student C

Read your information and use the questions in exercise 1 page 9 to find out about Christine's other friends.

Click on name to send email
Richard Hoffman (born 1958)
Hi, everybody. I spent the last 15 years in the Army, but I left in January of this year. I'm now working at Heathrow Airport as an Immigration Officer. I'm living in West London and would love to see old friends again. Especially the girls!
P.S. I'm still free and single.

3A Speaking exercise 1   page 27

Student C

Read your rolecard and decide what you want to say to your flatmates.

> You share a flat with the other students in your group. There are some problems in the flat and no one is happy.
>
> You stay at home a lot because you do not have a job. The other people in the flat never do any housework. You do it all. There are never any clean glasses when you want a drink. You can't hear the TV in the evening because Student B always listens to loud music.
>
> With your flatmates, make a list of four rules for the flat. *No smoking in the flat.*

5B Functional language exercise 6   page 49

Student A

Roleplay 1

> You are a passenger on a long-distance flight. You want to request some things from the flight attendant. Look at the ideas below and decide what you are going to say to the flight attendant.
>
> - You would like: a newspaper/a magazine; a cup of coffee/can of Coke; a sandwich/packet of peanuts.
> - You don't know how to use the headphones.
> - You feel cold.
> - You want to sleep but you can't close the window blind.

Roleplay 2

> You are the passenger. Listen to what the flight attendant asks you to do.

1B Grammar exercise 4   page 9

Student A

Ask and answer questions with your partner to complete the missing information.

Christine Smith left school in 1976. She studied (1) *business management* at Leeds University and then got a job at (2 *Where?*) _____. When she was in America, she met (3) *Adam* at a party at the White House. He worked for (4 *Who?*) _____. They started going out together and they got married (5) *two years later*. They now have (6 *How many?*) _____ children. Christine and her husband now live (7) *in West London*. She works for (8 *Who?*) _____ and he is writing (9) *his second novel*. Christine wants to get in touch with (10 *Who?*) _____ and promises to reply to all emails.

4A Reading exercise 2 page 37

Student B

Read about Pete and tick (✓) the sentences on page 37 that are about him.

Pete

Age: 35
Occupation: airline pilot

I am divorced. I have a daughter, but she lives with her mother in Australia, so I only see her from time to time. Because of my work, I am often away from home. I'm a very active person and I hate being bored. I play five-a-side football every Thursday evening and I play golf twice a month. I love old motorcycles (I've got a 1961 Moto Guzzi), music (Pink Floyd, Phil Collins, etc), skiing, good restaurants, fine wines and Havana cigars. Life is busy and full, but without love, it's also empty.

My perfect partner is intelligent, attractive and – most important of all – she is fun to be with. She likes some of the things that I like, but she also has a life of her own. She likes her work and she has lots of friends, but she wants more from life. I have so much to give – do you want to share my life with me?

4B Grammar exercise 4 page 39

Prepare five questions with the present continuous about the picture. Then close your books and ask your partner the questions.

6B Grammar exercise 3 page 59

Look at pictures A and B. How many differences can you find? Use the adjectives in the box to help you.

> beautiful   big   cheap   clean   cold   dirty
> early   expensive   happy   late   long   old
> short   small   tall   young   warm

The customers are older in picture A.

3A Speaking exercise 1 page 27

Student D

Read your rolecard and decide what you want to say to your flatmates.

> You share a flat with the other students in your group. There are some problems in the flat and no one is happy.
>
> When you got home yesterday, there was cigarette smoke in your room. You hate smoking! And there were some empty bottles of beer on the table. Who was smoking and drinking in your room? And why in **your** room? Student A is the only smoker in the house.
>
> With your flatmates, make a list of four rules for the flat.
> *No smoking in the flat.*

5B Functional language exercise 6 page 49

Student B

Roleplay 1

You are a flight attendant. Help the passenger.

Roleplay 2

You are a flight attendant. One of your passengers is very difficult. Look at the ideas below and decide what you are going to say to the passenger. Remember to be polite.

- The passenger is using her/his mobile phone which is not allowed during the flight.
- The passenger is snoring loudly and disturbing other passengers.
- The passenger is listening to very loud music on headphones and disturbing other passengers.
- The passenger has her/his legs stretched out in the aisle so it is difficult for people to pass.

7C Grammar exercise 3 page 70

Student A

Look at the *Things to do* list. Answer your partner's questions.

Have you ... yet?

Don't forget!

Check the mailbox
Write to the bank
Call the boss
Get some more paper
Speak to Trevor (in the Personnel dept.)
Do last week's accounts
Arrange a meeting with Sue & David
Read the horoscope!

1B Speaking exercise 2 page 9

Student D

Read your information and use the questions in exercise 1 page 9 to find out about Christine's other friends.

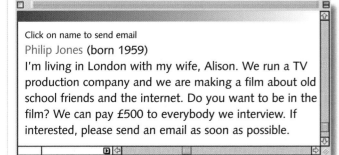

Click on name to send email
Philip Jones (born 1959)
I'm living in London with my wife, Alison. We run a TV production company and we are making a film about old school friends and the internet. Do you want to be in the film? We can pay £500 to everybody we interview. If interested, please send an email as soon as possible.

4C Functional language exercise 1 page 41

Pair B

Read the story of this film twice and then close your books.

My Best Friend's Wedding

Julianne and Michael are old friends. They agree to get married when they are 28 years old if they don't meet anyone else. Just before Julianne's 28th birthday, they speak on the telephone and Michael tells Julianne that he is in love with a girl called Kimmy and he's going to get married. The wedding is in four days. Julianne suddenly realizes that she is in love with Michael and she tries to stop the wedding. But everything she does goes wrong and Julianne realizes that Kimmy is really nice and that she is right for Michael. The film ends with Michael and Kimmy getting married.

3A Speaking exercise 1 page 27

Student E

Read your rolecard and decide what you want to say to your flatmates.

You share a flat with the other students in your group. There are some problems in the flat and no one is happy.

Two weeks ago you lost some CDs in the house. Now, you can't find your favourite DVD. Is someone borrowing your things? You know that Student C sometimes borrows things without asking.

With your flatmates, make a list of four rules for the flat. *No smoking in the flat.*

7D Pronunciation exercise 2 page 73

Student B

Dictate the addresses in column A to your partner and write the addresses your partner dictates in column B.

A	B
www.cnn.com	_____
www.onestopenglish.net/	_____
kerrphilip@macmillan.com	_____
r.dailly@doncaster.ac.uk	_____
straightforward	_____
www.aol.co.uk/msgview.adp	_____

Now check your answers with your partner.

4A Reading exercise 2 page 37

Student C

Read about Carl and tick (✓) the sentences on page 37 that are about him.

Carl

Age: 30
Occupation: unemployed

I lost my job (in a merchant bank) six months ago and thought it was the end of the world. I used to live for my work, all day and every day. I never had time for girlfriends! But now I am a different man. I don't have much money, but for the first time in my life I enjoy everything I do. I have new friends, new interests – it is a new me. I like being with other people, I love children and I would love to have a family. I love the country, the sea, the outdoors. I don't really like being in the city these days – I prefer to be with friends in the country, outdoors in the fresh air.

My perfect partner is open and kind. She likes being with other people and she enjoys lots of different things. She doesn't work too much and money is not very important: family and friends take first place. She wants a partner to share her life, but she is not in a hurry. Like me, she doesn't want to repeat the mistakes of the past.

7C Grammar exercise 3 page 70

Student B

Look at the *Things to do* list. Answer your partner's questions.

Yes, I have. No, I haven't. No, not yet.

Don't forget!
Check the mailbox ✓
Write to the bank
Call the boss
Get some more paper ✓ yes
Speak to Trevor (in the Personnel dept.)
Do last week's accounts
Arrange a meeting with Sue & David
Read the horoscope! ✓ done!

10A Speaking exercise 1 page 97

Take it in turns to choose one of the animals in the picture. Ask and answer *yes/no* questions to find out which animal it is.

Tapescripts

1A Speaking exercise 1 🔘 1.1

The Joneses are a typical English family. Mother Sally is 35 and she is a part-time secretary. Father David is 37 and works in an office. Sally is very busy with her job and the housework, so she doesn't have time for any hobbies. David likes doing things in the garden and repairing things in the house, but he sometimes goes to the pub with his friends. They have two children: Jason, who is seven and likes football and video games, and his sister, Jane, who is six, and likes playing with her Barbie dolls. They have a cat called Snowy.

There is no work or school on Saturdays and the family usually goes somewhere for the day – a walk in the country or a day at the beach. On Sundays, they visit friends and family. In the summer, they go on holiday to Spain for two weeks.

The family has dinner together at half-past six. The children's favourite dinner is chicken and chips, but Sally prefers spaghetti. On Sundays, they always have traditional roast beef or roast lamb. Sally cooks and David cuts the meat.

After dinner, they watch TV. They enjoy comedy programmes and soap operas and they always watch the Lottery results. One day they will win and move to a bigger house.

1B Listening exercise 3 🔘 1.3

C = Christine   A = Adam

A: Oh look at those red shoes! Hmm, cool …
C: What are you looking at, Adam? Why are you laughing?
A: And that lovely flowery dress. Love-ly.
C: Give me that. Where did you find it?
A: It was in this box.
C: Oh God, I look terrible.
A: No, you don't. You look lovely.
C: And look at Susan. Next to me on the floor.
A: Susan who?
C: Susan. My sister. Susan.
A: Susan! That's Susan? Never! How old were you?
C: I remember it well. It was 1973 – it was the year that Pink Floyd made *Dark Side of the Moon*. That's what we were singing! 1973 – it's more than thirty years ago! I was fifteen, and Susan, what, thirteen probably. Maybe twelve.
A: And who's the boy with the guitar and the lovely pink shirt? Boyfriend?
C: No. N.O. That's Nicholas, and he wasn't a boyfriend. He wasn't a friend. Well, maybe a friend of the family, but he wasn't a friend of mine. And anyway, Helga was Nicholas' girlfriend. That's her with the blonde hair. She was really in love with him. I could never understand it.
A: Helga? That's a funny name.
C: Yes, she was Swedish. Or her parents were Swedish. She was my best friend at the time. We did everything together.

A: Well, who was your boyfriend? Was it the boy in the yellow shirt?
C: Why do you want to know?
A: Well, I am your husband.
C: Hmm. I'll tell you later. I wonder where they all are now.
A: What do you mean?
C: I mean, Nicholas and Richard and Helga and him, what's his name, the one in the blue shirt, Philip, that was it. I mean, you know, where do they live? What do they do? Are they married, that sort of thing.
A: Well, there's one way to find out.
C: What do you mean?
A: Look on the internet. Your old school has probably got a website. Maybe it's got some information about all these old friends of yours.
C: Hey, that's a good idea. What's the name of that website? Old Friends United or something like that …

1D Functional language 1 exercise 1 🔘 1.10

M = Message   K = Kate

M: Thank you for calling Sayers Recruitment and Training. To listen to the menu, please press the star button on your telephone now. Thank you. For general enquiries, press 1 followed by hash. For business callers, press 2 followed by hash. To make an appointment with a careers adviser, press 3 followed by hash.
Thank you. You have reached the voicemail of:
K: Kate Woods
Hi, this is Kate Woods. I'm not in the office today, but you can call me at home on 0307 7 double 5 3046 or on my mobile 04 double 7 3201 double 8. That's 0307 7 double 5 3046 at home or 04 double 7 3201 double 8 for the mobile. You can also leave a message after the beep. Thanks.

1D Listening exercises 1 & 2 🔘 1.11–1.14

1   M = Message   D = Davina

M: This is 641480. I'm afraid there's no one to take your call right now. Please leave your name and number after the tone and I'll call you back.
D: Ah, yes, hello. Mr Trotter, my name is Davina and I'm, I'm interested in your, erm, advertisment. Could you call me back, please? Any time before 6 o'clock. The number is 0870 double 4 6091. Ask for Davina. Bye.

2   M = Message   B = Bella

M: Stuart here. I'm not home at the moment, so please leave a message after the beep.
B: Hello, good morning. This is Bella Moor, that's Moor, M- double O-R. I'm calling about the Kung Fu classes. You can call me back on my mobile, that's 0 double 47 3958 double 2. But I'll try to call you again later.

3   Re = Receptionist   R = Ruby

Re: Sayers Recruitment and Training. Can I help you?

R: Hello, yes, erm, I'm, er, I saw your advert and I'm looking for a job, I mean, I'm interested in a new job, and …

Re: Ah, yes, you need to speak to Mrs Sayers, but I'm afraid she's not in the office right now. Could I take your name and number and I'll ask her to call you back?

R: Er, yes, yes. Er, the name's Ruby, Ruby Tuesday and my number is 0308 double 5 71919.

Re: Thank you, Miss Tuesday. I'll pass on your message.

R: Thanks. Bye.

Re: Goodbye.

4   M = Message   S = Sara

M: This is 727 23 double 7. I'm afraid there is no one to take your call right now. Please leave your name and number after the beep and I'll call you back.

S: Oh, hello. This is a message for Mary Sharp. I'm interested in having English lessons because I need to prepare for an exam in Spain. Can you call me back? Some time this afternoon before six? My name is Sara and my number is 0308 3 double 4 7031.

2A   Listening exercises 1 & 2   🌐 1.16–1.18

1 Mr Miller taught biology and everybody, well, all the girls anyway, we all loved him. I was afraid of lots of the teachers, but with Mr Miller it was completely different. I was really fond of him, maybe a little more than fond, actually. He really cared about his students, you know what I mean? He was really interested in us, in us as people I mean, not just as students. We never missed his lessons. Well, the girls never missed his lessons, but some of the boys weren't very keen on him. I always got good grades in his classes and, you know what? When I left school, he helped me find my first job.

2 I didn't like my school at all. I was terrible at most subjects, but I was good at art. The teachers said I was stupid, but it wasn't true. They had a special class for all the difficult pupils and they put me in it. We were bored and we hated it. The teachers weren't interested in us, but we didn't worry about them. When I was sixteen, I took my exams and failed most of them – because I never worked in class and I didn't do my homework. We talked and played, and I only studied for one week before the exams. But I passed art. It was the only subject I was interested in. I'm a painter now. When people buy your pictures, they don't care if you have any exams or not.

3 I didn't really like school very much, but Fridays were OK. Friday was music day and I was good at music. I played the guitar and I sang well, but then everyone liked music lessons. One year, it was my last year at school, we had a new teacher and it was even better. Brilliant, I thought. The new teacher was young and we listened to rap and hip-hop. In the summer term we made a CD and we did a concert for the school. You know what, it was such fun that I didn't want to leave school.

2D   Listening exercises 1 & 3   🌐 1.23

    B = Bella   P = Patrick   ML = Mlle Lajolie

B: Good afternoon. Bonjour. Can I help you?

P: Er, yes. Bonjour. Please could I have some information about your school?

B: Certainly, sir. What would you like to know?

P: Well, could you tell me about your courses? I mean, for example, how many students are in a class?

B: There are fifteen students in a class. We have day-time classes and evening classes. And all our teachers are native French speakers. Do you speak any French?

P: Er, oui. Un petit peu.

B: Pardon?

P: Er, yes, well, my accent isn't very good. I think that I'm probably a beginner, actually. Do you have classes for beginners in the evenings?

B: Yes, our beginners' class is on Tuesdays and Thursdays.

P: Tuesdays and Thursdays?

B: Yes, that's right. Tuesdays and Thursdays.

P: And what time are the classes?

B: Between eight o'clock and half-past nine.

P: I see. And, um, how long does the course last?

B: It's a ten-week course. It starts next Tuesday. Actually, I'm in the class myself.

P: You're in the class? Jolly good, jolly good. And the teacher?

B: The teacher? Oh, yes, the teacher. It's Mademoiselle Lajolie. That's her over there.

P: Oh, excellent, excellent. Bonjour.

ML: Ouais, bonjour.

P: Oh, jolly good, jolly good. Erm, are there any social activities?

B: Oh yes, we have our French club on Friday evenings.

P: Marvellous. Good, well, um, is there a registration form or something? Oh, I almost forgot. How much are the course fees?

B: It's one hundred and fifty pounds for the ten weeks. And here's the registration form …

3A   Listening exercises 2 & 3   🌐 1.26

    A = Ali   C = Charlie

A: Hey, Charlie, do you have any time this week when I can come and look at your flat?

C: Yeah, what about this afternoon? There's nothing to eat in the flat, so I'm going to the shops on the way home to get some food.

A: Pizzas again?

C: No, I want to get some bread and some cheese, actually. Anyway, why don't you come with me and look at the flat after that?

A: Yeah, all right. Good idea.

C: So, things are still difficult at home? Still the same problems?

A: Er, well, yes and no. Things are worse. There's a new problem now. We've got twin cousins from London staying with us at the moment. They're sleeping in the room with me and my brothers. Fourteen-year-old twins!

C: Grim.

A: Yeah, and I've got some exams in a week or two. I get no peace and I can't do any work. It's driving me mad. Driving me mad. Maaaadddd.

C: Yeah, all right. Why don't you ask them to go to another room?

A: I can't ask my brothers to leave their own room!

C: No, not your brothers – your cousins. The fourteen-year-old cousins.

A: Oh, yeah? Ask some guests to leave the room! Oh, definitely, my parents will be very happy. Anyway, there's no space in the house. My mum's always in the living room watching TV. And I can't do my homework in there with the TV on.

C: Well, you know my flat's not very big. And there are five of us already! No peace there, I'm afraid. The library is the best place to work. Stay in the library after college and work there. We don't go to bed early and, well, I don't want to put you off …

A: No, it's not just that. I can't have any friends in my house. I get no independence. I mean, I love my mum and dad, but I think it's time to move.

C: And you really want to move in with us? I mean, we're happy to have you, but it's only a sofa in the living room. Oh, by the way, the kitchen's a bit dirty. I think it's my turn to do the housework. Haven't you got any better ideas for a place to stay?

A: No. Anyway, let's get that food.

C: Yeah, OK. Oh, have you got any cash on you? Money is a bit of a problem at the moment.

3D Listening exercises 1 & 2 1.27

E = Emma   L = Lucy   M = Mary   S = Stuart

E: Well, er, bye, Auntie Mary. Have a good journey. Lucy, give great-aunt Mary a kiss.

L: Don't want to.

M: It doesn't matter. Bye, bye, Lucy, see you soon, my dear. And thank you so much, Emma. It was wonderful to see you again. We had such a nice time, didn't we Lucy?

L: Huh.

E: Stop being so difficult, Lucy!

Platform 1 for the 14.25 to London. The fast train to London on platform 1.

M: Ah, that's my train.

S: 'Scuse me, ladies. Can you tell me the way to the football stadium, please?

E: Um, yes, it's, er, well, you go out of the station. Out of the station …

S: Yes, out of the station, then what?

E: Well, you go out of the station. Turn left. No, no, turn right. No, it's better to turn left.

S: Well, make up your mind. Is it left or right?

M: I think I can help you, young man.

S: Yeah?

M: Yes. You go out of the station. You see the cathedral in front of you. Turn right. Right. Have you got that, young man? Don't cross the road. Turn right again. At the end of the road, turn right again. You'll see the

castle. And a bridge in front of you. Cross the bridge and keep walking. Ten, fifteen minutes?

S: So, turn right out of the station, follow the road, turn right, then turn right again near the castle. Cross the bridge and keep walking. Is that what you said?

M: That's right, young man.

S: Well, thank you. Cheers.

M: You're welcome.

E: Mary?

M: Shh, dear. Wait a second.

E: But, Mary. The football stadium's the other way.

M: I don't know Newcastle very well, my dear, but I do know where the stadium is. I'm not stupid.

E: But, but …

M: Well, he wasn't very friendly, was he? Now, I must catch my train. Bye, bye, my dear. Bye, Lucy.

E: Give great-aunt Mary a kiss, Lucy.

3D Functional language exercise 1 1.28–1.30

1

Tony: Right, we're in front of the castle. What did that old woman say?

Stuart: Can't remember. Come on, Tony. Let's ask someone. 'Scuse me, how do I get to the stadium, please?

Man 1: The stadium? What, St James' Park?

Stuart: Yeah, that's right.

Man 1: Ah well, you go straight on …

Stuart: What, over the bridge?

Man 1: No, no, turn round and go straight on. Take the first street on the right and go past the station …

Stuart: But the station is the other way!

Man 1: Who lives here, you or me?

Stuart: Yeah, all right.

Man 1: So, you go past the station. Go straight on for about ten minutes. And that's it. About ten minutes after the station.

2

Stuart: Let's ask someone else.

Tony: Yeah, all right. 'Scuse me, can you tell me the way to the stadium?

Man 2: (Incomprehensible)

Stuart: Oh, thanks, mate.

Tony: What did he say?

Stuart: No idea! Difficult accent here, isn't it? Let's ask someone else.

3

Stuart: 'Scuse me, can you tell me the way to the stadium, please? Do we cross the bridge?

Woman: Cross the bridge? No, it's the other way. Go to the end of the road, straight on, straight on. You go past four, five, maybe six crossroads, and then you'll see the shopping centre on the right. And there's a church on the left. Take the first street on the left after the church. Go straight on. Go past the bus station and there's a metro station on the right. And the stadium is there. Well, more or less. You'll see it.

Tony: Did you get that, Stuart?

Stuart: Er, yeah, I think so.

4c Listening exercises 1 & 2 💿 1.37

OK, well, there's this guy, Joe, Joe Fox, and he's a really successful businessman. He's the boss of a big, I mean really big, bookshop in New York and he spends a lot of time on the internet, you know, chatting and stuff. And there's this woman, Kathleen, and she also works in the book business, but she's got this really nice little bookshop in New York that just sells children's books. Kathleen is going out with a guy, erm, I can't remember his name …

Anyway, she's going out with this guy and he writes for the newspaper, he's a journalist or something. But she spends a lot of time on the internet, too, and she's met this other guy in an internet chatroom, but she doesn't know his real name or anything about him, but they seem to have a lot in common and they get on really well. But this guy that she's met on the internet is … it's Joe Fox, but she doesn't know who he is and vice versa. Anyway, Fox's Books, that's Joe Fox's company, opens this huge new bookstore just around the corner from Kathleen's shop and they sell books much cheaper than Kathleen's shop, so her business quickly gets into trouble. The two of them, Kathleen and Joe, meet at a party and they have an argument about business. Yeah, they have an argument but he quite likes her, although he doesn't really think about it because he's thinking too much about this woman that he chats to on the internet. Anyway, Kathleen's business goes really badly and the bookshop has to close. So she feels really bad, and she's ill, she's got a cold, and she splits up with her boyfriend on the same day.

Her boyfriend tells her that he's not in love her, but it doesn't really matter because she's not in love with him either. Then Joe goes to visit Kathleen with a bunch of flowers because she's ill, but she tells him to go away, yes, she tells him to go away, but they talk a bit anyway, and they seem to get on quite well. On the internet, Kathleen still talks to the guy on the internet and they finally arrange to meet. So, one evening, she's sitting in a café waiting for him and he arrives, but when he sees that the woman who is waiting for him is Kathleen, he doesn't want to tell her that it's him, the guy on the internet. So, Joe now knows that Kathleen is the woman on the internet and he's really crazy about her, but she doesn't know who he is, and she still wants to meet her internet friend. So, it sort of carries on like that for a bit until she starts to fall in love with him, and then he finally tells her that he's her internet friend, and they're in the park, and they kiss, and, well, that's it. And they both live happily ever afterwards. Of course.

4d Listening exercises 1 & 2 💿 1.40–1.41

1   P = Patrick   D = Davina

P: Trotter here.
D: Oh, hello, Patrick. It's Davina.
P: Pardon?
D: Davina.
P: I'm sorry …
D: Davina. Davina Sayers.
P: Ah, Davina. Sorry, very bad line. I must get a new phone.
D: Well, yes, erm, I was just ringing to say thank you for a lovely evening. Marvellous. Thank you so much.

P: Oh, yes. I'm glad you liked it. Jolly good restaurant. Excellent food. And not too expensive. Lovely evening.
D: Well, yes, anyway, the thing is, erm …
P: Yes?
D: I was thinking, erm …
P: Yes?
D: Well, the thing is, some friends are coming to my house for dinner on Saturday, and, erm, well, would you like to come?
P: That's very kind of you. Er, Saturday, you say?
D: That's right. This Saturday.
P: Let me see. Saturday? Oh dear, I'm afraid I'm busy. Business dinner. An important client, unfortunately. Some other time, maybe.
D: Are you doing anything on Sunday?
P: Um, er …
D: Shall we say Sunday lunch? I know a very nice little restaurant near the river. At one o'clock, perhaps?
P: Ah, well, yes, but I'd rather not, actually. I'd love to, but not this weekend. I'm very busy in the morning. Afternoon, too, probably. I've got a lot of things to do. Problems at the office, you know.
D: Oh dear. I was so looking forward to introducing you to my friends. Oh well, never mind. What about next week? Do you have any time when you are free?
P: I'm really not sure. I know. Don't call me, I'll call you. All right?
D: Erm …
P: Anyway, must go. Lots to do. Cheerio.

2   S = Stuart   R = Ruby

R: Hello.
S: Hi, Rube. It's me. Stuart.
R: Oh, hi, Stuart. Did you have a good day at work?
S: Yeah, not too bad. There's a really gorgeous new girl in the Kung Fu class.
R: Thank you for telling me that, Stuart. I'm very interested in all the beautiful girls in your classes, I'm sure.
S: Oh, come on, love. Don't be like that. You were telling me at the weekend, you know, you were saying I should tell you more about my feelings. You know, my feelings, and things like that. Anyway, girl, what are you doing tonight, Rube?
R: Nothing special. Watching TV, I suppose. Why?
S: What about going out for a change?
R: Yeah, all right, that's a good idea. Got any ideas?
S: Yeah. Why don't we go down to the pub? I think some of the others will be there.
R: Why? Is there a football match on the TV?
S: Yeah, it's Wednesday.
R: What's special about Wednesday?
S: Champion's League.
R: Oh, right. Football. Why don't we do something different? It's always football on Wednesdays.
S: Like what?
R: I dunno. Let's go out for a meal, for example. There's that new pizzeria near the station.
S: Yeah, OK, why not? Let's do that. I know what. How about having a drink in the pub? Just the one.

R: Er, OK.

S: Then, let's get a taxi to the pizzeria.

R: Why don't we walk? I'd rather walk. It's not far and it's a lovely evening.

S: True, but I don't want to be home late. I want to get back for the match highlights on TV at half-past ten.

R: Stuart?

5B Listening exercises 2 & 3 🔘 1.42–1.44

1   C = Check-in assistant   M = Mike

C: Good afternoon, sir.

M: Morning. Oh, yeah, right, sorry, afternoon. Sorry, but I can't find my ticket. It's here somewhere. Hang on. Ah, here it is. Sorry about that.

C: Could I see your passport, please?

M: Yes, sure. I've got it somewhere. Here you are.

C: Thank you. That's fine. Do you have any bags to check in?

M: Er, no, no. Er, just this. Erm, excuse me, but I wonder if I could have a seat next to the window.

C: Er, yes, certainly. 23A. That's a window seat.

M: Oh, right. Thanks a lot.

C: You're welcome. Your plane is boarding in, erm, fifteen minutes at twelve-thirty. Fifteen minutes! You're a bit late – so no time for shopping, I'm afraid. It's departure gate 41. Have a nice flight.

M: Oh, yeah, right, thanks. Bye.

C: Goodbye now.

2   S = Security guard   M = Mike

S: Can you put any money or keys or mobile phone here, please, sir, and walk through the gate?

M: Sorry, what? Pardon?

S: Metal objects here, please.

M: Oh, right, yeah. The phone, too?

S: Yes, sir.

M: Sure. Sorry, I'm in a bit of a hurry.

M: Oh, no! Now what?

S: Can you stand over here and put your arms like that, please?

M: Oh, come on, I'm in a hurry. I've only got five minutes.

S: It's the Dublin flight, is it, sir?

M: Yeah, come on, we're not on a date.

S: Could you empty your inside pockets, please, sir?

M: Oh, it's my other set of keys. Here.

S: Put them on the desk there, please. Give me your jacket and then, can you walk through the gate again one more time?

M: Yup, OK, here you are. Oh, no! Not again.

S: I'm sorry, sir, but please stay calm. Could you put your hands in the air for me, please?

M: Oh, it's this comb. What's the time?

S: I'm afraid you can't take that comb on the plane, sir. It's a dangerous object.

M: What! Oh, well, you keep it.

3   F = Flight attendant   M = Mike   B = Bella

F: Would you like anything to drink?

M: Yes, I'd like a coffee, please. Strong. No sugar. No milk.

F: Certainly, sir. And for you, madam?

B: Just a glass of water for me, please.

F: Certainly, madam. That will be four euros fifty, please, sir.

M: It's not free? Oh, right. Right. Well, here you are. I'd like to have a receipt, please.

F: I'm afraid that we don't do receipts, sir. Here's your water, madam.

B: Many thanks.

M: Pardon?

F: I'm sorry, but we don't do receipts, sir.

M: Never mind. Ugh, horrible. That's not coffee. That's disgusting. Excuse me, can I get past? I need to go to the, er, you know, the, er, the …

B: The toilet? Sorry. Of course.

M: Sorry.

B: Whoops, oh mind the coffee!

M: Aaaagh!

B: Everything OK now?

M: Yeah, thanks. I'm sorry about that. It's just, it's just, well, you know, I get very nervous in planes. Do you mind if we talk? It helps if I can talk to someone. You know what I mean? I mean, if you don't mind. You look like the sort of person who understands.

5C Listening exercises 2 & 3 🔘 1.47

Presenter: Welcome to *The Holiday Programme*. Today, we continue our search for the Worst Hotel in Britain. In this programme, we look at the King Edward Hotel. Last year it was voted the worst hotel in Britain for service, cleanliness and facilities. Will the King Edward Hotel be the worst again this year? We sent our reporters, Nicki and Gavin Becks, for a weekend in Brighton to find out.

Nicki: We arrived in Brighton on Friday evening and drove straight to the King Edward Hotel. A big sign in the front window said 'Vacancies'. We rang the bell and waited. After about five minutes, the door finally opened and the manager appeared.

Manager: Yes?

Gavin: Hello. We'd like a double room for two nights, please.

Manager: It's late. Wait there and I'll see.

Nicki: It wasn't the friendliest welcome, but a few minutes later, a woman came to the door.

Woman: It's sixty pounds a night. No credit cards and you need to pay in advance.

Gavin: That's fine, fine. Here you are. Can we see the room?

Woman: I'll get the key. Hang on. Room 51, fifth floor. On the right.

Gavin:	Fine, thank you. Is that the lift over there?
Woman:	It's not working at the moment. The stairs are through that door.
Gavin:	Never mind. We'll walk.
Nicki:	The room itself was not too bad. There was a good view of the sea from the window, the bathroom was small but clean and the bed looked clean and comfortable.
Gavin:	We had a quick (cold) shower and got changed to go out for the evening. We walked downstairs and gave our key to the woman at reception.
Woman:	Everything all right?
Nicki:	Yes, the room's fine. The shower's cold, but …
Woman:	Oh, yes, I forgot about the shower. I'll ask my husband to fix it this evening.
Gavin:	That's kind of you. Thanks.
Woman:	What time are you coming back this evening?
Nicki:	I'm not sure. We're going to see a film and then maybe get something to eat afterwards. Why?
Woman:	We close the doors at eleven o'clock.
Gavin:	Eleven o'clock?
Woman:	Yes, the front door is locked at eleven o'clock.
Nicki:	We were happy to get out of the hotel. Brighton is a lively town on a Friday night and after the cinema, we had a few drinks in the old part of town before returning to the hotel. We got there at two minutes past eleven, and the door was locked. We rang and rang and, after fifteen minutes with no answer, we finally decided to give up and look for another hotel. Fortunately, there were vacancies at the Grand Hotel, which was only five minutes away.
Gavin:	The next morning after a hot shower, we returned to the King Edward Hotel. The manager was standing outside the front door when we arrived. Who do you think you are, he shouted. Waking up all the guests in the middle of the night! Next time you do that, I'll call the police.
Nicki:	It won't happen again, I said. We're going to stay at another hotel, thank you very much. At that, the man, who was holding our bags threw them at us. We picked up the bags and returned to the Grand. Now, there's a hotel that we liked …
Presenter:	Thank you, Nicki and Gavin. It certainly sounds as if the King Edward Hotel could win the competition for a second year. Let's wait and see. Next in the programme …

6B Listening exercises 1 & 2 🔘 1.50

J = Jilly M = Maura

| J: | Today, on the second day of our tour of Italy, we are in Bologna. Bologna, the capital of Emilia-Romagna perhaps the food capital of Italy, with its parmesan cheese, Parmigiano, Parma ham, mmm, Parma ham, its lasagne and tortelloni. Mmmm. But if you come to Bologna hoping to eat Spaghetti Bolognese, traditional, authentic spag bol, you will be disappointed. No Spaghetti Bolognese in Bologna? I must know more. I'm standing here in Bologna's main market and with |

me is Maura Giuliani, an expert on Italian food. Maura, why is there no Spaghetti Bolognese in Bologna?

M:	Well, we have a dish called Tagliatelle al Ragu, and the sauce is very similar to the sauce you call Bolognese. But we use tagliatelle, not spaghetti. Spaghetti comes from the south of Italy and we do not use it here. We do not eat Spaghetti Bolognese in Bologna – strange but true.
J:	Well, fancy that!
M:	And the sauce called 'Bolognese' that you buy in a bottle from your supermarket is even stranger!
J:	In what way?
M:	It is strange because it is made by strange men in white coats in strange laboratories. Their recipe is extremely complicated and very secret. It contains tomatoes from all over the world. It's got salt and sugar, lots of salt and sugar, chemicals, preservatives, artificial flavours. It's got chemical tomato flavour, chemical meat flavour and artificial colour. And what is in the flavours? Chemicals and more chemicals. When we make Ragu sauce at home, we use local, fresh ingredients that do not travel millions of miles before they go in your mouth. We make a simpler, more traditional recipe. It is healthier for you. And it tastes better. A lot better. But, and there is a but, it is slower to prepare. Good food is slow food.
J:	Yes, absolutely. I understand that you call yourself a 'slow foodie'. What exactly does that mean?
M:	Slow food is a movement that started in Italy back in 1986, but now has members in about 50 countries. Who are we? Well, it's quite difficult to say because all sorts of people are slow foodies. It's easier to say who we are not.
J:	And you are not …
M:	We're not McDonalds or Pizza Hut. We're not pasta sauce in a bottle. We're not a quick hamburger and chips for dinner. We think food is more important and more interesting than that. We're interested in making food more enjoyable, more traditional, better, slower. You can't really taste anything if you eat it fast.
J:	Maura, thanks. Looking at the food on sale at the market here is making my mouth water. Mmmm. There's a man over there selling some of those, what do you call them, um, those little balls of rice. I think I will eat some of them very, very, very slowly. After the market, Maura took us to a demonstration of pasta making.

6D Listening exercises 1 & 2 🔘 1.53

P = Patrick W = waiter

P:	Ah. Ah.
W:	Hello. *La Vie en Rose*. Can I help you?
P:	Er, yes, good afternoon. I'd like to book a table for ten, please.
W:	Oh dear, I'm afraid our last booking is at half-past nine, sir.
P:	No, no, no. Not ten o'clock. Ten people. I'd like a table for ten people on Friday at nine o'clock.

W: Oh, I'm sorry sir, silly me. Of course, of course. Ten people on Friday at nine o'clock. We all make mistakes, don't we?

P: Yes, that's right.

W: Yes, well, I'm afraid we don't have a table for ten, actually. We don't do big tables, I'm afraid. Do you know the restaurant? It's very intimate. I could put you on three smaller tables. There's a very romantic table for two next to the window, and two tables for four behind that.

P: Oh, well, that sounds marvellous. The name's Trotter. Patrick Trotter. I'll have the table in the window. The teacher and I. It's our French class's annual meal. We're going to practise our French. Hmm, yes, and the rest of the class on the other tables. Yes, perfect. Marvellous.

W: So, that's two tables for four and a romantic table for two on Friday at nine o'clock?

P: Yes, that's right.

W: Is that smoking or non-smoking, sir?

P: Non-smoking. Yes, non-smoking. And the name is Trotter.

W: Pardon?

P: Trotter. T – R – O – T – T – E – R. Major Patrick Trotter.

W: Oooh, Major!

P: Er, well, retired major, actually.

W: We look forward to seeing you on Friday night.

P: Yes, jolly good. See you on Friday, then.

W: By-eee.

P: Marvellous.

6D Functional language 1 exercise 2 1.54

W = Waiter   ML = Mme Lajolie

W: Hello. *La Vie en Rose*. Can I help you?

ML: Yes, good afternoon. I'd like to book a table for Friday, please.

W: Certainly, madam. For how many people?

ML: It's for ten people.

W: I'm afraid we don't have any large tables …

ML: Yes, I know. I've been before. Two or three smaller tables will be fine. If they're together …

W: Yes, well, let me see, we're quite busy on Friday. We've got another party of ten at nine o'clock. What time would you like, madam? Is seven o'clock too early?

ML: Seven o'clock? No. That's fine.

W: So, seven o'clock for ten people. Could I take your name, please, madam?

ML: Yes, it's Lajolie. I'll spell it for you. L – A – G. Oh, no, not G, J. L – A – J – O – L – I – E.

W: Well, we look forward to seeing you on Friday.

ML: Yes, thank you. Goodbye.

W: By-eee.

6D Functional language 2 exercises 1 & 2 1.57

W = Waiter   ML = Mlle Lajolie   B = Bella
S1 = Student 1   S2 = Student 2

W: Good evening, madam. Welcome to *La Vie en Rose*.

ML: Good evening. The name is Lajolie. I have a reservation for ten people. One person isn't here yet. Er, can you show him our tables when he arrives?

W: Certainly, madam. Let me show you to your tables. It's this way.

ML: Thank you.

W: It's these three tables here.

ML: Very nice. Bella, shall we sit at that table?

B: Yes, OK.

W: Can I take your coats?

B: Yes, thanks.

S2: Ta.

W: Would you like something to drink? Or would you like to see the menu first?

ML: Er, the menu, I think, please. Bella, what do you think?

B: Erm …

S2: No, let's have a drink. I'd like a …

ML: Oh, OK.

S2: I'll have a …

ML: Could we have a bottle of house red, please?

S2: Oh, OK. Good idea.

B: And a bottle of mineral water.

W: A bottle of mineral water – sparkling?

B: Please.

S1: Yup, fine by me.

W: One bottle of sparkling and a bottle of house red.

ML: Please.

S2: Excuse me, have you got an ashtray?

W: I'm very sorry, but this is a non-smoking table.

S2: What!?

B: Well, that was delicious.

S1: Yeah, it was good, wasn't it?

ML: Not too expensive, I hope.

B: Excuse me, could we have the bill, please?

W: Certainly, madam.

S2: I wonder where the other guy is. What's his name? You know, the major.

ML: You mean Mr Trotter.

S2: Yeah, that's right. 'Jolly good'.

ML: Don't be horrible. He's not that bad. Uh-oh, don't look now, but … Mr Trotter! You have arrived!

7A Listening exercises 1 & 2 1.58

J = Jerry   V = Valerio   M = Michelle   T = Tony

J: Welcome back to *Tell Jerry*. Today we're taking calls from people who've met famous people in their work. Our first caller is Valerio from New Jersey. Hello, Valerio.

V: Good afternoon, Jerry.

J: Hi, Valerio. How are you doing?

V: Not too bad, man …

J: Valerio, I understand you work as a chauffeur in New York.

V: It's my company, man.

J: OK. Er, have you ever met anyone famous in your job?

V: I sure have. Er, it's my company and I'm in charge. I keep all the stars for myself.

J: Er, Valerio, are you there?

V: Uh-huh.

J: Valerio, who have you driven in your car?

V: We get them all, man. Er, I've had more film stars than you can name.

J: Who was your last celebrity, Valerio?

V: I had, like, Madonna, I guess, er, two days ago. She was coming back from Britain. And I had Leonardo, er, what's his name, er, Leonardo Di Caprio the week before.

J: Have you ever spoken to any of the stars, Valerio?

V: Yeah, we say 'Good day, sir' or 'Good day, ma'am', but we're not paid to talk to them. It's not a yellow cab, you know what I mean? I've never had, like, a real conversation.

J: OK, thank you, Valerio. And over to our next caller. On the line is Michelle from Santa Monica. Hi there, Michelle, what do you do for a living?

M: Hi, Jerry. I'm a customer service assistant in a restaurant.

J: A customer service assistant?

M: Yeah, I'm a waitress.

J: OK, Michelle, have you met anyone really famous at work?

M: Brad Pitt and Jennifer Aniston.

J: Brad Pitt and Jennifer Aniston. Listeners, we have Michelle from Santa Monica on the line and Michelle has served Brad Pitt and Jennifer Aniston. Michelle, what were they like?

M: Mm, they were, you know, kind of cute.

J: Have you ever had any stars that were difficult customers?

M: Yeah, I've had some difficult people.

J: Can you tell us who?

M: Hey, no, I'll lose my job. But not many. Most of them are quiet – you know they just want to eat their dinner in peace.

J: Thank you, Michelle. Next caller. Thank you for calling *Tell Jerry*. This is Jerry – who is on the line?

T: Oh hello, Jerry. My name is Tony Lewington, calling from Manhattan.

J: Good afternoon, Tony. Tony, that's not an American accent.

T: I'm from Perth in Australia. I'm working for an ice cream shop in downtown Manhattan.

J: Tony the ice cream man, have you ever met anyone really famous in your work?

T: I've met a few, yeah. We had Tom Cruise and his girlfriend recently. And that other Tom, I can't remember his name, you know, in *Forrest Gump*. Tom …

Je: Tom Hanks?

T: Yeah, that's the one.

J: Have you ever spoken to one of the stars, Tony?

T: Oh, yeah. You know, you're getting an ice cream for someone, well, you talk to them, don't you? Well, I do. I've had a few good conversations.

J: What did you talk to Tom Cruise about?

T: Oh, we didn't talk. I was looking at his girlfriend.

J: Ah-hah! Be careful you don't get fired!

T: Hah. No worries.

J: OK. Thank you, Tony, from Perth in Australia.

7D Listening exercises 1 & 2 💿 2.2

D = Davina   R = Ruby

D: Come in.

R: Erm, Mrs Sayers?

D: Yes, that's the name on the door. And you are … ?

R: My name's Ruby. Ruby Tuesday. I've got an appointment.

D: Ah yes, Miss Tuesday. Come in.

R: Erm, it's Ms, actually. Not Miss.

D: Come in, my dear. Have a seat. Why don't you take your coat off?

R: I'm sorry I'm a bit late. I was making a copy of my CV.

D: You've brought it. Good. Could I see? Thank you. It's just the one page, is it?

R: Should I write some more?

D: Let's see. No, one page is probably enough. Do you have any qualifications?

R: No, not yet, but I'm thinking of going to evening classes. My boyfriend, Stuart, is a teacher at the college.

D: A professor of philosophy, is he?

R: Par-don?

D: Never mind. Now, what are you hoping to study?

R: Well, I'm quite interested in computers and the internet and things like that.

D: Well, a course in basic computer skills is a very good idea.

R: … and my manager says I've got very good people skills.

D: Yes, I see. So what exactly are you looking for? What kind of job would you like to do?

R: I dunno, really. I don't care, really. Anything is better than serving hamburgers all day. Know what I mean?

D: Hm, yes, well, I've never had that experience myself. But, to be honest, I think you should get a qualification before you look for a new job.

R: What? You mean you can't help me get another job?

D: No, not now. I mean, yes, we can find you another job, but you should think about your future career. Your life, young lady. Your life.

R: That's a laugh. What should I do with my life?

D: Well, I'd begin with your clothes.

R: My clothes?

D: Yes, look at you. You should improve your appearance, young lady. Why don't you buy a smart suit for interviews, for a start?

R: Oh, right.

D: And are all those earrings really necessary?

R: What's wrong with them?

D: They're very, erm, very fashionable. Very nice. But not a good idea for a job interview, I think. And your hair. What about having a little haircut?

R: A haircut?! I went to the hairdresser's yesterday, actually. Anything else?

D: Well, perhaps, one more thing.

R: Yes?

D: Well, if I were you, I'd arrive for interviews on time.

R: And if I were you, I'd … I'd … I'd

D: I'm only giving you a little bit of advice, young lady. Why don't you go away and think about it?

8A Speaking exercise 1 🔘 2.6–2.9

1 Right, er, well, there'll be more and more supermarkets … Er, you see more and more of the same kinds of shops everywhere, you know. Everywhere you go you see the same things, the same chains – so more supermarkets on the outside of the town. Er, the town centres will get quieter and quieter, no – there'll, there'll be less, um, less shops in the town centres and there'll be more bars and cafés and things like that, um, so people will … er, use their cars, I guess, more. Is that thirty seconds yet?

2 Everybody says that, er, you know, everybody will need English in the future, but I … I don't think this is true because, um, you know, you need, um, English for computers and the internet and that, but with … with, um … There's more and more Chinese people in the world, so, you know, we'll, maybe, we'll speak Chinese, we'll all need to speak Chinese because, um, 'cos … 'cos we will, and, er, um …

3 If you think about medicine now and you think about medicine, say one hundred years ago, the differences, um, are … are incredible because we can … we can do so many things now that we couldn't do then, like, you know, we've got a cure for polio, we've got a cure for lots of diseases, and … and transplants and things, so I guess in the future we'll, you know, carry on and we'll find cures for more and more things and we'll, um … That must be thirty seconds.

4 They get bigger and bigger, don't they? Well, no, not bigger, but more powerful, I mean. I mean, you can do anything really, now, um … Work, obviously, um, watch movies, play music, and, you know, they get smaller, and you can have little laptops or these little, er, these little things, you know, er, computers on your telephone, so, yeah they're more and more important. We'll all need them. They'll just be a part of our lives. Well, they are already, really. Is that time up?

8B Listening exercises 2 & 3 🔘 2.10

Back in 2001, American millionaire, Dennis Tito became the world's first space tourist. He paid 20 million dollars to fly to the International Space Station. A year later, the South African businessman, Mark Shuttleworth, wrote another 20-million dollar cheque to follow him. Others will probably follow soon, but who will it be? Perhaps, a pop star like Lance Bass of N'Synch? Or maybe another businessman? One thing is for sure: it certainly won't be you. Or perhaps it will be.

A European television consortium, Eurorbit, has announced plans for a new TV game show. The show, which will probably be called *Star Quest*, will have contestants from all the countries in the European Union. It will test the contestants' general knowledge, their skills and their ability to work in a team. Contestants will need to be fit and to speak English, but men and women of all ages are welcome to apply. The programme's organizers hope to film the thirteen-part show at different science museums around Europe – in London, Florence, Paris and at the New Metropolis Science and Technology Center in Amsterdam.

And the prize? The winner of the show will take his, or her, seat in a space ship some time next year. After training at the European Space Academy, the winner will blast off for an eight-day trip to the stars and a visit to the International Space Station.

Or perhaps not. Not everyone is happy with the idea. Will scientists in America at NASA refuse permission for the winner to visit the space station? They were unhappy with Dennis Tito's trip and say that this kind of space tourism is too dangerous. 'This idea is so stupid,' said one expert at New York University. However, a spokesman for Eurorbit said that the Americans will probably agree some kind of deal. Whatever happens, he said, the winner of the competition will definitely go into space. But it's possible that they won't be able to visit the space station.

The organizers of the programme are taking applications now. So if you want to be the next space tourist, send your request to contestant@eurorbit.com. That's contestant@eurorbit.com. And good luck!

8C Listening exercises 1 & 2 🔘 2.12

ML = Mlle Lajolie   B = Bella

ML: Bella.
B: Yes?
ML: Could you give me a hand with this?
B: With what?
ML: I want to send an email.
B: Yes, of course. What's the problem?
ML: Erm, I'm not too sure what I'm doing. Do I click on this?
B: Oh, no. Don't do that! Let's have a look. Where are you? Are you online?
ML: What do you mean?
B: Are you connected to the internet?
ML: I don't know.
B: Here, look, first of all, click on that button there. That connects you to the internet.
ML: Oh right. Like this?
B: Yes, that's right. No, do it again. Again, do a double click.
ML: Oh right.
B: OK. Now you're online. Now, after that click on the email icon.
ML: What's that?
B: The email icon? It's for your mail.
ML: Oh right. Single click or double?
B: Single, I think. It doesn't matter.
ML: Oh, look.
B: Right. Then, click on 'Write Mail'. OK?
ML: It's easy, isn't it? Now what?
B: OK, you see the little picture of an address book? You type your address there next to the icon.
ML: I don't know what my email address is.
B: Not your address, silly! The person you're writing to.
ML: Oh right. Oh, where did I put that address? Ah, here it is.
B: That's a school address. I know that school.
ML: Bella, you won't tell anyone, will you?

B: I won't tell anyone. Why are you writing to them?

ML: I'm applying for a job. I spoke to the director this morning and he asked me to send my CV.

B: You're not leaving us?

ML: Erm, well, the money's better and …

B: Oh, poor Mr Trotter. He'll be so unhappy.

ML: Huh! Not me. I'll be very pleased not to see that – mm … not to see him again. Anyway, you won't say anything, will you?

B: Promise.

ML: So, what next?

B: Well, next you write your message. There in the big space.

ML: Oh, OK. 'Dear Sir, With reference to our telephone conversation this morning, I am writing to you … OK. Done.

B: Right. Where's your CV?

ML: Oh, it's on disk.

B: Oh, OK. Have you put it in the machine?

ML: Yes.

B: OK. Click on 'Insert'. Then we need to find your document. Your CV. Ah, there it is. OK, you click on that. And afterwards click on 'Attach'. That's it.

ML: That's it?

B: Yes, click on 'Send' and then finally you log off.

ML: Log off?

B: Yes, log off. Go back to that button there to leave the internet.

ML: Brilliant. Thanks. When will they get it?

B: What? Your mail? They've already got it.

ML: Really?

8D Listening & speaking exercise 1 🔘 2.13–2.17

1 Looking for a laugh? Buy one of these freaky green hands and put it on your desk at work. Just watch your colleagues' faces when you talk to the hand and it starts walking!

2 Now you can write secret messages with our special invisible ink. The ultraviolet light means you can read them, too!

3 You can't find your keys? Again! With a light that shines for ten years, you'll never lose them again. And, if you like, you can play at Star Wars, too!

4 Feeling thirsty? Well, here's your own personal water machine for your desk in the office. It holds eight cups. With this in front of you, you can be sure you'll drink all the water you need.

5 Did you know that colours can change the way you feel? Do you sometimes wake up in the morning feeling (and looking!) grey? With one of these, you can wake up in the morning to a bright, colourful tomorrow.

9A Speaking & listening exercises 2 & 3 🔘 2.18

N = Nick   S = Sarah

N: Now for our weekly look at what's on. Sarah, what have you got for us this week?

S: Well, probably the most exciting concert of the summer is happening on Friday, Saturday and Sunday this week

at half-past seven. Robbie Williams. The gorgeous, talented and wonderful Robbie Williams is in town for three nights at the Wembley Arena. If you haven't got tickets, you'll be disappointed, but we've got two tickets to give away in this week's competition. Stay tuned for more details of the competition after the news. Also this week, at my favourite club in London's West End, there's a special Brazilian night with top Brazilian DJs playing the latest tech-funk from the country's coolest clubs. That's in addition to the usual line-up of the regular DJs with a mix of house, techno and hip hop. That's all on Saturday night Downstairs at The Sound Barrier in Oxford Street. Doors open at ten o'clock and you can dance until four in the morning. The place to be for a really cool night out.

N: Tech-funk at The Sound Barrier. Sarah, I know you think I'm a little boring, but what exactly is Brazilian 'tech-funk'?

S: Why don't you come and find out?

N: I'll be too tired, I think. A little after my bedtime. What else have you got for us?

S: Well, there's a fascinating afternoon of dance at Canary Wharf. It's part of the Greenwich Festival and they've got groups from Switzerland, France and an excellent group called Increpacion, er, I think that's how you pronounce it, from Spain. It sounds very interesting, and it's free. A great afternoon out for all the family. Let's hope the weather stays fine. That's Saturday at Canary Wharf between one and five.

N: Yes, sounds very interesting.

S: And if you're interested in dance, don't forget that you can still see London's most popular and most enjoyable musical – *Fame* – at the Aldwych Theatre. Performances are on at half-past seven Monday to Saturday, with an afternoon show on Saturdays at half-past three. No shows on Sunday.

N: Have you seen it yet, Sarah?

S: I've been twice! And you?

N: Er, no. Not my kind of thing, actually.

S: The next thing I've got is something for you. This Friday, there is a performance of Verdi's Requiem at the Royal Festival Hall. With the London Philharmonic. Half-past seven, Friday.

N: Ah, yes, a beautiful piece of music.

S: Isn't it a bit depressing going to listen to a requiem?

N: Pardon?

S: Right, what next? Yes. I went to an exhibition at the National Gallery last week which was absolutely fantastic. It's paintings by the Spanish impressionist, Pizzarro.

N: Pissarro.

S: Yes, paintings that the artist did when he was living in London. I was quite surprised – they were really nice. So, for a afternoon of art and culture, check out this exhibition at the National Gallery. Every day from nine in the morning to six o'clock. Ooh, and one last idea. A fun idea for all the family. The Moscow State Circus is in Alexandra Park this week from Tuesday to Sunday. I saw them a few years ago and they're one of the best circuses around.

N: Thank you, Sarah. You've got a busy weekend in front of you. Time now to go over to the news room, but stay tuned for details of our competition with two tickets to Robbie Williams at …

9D Pronunciation exercise 3 🔊 2.24

On the seventh of August, we have the Cuban salsa band, Los Van Van. Then, for two nights, on the twelfth and thirteenth of August, we have Justin Timberlake. Craig David is coming on the twenty-second of August, and we have the Red Hot Chili Peppers on September the third and fourth. For lovers of classical music, there is an evening with Cecilia Bartoli on September the twenty-first. Also, beginning on October the twenty-seventh and finishing on October the thirty-first, you can see Tchaikovsky's *Swan Lake*. Shakira is coming on the third of November, and on the fifth of November we have Handel's *Messiah*. The sixteenth of November is *A Night with Mr Bean* and on November the twenty-second, the Wynton Marsalis Septet are in town. Enrique Iglesias is coming on the second of December, and on the fourth of December there is a special tribute to the Beatles. From December the seventeenth to the twenty-fourth, we have our children's show, *Beauty and the Beast*, and finally on the thirty-first of December, there is the Johann Strauss New Year concert.

9D Listening exercises 3 & 4 🔊 2.25–2.28

1   BO = Box Office   M = Mary

BO: Metropolitan Box Office. This is Trevor speaking. Can I help you?

M: Yes, hello. I'd like to book three tickets for *Beauty and the Beast* please.

BO: Certainly, madam. How many tickets do you want?

M: Three please.

BO: Three tickets for *Beauty and the Beast*. And what date would you like?

M: The Tuesday before Christmas, December the twenty-third, please.

BO: Would you like the matinee or the evening performance? The matinee starts at two o'clock.

M: Oh, the matinee, the matinee. It's for a young child, you see. My great niece.

BO: Just one second, please. We've only got tickets in the rear circle for that date, madam.

M: Hmm. Monday the twenty-second?

BO: The twenty-second. Yes, we've got all tickets available for that date. What sort of seats would you like?

M: Oh, the front of the stalls. Definitely.

BO: So, that's three seats at the front of the stalls for the twenty-second of December. Those seats cost thirty pounds each.

M: Fine.

BO: Could I take your name please, madam?

M: Yes, it's Mary Sharp. S-H-A-R-P. Sharp.

BO: Thank you, Mrs Sharp. And you're paying by credit card?

M: Yes. Visa.

BO: Could I take your card number, please?

M: Yes, it's 814 double 66 282.

BO: Thank you. And the expiry date?

M: Yes, the expiry date is 07/09.

BO: Thank you, Mrs Sharp. That's three tickets for the matinee performance of *Beauty and the Beast* on Monday the twenty-second of December. That will be ninety pounds plus a booking fee of three pounds, so ninety-three pounds altogether.

M: Lovely.

BO: Could I take your address, please?

2   BO = Box Office   B = Bella

BO: Metropolitan Box Office. This is Trevor speaking. Can I help you?

B: Hello, good afternoon. I'd like two tickets for Winston Marsala, please.

BO: Wynton Marsalis?

B: Yes, that's the one.

BO: Wynton Marsalis Septet, Saturday the twenty-second of November. Half-past seven.

B: Have you got anything in the circle?

BO: Front or rear?

B: How much are the seats at the front?

BO: I've got two right in the middle at the front for twenty-eight pounds. And there's a booking fee in addition to that. It's one pound per ticket, so that's fifty-eight pounds altogether. Could I take your details, please?

B: Yes, the name's Moor. M, double O, R. And the first's name's Bella.

BO: Bella Moor.

B: I've got a Visa. And the card number is 204 205 009. Expiry date 03/09.

BO: Thank you, Mrs Moor.

B: Ms.

BO: Sorry. Ms Moor.

B: Would it be possible to send the tickets to someone else? They're a present.

BO: Yes, certainly. If you'd like to give me the details.

B: Yes, the name is Mr Mike Marks, that's M-A-R-K-S, and his address is Flat 4, number 27 Park …

3   BO = Box Office   S = Stuart

BO: Metropolitan Box Office. This is Trevor speaking. Can I help you?

S: Yeah, I want a ticket for the Red Hot Chilis on the fourth of September.

BO: The Red Hot Chili Peppers? I'll just check for you. September the fourth … No, I'm sorry, sir, we're sold out.

S: What about the other day? The third.

BO: Yes, we've got a few tickets left in the rear stalls.

S: Oh, great. How much are they?

BO: Just the one ticket is it, sir?

S: Yes, just the one.

BO: That'll be thirty-six pounds, including the booking fee of one pound.

S: How much?

BO: Thirty-six pounds altogether, sir.

S: Thirty-six quid? Forget it.

4   BO = Box Office   P = Patrick

BO: Metropolitan Box Office. This is Trevor. How can I help you?

P: Good afternoon. I'd like two tickets for the evening with Cecilia Bartoli.

BO: Yes, Cecilia Bartoli. Certainly, sir.

P: Yes, Cecilia Bartoli. The best seats you've got, please.

BO: I'll see what seats we've got available. We've got a couple of seats at the front of the circle at forty-five pounds each.

P: Marvellous.

BO: There's a booking fee of two pounds, so that'll be ninety-two pounds altogether.

P: Jolly good. Do you take American Express?

BO: That'll be no problem, sir. Could I take your details, please?

P: Yes, the name's Trotter. Major Patrick Trotter and the address is …

10c   Listening exercises 2 & 3   🔊 2.30

M = Martin   P = Presenter   S = Sunil

M: … so an excellent weekend for the top three in the Premiership with Arsenal, Chelsea and Manchester United all winning.

P: Thank you, Martin, and the full football results will be after the news at six o'clock. Now, the other big event this weekend was the New York Marathon. To bring us up to date with the news from New York, here's Sunil Gupta.

S: Yes, it's all over here in New York. This year's winner of the men's race was the Kenyan, Martin Lel, in a time of 2 hours, 10 minutes and 30 seconds. In an exciting finish, Lel pushed last year's winner, Rodgers Rop, into second place, with Christopher Cheboiboch taking the bronze and making it one-two-three for Kenya. Another Kenyan, Margaret Okayo, took the women's race in a time of 2 hours 22 minutes and 31 seconds. But the big event of the afternoon for the spectators in Manhattan's Central Park was the arrival on the line of the two Britons, Ranulph Fiennes and Mike Stroud. Fiennes and Stroud crossed the line together with an official time of 5 hours 25 minutes and 46 seconds and will surely be in the *Guinness Book of Records*.
For Fiennes and Stroud, this was an incredible seventh marathon in seven days in seven different continents. Their marathon marathon began last week in Patagonia in the deep south of South America. In the last week, they have been to the Antarctic, Sydney, Singapore, London and Cairo, completing a marathon at each stopover. Perhaps the most astonishing thing about this achievement is that Ranulph Fiennes suffered a heart attack earlier this year and had a heart operation just three months ago. Fiennes and his colleague, Mike Stroud have raised millions of pounds for the British Heart Foundation by completing the marathon in New York today. For Fiennes and Stroud, it's all in a day's work. On previous expeditions, they have raised more than four million pounds for a multiple sclerosis research centre and two million pounds for a breast cancer clinic. They have been to the North and South Poles, they have walked across the Andes, they have canoed up the Amazon, and in the 1990s, Fiennes discovered the lost city of Ubar in the desert of Oman. But at a party tonight in New York's Central Park to celebrate the end of the race, other runners were disappointed to find that Fiennes and Stroud were not there. A spokesman for the British Heart Foundation said, 'Both runners are completely exhausted and they have gone home. They caught a plane to London earlier this evening. Dr Fiennes has gone to join his wife before going into hospital for a check-up on his heart next week. Dr Stroud has gone to London for a day of rest before returning to work on Tuesday morning.' This is Sunil Gupta reporting from New York's Central Park.

P: Thank you, Sunil. And the time is now six o'clock Greenwich Mean Time.

10d   Listening exercises 1 & 2   🔊 2.33–2.34

1   D = Doctor   S = Stuart

D: Come in, come in, take a seat. Now, how can I I can help you?

S: Er, yeah, well, I'm not very well.

D: Well, you look a bit grey, Mr Simeon. Tell me what's the matter.

S: I've got a headache all the time.

D: Yes. And?

S: I've got a cold.

D: And a cough.

S: Yes, that's right.

D: Where else does it hurt?

S: Everywhere, really. My back, my chest, my neck. To be honest, I feel awful.

D: OK. I'll have a look at you. Take off your shirt.

S: What?

D: Your shirt, Mr Simeon.

S: Oh, right.

D: And put this in your mouth. I want to see if you've got a temperature.

S: Do you think … ?

D: Don't talk now. Ssh.

S: Hmmm

D: Hmm, let's see. Mm … 39°. It's quite high.

S: Nothing serious, is it? What's wrong with me?

D: Oh, flu, I think.

S: Oh! I thought it was maybe something serious.

D: Flu can be serious, Mr Simeon, but it's nothing to worry about. OK, put your shirt back on. Now, you'll need to take four or five days off work. Rest as much as possible, stay in bed. You should take some aspirin or paracetamol for the pain. And you should eat lots of fruit and vegetables. You need lots of vitamin C. Is there someone who can look after you? I can't remember. Are you married?

S: No.

D: Oh, no, that's right. You've got a girlfriend, haven't you? Ruby, isn't it?

S: Not at the moment. She left me.

D: Ah! I am sorry. Do you feel depressed?

S: Depressed? Me? Never!

D: Well, you need someone to look after you. Your mother, perhaps? But I'll give you a prescription for some strong paracetamol. All right?

S: Is that it? No antibiotics or anything?

D: No, no antibiotics. Just lots of rest. And I'll give you a letter for your work.

S: Oh, right. Thanks.

2   D = Doctor   M = Mike

D: Next. Ah, Mr Marks.

M: Yeah, uh, hi.

D: How can I help you?

M: Oh, sorry. That's my phone. Mike here. Oh, hi.

D: Mr Marks?

M: Yeah?

D: Er, perhaps you can call the person back?

M: Yeah, sorry. Sorry. Listen, Bella, I'm in a meeting right now. Can I call you back? OK, speak to you later. Sorry about that, doctor.

D: Right, well. Perhaps, if you're not too busy … What seems to be the matter?

M: Yeah, sorry. Um, I've, er, I've had a stomach ache for a few days. Oh, sorry. I'll switch it off. Yeah, it's my stomach. It really hurts. Is there anything I can take for it?

D: So, you've got a stomach ache. Are you eating normally?

M: What do you mean?

D: I mean, are you eating normally? What did you have for lunch, for example?

M: Lunch? Erm, nothing much. I just had a coffee, I think.

D: A coffee? Nothing to eat? And breakfast?

M: Coffee. Oh, and a piece of chocolate.

D: Mr Marks. You cannot be serious. You say you have a pain in your stomach. You have a pain in your stomach because you have eaten nothing all day.

M: Well, I'm not very hungry at the moment.

D: I can see that.

M: I've got a meeting in New York later in the week. And, well, I hate flying, and every time I think about getting in the plane, my stomach hurts and sometimes I get a headache, sometimes I feel cold, sometimes I feel hot, or hot and cold, you know, and I'm not hungry, and I think of that plane, and I think oh no I can't, I can't, I mean, you know, what if the plane crashes or something, and then I get this really, really big, big headache, and my eyes hurt, here, my eyes, behind the eyes, you know, it's really painful …

D: Calm down, calm down. Mr Marks, I don't think that it's a very good idea for you to go to New York for that meeting. Not right now.

M: What?

D: I don't think you should travel at the moment.

M: What? Not go to New York?

D: No.

M: Oh. Brilliant. Will you give me a letter for my boss to say that I'm ill?

D: Yes.

M: But you won't say that it's because I'm afraid of flying.

D: No, I will say that you are not well enough to travel. Your headaches and your lack of appetite point to stress and I will say that you are suffering from stress. And I'll also make an appointment for you to see a specialist. Someone who can help you with your fear of flying. Now, you need to eat. A good, healthy meal. That's the most important thing.

M: I'm going out for dinner tonight. New girlfriend.

D: Good. But have something now. Go and buy something to eat when you leave here, OK?

M: That's it? No prescription? No medicine?

D: No. Er, yes. I mean, yes, that's it and, no, no medicine. Not for now. Get something to eat. OK?

M: Yeah, OK.

D: All right, now, come back and see me in ten days.

M: Yeah, yeah. Right.

D: Goodbye, Mr Marks. See you in ten days.

M: Yeah, yeah, thanks. Sorry. Bye. Bye.

11A Listening exercises 2 & 3   2.40–2.41

Susan   I was just starting in business. It was a small advertising agency that I ran with my sister and in those days it was hard for a woman to run a business. Most, maybe all, of our clients were men and we took them out, we entertained them. We took them to restaurants, we took them to ball games, we took them out to make them feel good and we wanted them to take us seriously. But most of them were just boys, really, and they thought we were out on a date. You know, they were our clients but they wanted to pay. Then, one evening when I was out with a client, there was a woman at the table next to mine, and when the check came, she held up this little card, American Express, I guess it was, and the waiter said 'Yes, ma'am' Gee, I wanted one of those baaaad. Next day, I spoke to my sister. At first she said no, but after a few weeks she finally agreed and we applied for a card. I remember the first time I used it. When the check came, my client looked at me in the eyes and said 'I'll take care of that, honey', but I already had my card in the air. Hell, was he impressed! He signed the contract right there in the restaurant. It was the best investment we ever made.

Katy   What did I really want when I was younger? Hah, the same as now! But I want more now! No, seriously, but we don't change as we get older, do we? Well, I don't anyway. No, what I wanted was independence. I was still living with my parents and it took me ages, bloomin' ages, to get into town for a night out. And the last train home was really early, so I had to leave just when the evening was getting going. I mean, there you are with some really gorgeous bloke, and you look at your watch and it's half-past nine or something. 'Sorry, but my last train goes in twenty minutes.' It was driving me mad. I was saving up to buy a Mini, but when I saw my first Capri, I took one look at it and knew that was what I wanted. It took me two years to get enough money, but in the end, there I was, the owner of my very own Capri Mark I 1600 sex bomb, metallic yellow with very sexy sports wheels. So, finally, I had what I needed to go out when I wanted, where I wanted and with who I wanted. I've done hundreds of thousands of miles in it. I've still got it, actually.

11A Functional language exercise 1 💿 2.42–2.43

1 Good afternoon, I'm looking for a – I'm sorry I don't know the right word. It's a kind of computer, a little one that you can put in your pocket. You know, it's a thing you send emails with, I think. In fact, I'm not really sure what you do with it. But you know what I mean. A little computer. It's a present for my grandson.

2 Good morning. I'm looking for some, erm, what do you call them? You know, they're a sort of shoe. Well, not really a shoe, but, erm, well, yes they're a sort of shoe, really. You use them to go to the beach. In the summer. You see all the young people wearing them. Do you know what I mean?

11D Listening exercises 2 & 3 💿 2.47

B = Bella   ML = Mlle Lajolie   P = Patrick

B: Do you mind if we do just one more shop?

ML: No, I don't mind. I'm enjoying myself.

B: That's because you're not looking for anything special. And you can buy anything. It's easy for you. It all looks good on you.

ML: Well, I find it easier than you – but what about that black dress you tried on in the last shop? It really suited you. Why didn't you get it?

B: It didn't suit me at all. I looked like a waitress in a cheap restaurant.

ML: You did not. You looked great.

B: I did not. The only thing I've really liked was that red dress in H & M. But every time I find something that I like, it doesn't fit me. I mean, they have my size, but they never seem to fit.

ML: It's difficult with dresses, isn't it?

B: Difficult? Impossible, more like. I always look fat in dresses. Maybe, I'll just get a top that goes with my black skirt. What do you think?

ML: It might be easier. I saw some nice ones in the window of Zara.

B: What colour suits me best?

ML: Maybe green to go with your eyes?

B: Green?

ML: Yes, there was a really nice green top in the Zara window.

B: I don't think Mike likes green.

ML: Huh! What does he know about clothes? His jackets are always three sizes too big, and his trousers don't fit him either.

B: He likes the relaxed, casual look. I think it suits him.

ML: Oh, well. What about, I don't know, maybe something silver or gold?

B: That's a thought. You don't think that silver or gold are a bit, you know … ?

ML: No, they'd look really good with that skirt. Gold, maybe, because you've got some really nice gold jewellery. But silver would be OK, too.

P: Afternoon, ladies.

ML: Oh, God, it's that awful man.

B: Hello, Mr Trotter.

P: Bonjour. Bonjour. Done some shopping, I see. Any bargains?

ML: I'm sorry, Mr Trotter, we're in a bit of a hurry. We were just going. There are a few things we need before the shops close.

P: Let me carry your bags, my dear.

ML: That will be quite all right, thank you. Come on, Bella. Goodbye, Mr Trotter.

P: Yes, well, jolly good. See you at the party this evening?

B: Yes. Byee.

ML: He's not going to the party, is he?

B: I'm afraid so. It's for the students as well as the staff.

ML: If he tries to chat me up one more time, I'll, I'll –
Come on, let's find a top for you.

B: Ooh, look.

ML: Oh, yes, that looks nice. That would suit you. Let's hope they've got your size. Shall we go in and have a look?

B: Yes. Did you see what Mr Trotter was wearing!?

ML: I try not to look at him.

B: I know you like him really.

ML: Bella. Come on, let's have a look at those tops.

12A Listening exercises 1 & 2 💿 2.54

They said he couldn't do it, but early this morning, the American adventurer, Steve Fossett, finally got out of his helium-filled balloon at Lake Yamma Yamma in Queensland, 700 miles north of Sydney. After six attempts, Steve Fossett has become the first person to fly solo round the world. The journey, of more than 20,000 miles, took him just under fifteen days, although he had a few problems on the way and he almost called the attempt off.

Steve took off from Northam in Western Australia on June 19th. He had to put off his departure for three hours because of a problem with wind, but he finally got going, flying past Sydney and New Zealand before starting the long journey over the Pacific to Santiago in Chile. At a news conference, Steve said, 'I had some exciting moments.' At one point, he was flying low when his burner control stopped working. On another occasion, there was a small fire in the balloon. But compared to his earlier attempts, these were small problems. The difficulties were sorted out and Steve was able to carry on with his epic journey.

Steve now plans to give up ballooning, but he has one or two other interesting hobbies. Way back in 1985, he swam across the Channel between England and France. He took part in the Alaska Dog Race in 1992, and in 1996 he raced in the 24-hour Classic at Le Mans in France. He holds the Round the World record for small aeroplanes – in both directions – and in 2001, he sailed across the Atlantic in four days seventeen hours, beating the previous record by an incredible 43 hours. Oh, and I almost forgot, he holds another eight world records for speed sailing.

His latest interest is gliding. He already has the world records for 500 and 1000 kilometres. What next? Well, his next project is to fly a glider to the edge of space. The edge of space in a glider? It sounds crazy, but adventure is a way of life for this extraordinary, quiet man. Channel Five will be showing a documentary about the life and achievements of Steve Fossett this evening at nine-fifteen and there will be …

12c Vocabulary exercise 5 🔘 2.57

The most widely-spoken language in the world is Mandarin Chinese with approximately 1 billion speakers. Next comes the Indian language family of Hindi, Bengali, Punjabi and so on. More than half a billion people speak one or more of these languages. After that, we have English which also has more than 500 million speakers (including speakers of English as a second or third language). The next language on our list is Spanish, with speakers in Spain, Central and South America. Next is Russian, followed by Arabic. At number seven on our list is Portuguese with about 200 million speakers and finally, at number eight, is French with about 130 million.

12d Listening exercises 1 & 2 🔘 2.61–2.64

1   **B = Bella   M = Mike**

B: Mike, where have you been? I was really worried.
M: Bella, I've had a terrible day. Awful.
B: Why? What happened?
M: A worm got through my firewall and disabled my C drive.
B: Mike, what are you talking about? I don't understand a single word.
M: Oh, yeah, sorry. Computers. I got a virus. It's destroyed everything. Everything.
B: Oh God, we had one of those viruses at work. Why do people send those things? Do they think it's funny? They must be mad.
M: Oh, definitely. Mad. Criminals. And they're dangerous.
B: Why don't the police do something to stop them?
M: I dunno, Bell. Maybe, they're too busy with other things.
B: Anyway, I'm really sorry. Come on, let me get you a drink. Forget about it. Are we going to dance later?

2   **P = Patrick   ML = Mlle Lajolie**

P: Ah, I was hoping to see you. Marvellous party, don't you think?
ML: Oh, it's you.
P: Can I get you a drink? Would you like a crisp?
ML: Pardon?
P: A crisp. Jolly good, if you ask me. Cheese and onion flavour, I think.
ML: Mr Trotter, I do not eat junk food.
P: I know, I know. You want to keep looking good, eh?
ML: No, Mr Trotter. I eat natural, organic food because I care about the future of this planet. I like to know what I am eating and I do not wish to eat genetically modified potatoes with chemical flavours.
P: You eat all that organic stuff, do you? I've always thought that it's a waste of money. All tastes the same to me.
ML: Well, that is not the way I see it. Now, will you excuse me? There's someone I want to talk to.
P: Oh, well, see you later.

3   **R = Ruby   D = Davina**

R: 'Scuse me, can you pass the crisps, please?
D: Certainly. Here you are. Ah, it's, erm, I believe we have met.
R: Ruby.
D: Ah, yes, Ruby.
R: I came for some job advice. You said something about my clothes.
D: Ah, yes, Ruby.
R: Would you like to give some money to the homeless this Christmas? It's for Christmas presents for homeless children.
D: Oh, absolutely, absolutely. What a good idea. Is one pound enough, do you think?
R: Well, it's not exactly generous. Do you know how hard their lives are? Living on the street.
D: Yes, yes, I see what you mean, but I don't have any more change.
R: Some people give notes.
D: You are extremely pushy, young lady. Here. Take ten pounds. It is for a good cause after all. We should all help the poor. Not everyone is as fortunate as myself. Now, who is that handsome young man standing over there?
R: Him?! That's Stuart. My ex.
D: What a marvellous example of a man.
R: You must be joking! He's a monkey. You can have him!
D: What are you suggesting, young lady?

4   **S = Stuart   M = Mary**

S: 'Scuse me. Have we met before?
M: I don't think so, young man. I always remember a face.
S: Oh, I just thought …
M: I never forget a face, young man. And certainly not a handsome young man like you.
S: Oh, right. Nice weather, innit?
M: It's certainly very hot. But I wouldn't call it 'nice'. There's nothing nice about global warming.
S: Global what? You mean all that stuff about the planet getting hotter? I don't care about that.
M: Well, I disagree, I'm afraid. I think we should all be extremely worried.
S: Nah. I'm not sure about that. I read in the newspaper that it's not true that it's getting hotter. It's just a bit hot that's all.
M: You shouldn't believe everything you read in the newspapers, you know.
S: Yeah, well, that's the problem, innit? People like you and me don't know what to believe.
M: Well, I'm telling you that you should be worried.
S: What do you know about it?
M: I'm a climatologist.
S: A what?
M: A weather scientist, young man.

1 | Review

1 Complete the questions with a word from the box.

how (x2)   what (x3)   when   who   why

1 _____ is her name?
2 _____ was she born?
3 _____ many brothers and sisters does she have?
4 _____ colour is her hair?
5 _____ languages does she speak?
6 _____ is she famous?
7 _____ rich is she?
8 _____ was her grandfather?

2 Match the answers below to the questions in exercise 1.

1 because she is very rich
2 in 1985
3 reddish brown
4 Athina Roussel
5 she has more than $2 billion
6 Swedish, French and English
7 the Greek businessman, Aristotle Onassis
8 three

3 Write questions for the sentences below.

1 What did Athina's mother give her for her second birthday?

1 Athina's mother gave her a zoo for her second birthday.
2 Her mother died in 1988.
3 Athina lived in Switzerland.
4 Her father and step-mother have a house in Lausanne.
5 Athina's first boyfriend was Alvaro Alfonso de Miranda Neta.
6 He comes from Brazil.
7 Athina calls him Doda.
8 Athina is very popular in Greece.

4 Rearrange the words to make questions.

1 a   common   do   have   him   in   lot   with   you ?
2 are   best   friend   his   you ?
3 go   he   school   to   did   with   you ?
4 at   friends   good   school   were   you ?
5 married   he   is ?
6 live   you   near   he   does ?
7 did   him   see   yesterday   you ?
8 English   speak   can   he ?

5 Match the short answers below to the questions in exercise 4.

a No, he doesn't.
b No, I didn't.
c No, I'm not.
d No, we weren't.
e Yes, he can.
f Yes, he did.
g Yes, he is.
h Yes, I do.

6 Think of a (male) friend. Work in pairs. Ask and answer the questions in exercise 4.

7 Each of the telephone messages below has two words missing. Insert the missing words.

1 I'm afraid is ⟨*there*⟩ no one to take your call right now.
   Please leave ⟨*your*⟩ name and I'll call you back.
2 Hello, this 2470362. There's no one at home the moment. Please leave a message after the beep.
3 Hello, my name is Sayers and I'm calling your advertisement in the newspaper. My number is 446091. Could call me back later, please?
4 This Ruby here. I'm not at home right now. Please leave your message and I'll try call you later. Many thanks.
5 Ruby, are you there? Ruby? It's Stuart. Can you give me a call at work some time afternoon? Or you can call me my mobile. It's urgent, OK?

8 Look at Sean Connery's family tree and decide if the sentences are true (T) or false (F).

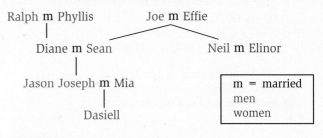

1 Diane is Mia's mother-in-law.
2 Effie is Jason Joseph's grandmother.
3 Elinor and Diane are cousins.
4 Elinor is Effie's aunt.
5 Jason Joseph is Neil's nephew.
6 Mia is Sean's niece.
7 Phyllis is Diane's mother.
8 Sean is Ralph's son-in-law.

2 | Review

1 Complete the text. Put the verbs in brackets into the past simple or the past continuous.

A few years ago, a student (1) _____ (*work*) for a telephone pizza company in the evenings after college. One day, she took a pizza to the richest man in town. The man (2) _____ (*pay*) the money, took the pizza and (3) _____ (*go*) into his house. He (4) _____ (*open*) the pizza box when the door (5) _____ (*ring*) again. He went to the door and saw that the student was still there. Clearly, she (6) _____ (*wait*) for something. 'What do you want? A tip?' the man (7) _____ (*ask*). 'No, sir,' replied the student. 'When I (8) _____ (*put*) the pizza on my bike, I spoke to the boy who brought your pizza yesterday. He said you didn't give tips.' 'That's not true,' the man (9) _____ (*reply*). 'In fact, I'm very generous. Here, take five dollars.' 'That's very kind of you, sir,' said the student. 'I needed the money to buy a book for my course at college.' 'What are you studying?' asked the man. 'Psychology, sir.'

2 Read the information about Trinity College in Dublin. Write six questions about the text in the past simple. Begin your questions with:

When
What   did ...?
Where

When did Trinity College open?

Trinity College, Dublin, became the first Irish university when it opened in 1594. All the students studied the same subjects – Latin, Greek, mathematics, science and philosophy. In 1834, the university allowed students to study specialized subjects. Eight years later, the university opened a department of engineering. In 1925, the first students entered the university's business school.

At the beginning, Trinity College was only for Protestants. The first Catholic students arrived two hundred years later. Many famous writers studied at Trinity. Jonathan Swift (who wrote *Gulliver's Travels*) and Bram Stoker (who wrote *Dracula*) both went there. The first women did not enter Trinity College until 1904. Mary Robinson, who became the first woman Irish president in 1990, studied law at Trinity in the 1960s.

3 Work in pairs. Close your books. Ask and answer the questions in exercise 2.

4 Change the sentences below so that they are true for you. Use *used to* or *didn't use to* with the correct form of the verb in italics.

1 I used to go to a school near home when I was young.

1 I *went* to a school near home when I was young.
2 I *sat* at the front of the class.
3 I *was* the teacher's favourite pupil.
4 I *did* extra homework every day.
5 We *had* sport every Wednesday afternoon.
6 I *enjoyed* sport.
7 I *got* very good grades in all my subjects.
8 I *liked* English lessons.

5 Complete the first word of the questions below:

1 _____ I have some information about your English courses, please?
2 _____ there any examinations I can take?
3 _____ you have a school in the centre of town?
4 _____ long do the courses last?
5 _____ you tell me anything about the teachers?
6 _____ much do the courses cost?
7 _____ there a library that students can use?
8 _____ time is the class for beginners?

6 Match the sentences below to the questions in exercise 5.

1 The tuition fees are all on this piece of paper.
2 They're all very experienced and qualified.
3 Usually about ten weeks. We have the same terms as state schools.
4 We're very flexible and we have many different timetables.
5 Yes, certainly. And we usually get very good results.
6 Yes, certainly. There's a meeting for new pupils this afternoon, if you're interested.
7 Yes. We also have a language laboratory and multi-media centre.
8 Yes. We have eight different locations. You can choose.

3 | Review

1 In the newspaper article below there are eight mistakes. Correct the mistakes.

Melbourne is the world's best city

The Australian city of Melbourne is the best place in the worlds to live,

The Australian city of Melbourne is the best place in the worlds to live, says a report from the Economist Intelligence Unit. The EIU looked at more than one hundred city around the world.

Melbourne got high grades for educations, entertainments and culture, housing, healths and weather. Because of this, more and more visitor were coming to Melbourne.

Other Australian cities also did well, but the report showed that there was more crimes in Sydney.

The best European cities were Vienna and Geneva, but Paris (28), Madrid (45=) and London (45=) were much lower in the list because of problems with crime, the weathers and the prices in the shops.

New York and Washington had similar difficulties, but were lower in the list.

---

2 Complete the dialogue with *some, any* or *no*.

A: I'm phoning you about the flat you advertised in the newspaper. Are there (1) _____ rules I should know about?

B: Er, yes. You can't have (2) _____ pets. (3) _____ dogs, (4) _____ cats. We've had (5) _____ problems with animals in the past.

A: Oh, fine. I've got (6) _____ friends coming to visit me at the weekend. Is that OK?

B: That's (7) _____ problem. Visitors are very welcome until ten o'clock.

A: And after ten?

B: No. You can't have (8) _____ guests in your room after ten. House rules, I'm afraid.

A: Do you have (9) _____ other rules like that?

B: There are (10) _____ other little things, but nothing important.

A: OK, well, I'm going to look at (11) _____ other flats this afternoon. I'll give you a call this evening.

B: OK, speak to you later.

3 In three of the sentences below, *of* is not necessary. Cross out *of* where it is incorrect.

1 Did you know that there are many of places in the world called London?
2 Most of them are in North America.
3 Many of them are very small towns.
4 However, some of them, like London, Ontario, are big.
5 There are also some of places called London in Africa.
6 Most of people in London, England, have never heard of these other places.

4 Choose the best quantifier to complete the sentences.

1 My flat's really nice but the neighbours make *a lot of / not enough / too many* noise.
2 There's *a few / not many / too much* traffic in my street.
3 My flat's quite small and there's *a lot of / not enough / too many* space when we have visitors.
4 I often invite *a few / not much / too much* friends for dinner in the evenings.
5 I'm looking for a new flat because this one costs *a little / not enough / too much* money.
6 I like going out so I only spend *a few / a little / a lot of* time at home.
7 I've lived in *many / not much / too much* different places, but this is my favourite.
8 There's *a few / not much / too many* nightlife in this part of town.

5 Look at the map on page 32 and complete the directions from the train station to the bars and restaurants near the river.

of	bridge	to (x2)	out	go	take	on

When you come (1) _____ of the train station, turn right. Walk along this road and then (2) _____ the first street (3) _____ your right. You go under a (4) _____ and then you come to the castle. (5) _____ left and follow this road. Keep to the right and you'll come (6) _____ the river. The bars and restaurants are on the other side (7) _____ the Tyne Bridge next (8) _____ the river.

6 Work with a partner. Choose one of the places in the box. Give directions to this place from your school, but do not say the name of the place. Your partner must guess which place you are talking about.

art gallery	bus station	cinema	museum
nightclub	park	shopping centre	theatre

4 | Review

1 Each of the advertisements below contain three mistakes. Correct the mistakes.

Do you like going to museums? Does you want to talk about philosophy and politics? Do you have a large collection of books? No? Good! My ideal man doesn't has time for all that. He is tall and handsome and enjoy sport of all kinds.
Box 788367

My perfect man is the strong, silent type. He not find it easy to say how he feels and most people doesn't understand him. But he know that somewhere, he will find the woman of his dreams. It's me.
Box 468835

Do the modern world drive you mad? Do you believe in a better, more natural way of life? I have a beautiful house in the mountains, but I am need someone to share it with me. If you wants a change and you like the outdoor life, get in touch.
Box 794662

2 Put the words in brackets in the correct place in the sentences.

1 We don't go out on our own. (*often*)
2 We have arguments about little things. (*sometimes*)
3 We share all the housework. (*usually*)
4 We speak on the phone. (*six times a day*)
5 We talk about our day at work. (*every evening*)
6 We tell each other all our secrets. (*always*)
7 We want to have children. (*never*)
8 We wear the same colour clothes. (*often*)

3 Complete the phrases with *in, on* or *at*.

1 _____ 1917
2 _____ Friday afternoon
3 _____ lunch time
4 _____ October
5 _____ the start of the lesson
6 _____ the weekend
7 _____ February 29th
8 _____ half past two
9 _____ New Year's Day
10 _____ Sunday
11 _____ the summer holidays
12 _____ the winter

4 Put the verbs in brackets into the present simple or the present continuous.

A: _____ (*you / have*) a boyfriend at the moment?
B: Yes, I _____ (*go*) out with a guy called Paul.
A: Paul? Paul what? _____ (*I / know*) him?
B: No, I _____ (*not / think*) so. He's a journalist.
A: Really? Who _____ (*he / work*) for?
B: The BBC. He _____ (*make*) a TV programme about online dating.
A: That's interesting! I _____ (*see*) a guy that I met online.
B: Really? _____ (*you / want*) to meet Paul? He'd love to talk to you.

5 Rearrange the words to make questions.

1 also are English friends studying your ?
2 come does from Scotland teacher your ?
3 do go often restaurants to you ?
4 are jeans today wearing you ?
5 do like your parents travelling ?
6 at is it moment raining the?

6 Match the short answers to the questions in exercise 5.

a No, I'm not.   d Yes, I do.
b No, they don't.   e Yes, it is.
c No, they're not.   f Yes, she does.

7 Now give answers that are true for you to the questions in exercise 5.

8 In each suggestion/response below, there is one word missing. Insert the missing word.

1 How tomorrow? Dinner at my place tomorrow?

2 I'd rather. I'm always tired afterwards.

3 It's kind you, but I have an evening class this evening.

4 Well, why don't meet after your class?

5 Would you like come to dinner this evening?

6 Yes, why not? I'd love.

9 Rearrange the lines in exercise 8 to make a dialogue. Practice the dialogue with a partner.

5 | Review

1 Philip has planned a weekend in Poland. Continue the description of his plans using *going to* + infinitive or present continuous.

Friday evening
  Arrive in Krakow – find a hotel
Saturday morning
  Visit the city centre, the cathedral and the castle
  12.30 Meet Grzegorz for lunch (Wierzynek restaurant)
Saturday afternoon
  Catch minibus to Wieliczka salt mine
Saturday evening
  Go to Beethoven concert (Philharmonica Hall)
  Dinner – find a good restaurant in the old town
Sunday
  9.30 Visit Historical Museum (with Marek)
  Have picnic with Marek (and his friends) in the Wolski Forest
  18.30 Fly home

He is arriving in Krakow on Friday evening and then he is going to look for a hotel. On Saturday morning, he …

2 Make questions/sentences from the prompts. Use *going to* + infinitive or the present continuous.

1 A: how / he / get / to Krakow ?
  B: he / catch / a plane / from Heathrow
2 A: he / buy / a guide book ?
  B: no / his friends / show him around
3 A: he / visit / other Polish cities ?
  B: no / he / not have / enough time
4 A: why / he / stay / only two days ?
  B: he / go back / to Poland / next year

3 Choose the correct form to complete the dialogues.

1 A: Have you got a single room for two nights?
  B: I think so. *I'll just check / I'm just going to check.*
2 A: Would you like a room with a view? It's a bit more expensive.
  B: No thanks. *I'll have / I'm going to have* the cheaper room.
3 A: Do you want to book a table for dinner?
  B: No thanks. *I'll have / I'm going to have* dinner with some friends.
4 A: Could you give me a wake-up call in the morning?
  B: Yes, sir. *We'll do / We're going to do* that for you.
5 A: Do you need a taxi?
  B: No thanks. A friend *will come / is coming* to pick me up.

4 Complete the sentences. Put the verbs in brackets into the correct form.

1 I'm interested in _____ (*hear*) more about your special offers.
2 I would like _____ (*spend*) a couple of weeks in the Swiss Alps.
3 I want _____ (*climb*) a few mountains.
4 I hope _____ (*do*) some sky diving as well.
5 I intend _____ (*take*) my own equipment.
6 I'm planning _____ (*go*) there in the late spring.
7 I'm looking forward to _____ (*hear*) from you.

5 In the dialogue below there are six mistakes. Correct the mistakes.

A: Good morning, sir. How can I help you?

B: Yes, I've got a ticket to London for tomorrow morning and I wonder if could I change it for a flight in the evening.

A: I'll see what I can do. Could I to see your ticket and passport, please?

B: Yes, of course. Here you are.

A: No problem. About what time do you want to leave?

B: I'd like take the last flight, please.

A: I'm afraid but the last flight is fully booked, but we have a seat on the 19.35.

B: That's fine. Can I having a window seat, please?

A: I sorry, but I can't do that for you now. Ask when you get to check-in.

B: OK.

A: Could you just sign here, please?

6 Complete the sentences with a word from the box.

---

air conditioning   facilities   lift   location
room service   shower   twin

---

1 The hotel has excellent _____ with a fantastic gym and sauna.
2 It has an incredible _____ near the cable car station.
3 We asked for a room with a _____ and toilet.
4 We wanted a double room but they only had one with _____ beds.
5 The _____ didn't work and, unfortunately, our room was on the sixth floor.
6 It's very hot here, but all the rooms have _____.
7 In the mornings, we telephoned _____ and had breakfast in bed.

6 | Review

1 Replace the adjectives in the sentences below with their opposites. Choose from the adjectives in the box.

artificial	authentic	boring	delicious	empty
expensive	traditional	slow	unhealthy	weak

1 We had an extremely cheap meal last night.
2 The food was quite interesting, especially the dessert.
3 It was a very healthy menu, too.
4 Everything was really modern.
5 The service was a bit fast.
6 I'm not surprised that the restaurant was fairly full.

2 Put the adjectives in brackets into the comparative form. Then complete the sentences with your own ideas.

1 It's often _____ (cheap) to do your shopping at the market than …
2 Pizza is usually _____ (popular) with children than …
3 For breakfast, it's _____ (good) to eat fruit and yoghurt than …
4 Fruit and vegetables are _____ (healthy) for you than …
5 I often have a _____ (big) lunch on Sundays than …
6 I think that Chinese food is _____ (interesting) than …
7 Having a healthy diet is _____ (important) than …
8 It's _____ (easy) to cook pasta than …

3 Complete the questions. Put the adjectives into the superlative form.

1 What is _____ (good) night to go out in your town?
2 Who is _____ (strong) student in your class?
3 What is _____ (bad) time of day for you?
4 Which is _____ (busy) street in your town?
5 Which is _____ (expensive) shop in your town?
6 Which is _____ (hot) month of the year?
7 Who is _____ (calm) person you know?
8 Who is _____ (famous) person in your country?

4 Work in pairs. Ask and answer the questions in exercise 3.

5 Some of the recipes below are very strange. Put a cross (x) next to the strange recipes.

1	bacon and eggs	7	lemon sorbet
2	caviar doughnuts	8	pasta and tomato sauce
3	chicken and rice	9	peanut butter crisps
4	chocolate cookies	10	potato salad
5	coffee noodles	11	steak and chips
6	ham and yoghurt	12	strawberry ice cream

6 Put the adjectives in brackets into the correct form.

Ristorante Palio

For a good, honest meal, you won't find
(1) _____ (good) than this. It serves traditional Italian food and it's (2) _____ (authentic) than other Italian restaurants in town. The service is
(3) _____ (slow) than we would like, but it's a lot (4) _____ (friendly).
★★★

The Cut

The Cut is probably (5) _____ (fashionable) restaurant in the centre of town. It's got (6) _____ (loud) music and (7) _____ (uncomfortable) chairs, but it seems that everyone wants to go there. The prices are (8) _____ (high) than the other restaurants in the area, but for (9) _____ (unforgettable) night out, this is the place to go.
★★★★

7 Put the sentences into two groups:
1 making a reservation for a restaurant
2 in a restaurant

a Certainly, madam. For how many people?
b Have you got anything for nine o'clock?
c Hello. We have a reservation for two people. The name is Wilson.
d I'd like to book a table for this evening, please.
e It's just for two people.
f Lovely. It is a non-smoking table, isn't it?
g No, thanks. Just the menu, please.
h This is the Taj Mahal. How can I help you?
i What time would you like?
j Yes, madam. A table for two at nine. We look forward to seeing you.
k Yes, madam. Let me show you your table. It's over there, by the window.
l Yes, madam. Would you like something to drink now?

8 Now put the sentences in exercise 6 in the correct order to make two dialogues.

Dialogue 1 __ __ __ __ __ __ __
Dialogue 2 __ __ __ __ __

7 | Review

1 Complete the sentences. Put the verbs in brackets into the present perfect simple.

1 She _____ (apply) for the senior manager's job, but she doesn't have much experience.
2 She _____ (be) very stressed at work and she gets angry very quickly.
3 She _____ (already / leave) – she hates waiting.
4 She _____ (do) lots of different training courses, so she can do almost anything in the office now.
5 She _____ (never / need) to ask for help from the boss.
6 She _____ (think) of some unusual new ways to recruit staff.

2 Choose the correct word to complete the sentences.

a She hasn't got a lot of *patience / patient*.
b She's extremely *skilled / skills*.
c She's got a lot of *imagination / imaginative*.
d She's probably too *ambition / ambitious*.
e She's very *emotion / emotional* at the moment.
f She's very *independence / independent* at work.

3 Match the sentences in exercise 2 to the sentences in exercise 1.

4 Complete the sentences. Put the verbs in brackets into the present perfect simple or the past simple.

1 I _____ (drive) the president to the airport yesterday.
2 I _____ (not / give) him his medicine yet.
3 I _____ (be) on the cover of three different women's magazines.
4 I _____ (make) six films but I usually work in the theatre.
5 I _____ (never / have) a customer who was so hungry.
6 In my last job, I _____ (work) for the company that is building a bridge over the river.
7 Last week, I _____ (write) an article about the salaries of top businessmen.
8 You are the best student that I _____ (ever / have)!

5 Match the sentences in exercise 4 to one of the jobs in the box.

| actor | chauffeur | engineer | journalist | model |
| nurse | teacher | waitress | | |

6 Work in pairs. Choose four more jobs and write a sentence (as in exercise 4) for each one. Your partner must guess the job.

7 Complete the sentences with a word from the box.

| apply | career | company | course | fired |
| leave | living | salary | unemployment | |

1 Why did you _____ for this job?
  a) Because I've got no money and the _____ is good.
  b) I've always wanted to work for this _____.
2 Why did you _____ your last job?
  a) My boss hated me and I was _____.
  b) Because I wanted a more interesting _____.
3 What do you do for a _____ at the moment?
  a) I'm between jobs, but I'm doing a training _____ in personnel management.
  b) I get _____ benefit.

| horoscope | manager | experience |
| charge | responsible | get |

4 Have you ever been in _____ of other people?
  a) Yes, I was _____ for a team of five people in my last job.
  b) No, I haven't. I've never been a _____.
5 Why do you think you should _____ this job?
  a) My _____ said this was my lucky day.
  b) I think I have the right _____ and personal qualities.

8 Choose the best answers to the questions in exercise 7. Then work in pairs and practise the interview with your partner.

9 Complete the dialogue with a phrase from the box.

| do you think I should | how about | if I were you |
| what should I | why don't you | you should |

A: I hate this job. (1) _____ leave?
B: Not yet. (2) _____ wait until you find another one.
A: I haven't got the time at the moment.
B: (3) _____ taking a day off so you can look for something else?
A: (4) _____ I tell the boss?
B: (5) _____ ring and say you're not well?
A: I can't do that!
B: Why not? I'd take a few days off (6) _____.

8 | Review

1 Rearrange the words to complete the (unsuccessful) predictions.

1 a   be   not   popular   way   will
The telephone _____ of communicating. (1876)

2 able   be   machines   never   will
Heavy _____ to fly. (1895)

3 actors   hear   to   want   won't
People _____ talking in films. (1927)

4 be   four   might   possible   sell   to
It _____ or five computers. (1943)

5 future   may   more   no   the   weigh
Computers in _____ than 1.5 tons. (1949)

6 never   television   the   use   will
We _____ for entertainment. (1955)

7 a   computer   people   that   want   will
I don't think _____ in their homes. (1977)

2 In four of the sentences below there are grammatical mistakes. Correct the mistakes.

1 Computers will definitely get smaller and smaller.
2 English definitely won't be an important language fifty years from now.
3 It won't be possibly necessary to find new sources of energy.
4 Military engineers will probably develop more powerful lasers.
5 Scientists maybe will find a way to travel in time.
6 The world's population will possibly double before the end of the century.
7 There won't be probably another world war.
8 We perhaps will make contact with aliens in the next few years.

3 Decide if the sentences describe predictions or plans. Then choose the correct verb form to complete the sentences.

1 *Are you going to / Will you* watch the football on TV this evening?
2 Do you think the talk *is going to / will* be interesting?
3 *I'm going to / I'll* check my email when I get home.
4 *It's going to / It will* be more difficult for young people to find a job.
5 New kinds of medicine *are going to / will* make us all live longer.
6 *We're going to / We'll* buy a new car next month.
7 Why *is she going to / will she* live in Japan?
8 *You're never going to / You'll never* see a more frightening film.

4 Put *if* in the correct place in the sentences below.

1 He won't like it you do that.
2 I have time, I'll come and see you.
3 I need some money, I'll ask the bank.
4 I'll help you you like.
5 They'll be very sad you go away.
6 We don't leave soon, we'll be late.
7 We'll miss the plane we don't hurry.
8 You'll be ill you eat that.

5 Choose the correct verb form to complete the text.

If the world's population (1) *continues / will continue* to rise, it (2) *becomes / will become* more and more difficult to feed everyone. Some scientists think that genetically modified (GM) food is the answer. But not everyone agrees. We will need more research before we (3) *know / will know* if GM food is really safe, they say. For example, what (4) *happens / will happen* to ordinary plants and animals if we (5) *grow / will grow* GM food on our farms? The GM companies say there is no danger. They say that when farmers (6) *use / will use* GM crops, they (7) *need / will need* fewer chemicals on their farms. And if we (8) *use / will use* fewer chemicals, our food (9) *is / will be* healthier to eat.

6 Put the instructions below in the correct order.

☐ all, click on 'Tools' on the main toolbar. Next,
☐ that says 'current selection'. After that, choose the dictionary that
☐ the word that you want to translate and click on the button
☐ select 'Language' and click on 'Translate'. You
☐ you will see the translation in the box.
☐ You can probably use your computer to translate words into English. First of
☐ you want to use. Finally, click on the 'Go' button and
☐ will then see a 'Translate' window on your screen. Highlight

7 Choose the best adjective to complete the questions about your town.

1 What is *important / impossible* for a visitor to know?
2 Where is it *unhealthy / unusual* to see tourists?
3 Where is it *easy / healthy* to park in the centre of town?
4 When is it *legal / usual* for people to eat?
5 Where is it *illegal / possible* to buy English books?
6 When is it *difficult / safe* to find a taxi in your town?
7 At what age is it *healthy / legal* to go to a nightclub?
8 When is it *dangerous / important* to walk in the park?

8 Work with a partner. Ask and answer the questions.

9 | Review

1 Choose the correct word to complete the sentences.

1 At what time in the evening do you usually get *tired / tiring*?
2 Do you ever get *annoyed / annoying* with your best friend? Why?
3 What do you do when you are *bored / boring*?
4 What's the most *excited / exciting* thing you've ever done?
5 When was the last time you felt really *frightened / frightening*?
6 Where was your most *disappointed / disappointing* holiday?
7 Who is the most *interested / interesting* person you've ever met?

2 Work in pairs. Ask and answer the questions in exercise 1.

3 Complete the text. Put the verbs in brackets into the present simple passive.

China Central Television (CCTV) (1) _____ (*own*) by the Chinese government. It receives some money from the government but programmes (2) _____ (*pay*) for with advertising money. It has thirteen different channels and these are called CCTV-1, CCTV-2, CCTV-3, etc. Programmes (3) _____ (*make*) in three different languages: Mandarin, Fujian dialect and English.
The most popular programme is the news, which (4) _____ (*watch*) by more than 300 million people every day. Soap operas are also very popular and the stars of the shows (5) _____ (*know*) to millions of people.
The English language programmes (6) _____ (*show*) on CCTV-9. It has a variety of programmes, including news, business news, documentaries and sport. For foreigners it is interesting because current affairs (7) _____ (*look*) at from a Chinese point of view.
CCTV (8) _____ (*see*) by many viewers in the USA.

4 Complete the questions with a verbs from the box. Use the past simple passive.

| call direct hit play receive save win build |

1 When and where _____ the *Titanic* _____?
2 What _____ the captain of the ship _____?
3 How many warnings about icebergs _____ _____ by the ship?
4 When _____ the ship finally _____ by an iceberg?
5 How many people _____ _____ from the ship?
6 Who _____ the film _____ by?
7 Who _____ the main roles in the film _____ by?
8 How many Oscars _____ _____ by the movie?

5 The information below gives you the answers to the questions in exercise 4. Use the information to make sentences about the *Titanic*.

1 *The Titanic was built in 1911 in Belfast.*

1 in 1911 in Belfast
2 Edward Smith
3 six, or possibly seven
4 at 11.40 pm on April 14th 1912
5 about 700
6 James Cameron
7 Kate Winslet and Leonardo DiCaprio
8 eleven

6 Complete the text. Put the verbs in brackets into the correct present simple form: active or passive.

The Simpsons is probably the most popular TV show in the world. It (1) _____ (*watch*) in more than 70 countries around the world. It's also expensive to buy. In the UK, Channel 4 (2) _____ (*pay*) £700,000 for every episode.

The show's creator, Matt Groening, (3) _____ (*write*) other cartoons for TV and newspapers. In one episode of *The Simpsons*, we (4) _____ (*see*) Groening signing books. He (5) _____ (*introduce*) as the creator of the TV show, Futurama.

The characters in *The Simpsons* (6) _____ (*base*) on Groening's own family. Groening's father, for example, (7) _____ (*call*) Homer and his mother Margaret. The main characters (8) _____ (*play*) by a team of actors. It (9) _____ (*think*) that these actors (10) _____ (*earn*) more than $250,000 for every episode. From time to time, famous Hollywood actors like Mel Gibson or Danny DeVito (11) _____ (*star*) in the show.

7 Rearrange the lines to make a dialogue at a box office.

☐ Certainly, I'll see what we've got available. Which show do you want –the Friday or the Saturday?
☐ Could you hold on and I'll check for you? No, I'm afraid that's sold out, but we've got seats in the stalls for the Saturday.
☐ Fine. Can I pay by credit card.
☐ Hi. I'd like ten tickets for the Beenie Man concert, please.
☐ OK, that's ten tickets for Beenie Man on the Saturday. That will be £180 altogether, sir.
☐ That's fine. Ten, please.
☐ The Friday. Downstairs in the stalls if that's possible.
☐ Yes, of course. Could I take your details please?

10 | Review

1 Complete the sentences with *for* or *since*.

1 She's seen many different specialists _____ the illness started.
2 She hasn't had a cough _____ she was a child.
3 She's had high blood pressure _____ the last few days.
4 She's lost a lot of weight _____ the beginning of the year.
5 She's felt exhausted _____ a week or two.
6 Her back has been painful _____ about ten days.
7 She's taken five days off work _____ the problems began.
8 She hasn't taken antibiotics _____ a long time.

2 Complete the text. Put the verbs in brackets into the past simple or the present perfect simple.

When Valerie Brasseur (1) _____ (*finish*) nursing school, there was only thing that she (2) _____ (*want*) to do. For the last six months, Valerie (3) _____ (*be*) in the Sudan where she is working as a nurse for the organization Médecins Sans Frontières (Doctors Without Borders).
A group of French doctors (4) _____ (*begin*) the organization in 1971. Since then, MSF (5) _____ (*provide*) medical help in more than 80 countries around the world. Because the staff work in countries at war, MSF (6) _____ (*never / be*) out of the news and, in 1999, it (7) _____ (*win*) the Nobel Peace Prize.
Valerie (8) _____ (*know*) about MSF since she was 18 – the year that she (9) _____ (*leave*) home and (10) _____ (*go*) to nursing school. It was also the year that her parents (11) _____ (*begin*) to work for the organisation. Because Valerie is in the Sudan and her parents in Central America, she (12) _____ (*not / see*) them for over eighteen months.

3 In the dialogue below there are six grammatical mistakes. Correct the mistakes.

A: Good morning, Mr Riley. I didn't see you for at least two weeks. What's wrong with you?

B: It's my chest, doctor. It's been really painful.

A: How long do you have the pain?

B: Since I stopped smoking.

A: When exactly have you stopped smoking?

B: Oh, I stopped the day before yesterday.

A: So you haven't had a cigarette since two days?

B: Yes, I've found it very difficult.

A: Where exactly does it hurt?

B: Here and here and here. I feel awful.

A: Anything else?

B: Well, I am under a lot of stress in the last few days.

A: I see. Take off your shirt. I'll have a look at you. Yes, it's as I thought. It's normal, I'm afraid, when people stop smoking.

B: Can you give me a prescription for it?

A: No, but come back and see me if the pain hasn't been away in the next few days, OK?

4 Choose the best way to continue the mini-dialogues below.

1 She's been to see the doctor.
   a) What did the doctor say?
   b) What time did she leave?
2 I went to the station this morning to say goodbye to my parents.
   a) Where have they been?
   b) Where have they gone?
3 Where has your boss gone?
   a) I don't know. He didn't want to say.
   b) He's just had a week's holiday in Tunisia.
4 I played golf at the new club near the river at the weekend.
   a) Oh, I've been there, too.
   b) Oh, I've gone there, too.
5 So, is this the first time you've seen the new hospital?
   a) Yes, I've been away a long time.
   b) Yes, I've gone away a long time.

5 Complete the questions with a word from the box.

check-up   operation   pressure   specialist
suffer   symptoms   treatment   weight

1 Do you ever _____ from stress?
2 Have you ever been to hospital for an _____?
3 How long do you have to wait for an appointment with a _____ doctor?
4 How often should you see a doctor for a _____?
5 What are the _____ of flu?
6 What is the best _____ for a hangover?
7 What is the best way to lose _____?
8 What should you do if you have high blood _____?

6 Work with a partner. Ask and answer the questions in exercise 1.

11 | Review

1 Combine the pairs of sentences with an infinitive of purpose and make any necessary changes.

1 *He needs a new suit to wear for his interview.*

1 He needs a new suit. He'll wear it for his interview.
2 He bought a new car. He wanted to impress his girlfriend.
3 She called the restaurant. She booked a table for this evening.
4 He spoke to his boss. He asked for a pay rise.
5 She went to the changing-room. She tried on the jeans.
6 She's started swimming. She's hoping to get fit.
7 He used a thesaurus. He found a better word.
8 She always reads the newspaper. She looks at her horoscope.

2 Choose the best explanation for the signs.

1 CREDIT CARDS WELCOME

   a) You can't pay by credit card.
   b) You don't have to pay by cash.
   c) You have to pay by cash.

2 WE NOT ACCEPT CHEQUES UNDER £20

   a) You can pay by cheque if it's more than £20.
   b) You can't pay by cheque if it's more than £20.
   c) You have to pay by cheque if it's more than £20.

3 BUY 2 PACKETS – GET 1 FREE!

   a) You can't buy more than two packets.
   b) You don't have to pay for the third packet.
   c) You have to buy three packets.

4 NO DOGS ALLOWED

   a) You can't bring dogs in here.
   b) You don't have to bring dogs in here.
   c) You must have a dog.

5 STAFF TOILET ONLY

   a) Customers can use this toilet.
   b) Customers have to find another toilet.
   c) Staff can't use this toilet.

6 BUY NOW, PAY LATER (12 MONTHS FREE CREDIT)

   a) You can't pay later.
   b) You don't have to spend anything now.
   c) You must pay now.

3 Match the sentences 1–5 to the sentences a–e.

1 At my primary school, all the boys had to wear a uniform.
2 When it was cold in winter, we didn't have to wear shorts.
3 The girls couldn't wear trousers.
4 We couldn't wear trainers.
5 The teachers had to wear black gowns.

a Some of them also wore a funny hat, but they didn't have to.
b The school rules said we could only have black shoes.
c It was grey shorts, a grey jacket and tie.
d They had grey skirts or a grey dress in the summer.
e We could wear trousers instead.

4 Rewrite the sentences with the present or past form of *can/can't, have to/don't have to*.

1 A few years ago, it was possible to smoke almost anywhere.
   You _____.
2 Was it necessary for you wait a long time?
   Did _____.
3 It isn't necessary to say 'Sorry' all the time.
   You _____.
4 It was impossible to find anywhere to park my car.
   I _____.
5 It was necessary to get a new car after the accident.
   We _____.
6 It's necessary for me to work overtime this evening
   I _____.
7 Hats are not allowed in many churches.
   You _____.

5 Correct the mistakes in the sentences below.

1 Can you tell me where the change room is, please?
2 Do you like shopping for clothe?
3 excuse me, have you got this suit on a darker colour?
4 I like this top. Can I try on it?
5 I really like your jeans. Where did you get it?
6 I'm sorry, this doesn't suit. Can I try another size?
7 She's gone to the department store to buy some underwears.
8 What size trouser do you take?

12 | Review

1 Complete the sentences with a preposition from the box.

> across   along   around   out of   over   past
> through   into

1 How long does it take a supersonic jet to fly _____ the world?
2 Schumacher got _____ his car and waited for the race to begin.
3 She plans to swim _____ the Straits of Gibraltar between Spain and Morocco.
4 The bus drove _____ the bus stop without stopping.
5 The prisoners climbed _____ the wall and escaped from the prison.
6 There was a lot of traffic in the city centre and it was difficult to get _____.
7 What time do you get _____ class after your lesson?
8 You need to drive _____ this road for about five miles.

2 Complete the phrasal verbs in the sentences below.

1 Marco Polo's family called _____ their plan to travel to China by sea and decided to go by land instead.
2 Columbus had many problems crossing the Atlantic, but he decided to carry _____ .
3 Roald Amundsen gave _____ his attempt to go to the North Pole because of the start of the First World War in 1914.
4 Amelia Earhart often had to put _____ her flights for a few days because of the weather.
5 Humboldt often needed to sort _____ diplomatic problems before he could travel.
6 Neil Armstrong's Apollo 11 mission took _____ from the Kennedy Space Centre in Florida.

3 Choose the correct form to complete the sentences.

1 Do you know anyone *which is / who is / who are* homeless?
2 Hungary is a country *that has / that have / who have* no sea coast.
3 I never eat food *that is / which are / who is* genetically modified.
4 I was surprised that there were some people *that has / who has / who have* never heard of Marco Polo.
5 It's a journey *that take / which takes / who takes* more than five days.
6 The newspaper showed pictures of protesters *that was / which were / who were* in the trees.
7 There are many mysteries *that has / which has / which have* never been solved.
8 There are some English accents *that is / that are / which is* very difficult to understand.

4 Read the newspaper article below. Put the relative clauses a–h in the gaps 1–8.

a that led to Jaschan's arrest
b that protects them from the Sasser worm
c that were found in his home
d who were responsible for another virus, Netsky
e who has admitted creating the Sasser computer virus
f who have problems with their computers
g who knew the identity of the virus creator
h which closed down their machines

Police arrest virus writer

German police have arrested Sven Jaschan, a teenager (1)_____. They have also taken a number of computers and disks (2) _____.

The virus first appeared on the internet on May 1 of this year. Millions of computer-users around the world were hit by the virus (3) _____. Some businesses had to close temporarily so that they could install software (4) _____.

It is understood that the police received a phone call from someone (5)_____. Microsoft said that they would pay for information (6) _____.

Jaschan, an 18-year old high school student from Rotenburg, wrote the virus alone. However, police believe that he was also part of a group of people (7) _____.

Jaschan's mother runs a company from the family home. The company provides help to people (8) _____.

5 Complete the sentences with a word from the box.

> conservation   engineering   global   homeless
> organic   poverty   viruses   wage

1 The government should increase the minimum _____.
2 We shouldn't worry too much about _____ warming.
3 People who design computer _____ must be crazy.
4 I think _____ food is a waste of money.
5 There's always a strong connection between _____ and crime.
6 Animal _____ is not a very important issue.
7 Genetic _____ is the solution to the world's food problems.
8 There will probably be more and more _____ people on the streets.

6 Work in pairs. Discuss your responses to the opinions in exercise 5.

Macmillan Education
Between Towns Road, Oxford OX4 3PP
A division of Macmillan Publishers Limited
Companies and representatives throughout the world

ISBN 1405 01057 6

Designed by Oliver Design

Illustrated by Paul Collicutt pp47, 58; Mark Duffin pp12, 13, 29, 51, 56, 60, 62, 76, 80, 101, 106, 126; Andy Hammond pp20, 21; Joanna Kerr pp100, 108 and Monica Laita pp38, 39 of New Division; Simon Lubach pp98, 99; Ed McLachlan pp23, 33, 42, 48, 49, 63, 72, 80, 102, 112; Philip Pepper pp11, 27, 69, 87, 127, 129, 130(r); Annette Marie Percy p43; Chris Robson pp102, 103; Derek West p32 and Gary Wing pp71, 130(l).

Cover design by Macmillan Publishers Limited

Cover photographs by:
Top Line (left to right), Corbis / R Holmes, Bridgeman, Popperfoto, Picture Disk, Image Works, Corbis (+bl).
Bottom Line (left to right) Digital Vision, Press Association, Corbis RF(+br), Image State RF, Topham, Science Photo Library / A Pasieka.
Back Cover (left to right) Digital Vision, Corbis RF , Corbis RF, Haddon Davies, Image State RF, Picture Disk.

Author's acknowledgements
The author would like to thank Katy Wright.

The author and publishers would like to thank the following people for their help and contribution:
Carolina Mussons, Mari-Carmen Lafuente, Eliseo Picó Mas, Carmen Roig-Papiol and Lourdes Montoro, EOI Sta Coloma de Gramanet, Barcelona. Maggie Hawes, Tony Isaac, Tom Radman and Anita Roberts, British Council, Barcelona. Rosie Dickson and Sarah Hartley, Merit School, Barcelona. Christina Anastasiadis, Andrew Graydon, Steven McGuire, Alan Hammans, Heather Shortland and Roger Edwards, International House Zurbano, Madrid. Guy Heath, British Council, Madrid. Ramón Silles, EOI Majadahonda. Javier Martinez Maestro, EOI Parla. Rosa Melgar, EOI Valdezarza. Susana Galan, The English Centre, Madrid. Yolanda Scott-Tennent Basallote, EOI Tarragona. Ceri Jones.
Marzenna Raczkowska. Yaffite Mor, Alicja Fialek and Ricky Krzyzewski, UEC-Bell School of English, Warsaw. Steve Allen, Joanna Zymelka, Marek Kazmierski, Przemek Skrzyniarz, Colin Hinde, Mireille Szepaniak, Gabriela Pawlikowska and Simon Over, English First, Warsaw. Fiona Harrison-Rees, British Council, Warsaw. Karina Davies and Katarzyna Wywial, Szkola Jezykow Obcych 'Bakalarz', Warsaw. Peter Moran and Joanna Trojanowska, International House, Krakow. Walter Nowlan, British Council, Krakow. Agnieszka Bieniek, Anna Galus, Malgorzata Paprota and Joanna Berej, U Metodystow, Lublin. Mr Paudyna, Alicja Grajek, Eliza Trojanowska and Monika Bochyn'ska, Studium Jezykow Obcych, Minsk Mazowiecki. Paola Randali. Paola Povesi. Roberta Giugni. Mirella Fantin. Rossella Salmoiraghi. Marco Nervegna and Rebecca Kirby, Linguaviva, Milan. Peter Sheekey, Oxford Group, Milan. Irina Kuznetsova, Elena Ivanova, Olga Kekshoeva and Yulia Mukoseeva, Tom's House, Moscow. Asya Zakirova, Tatyana Tsukanova, Natalia Brynzynyuk, Anna Karazhas, Anastasia Karazhas and Nadya Shishkina, Mr English Club, Moscow. Inna Turchin, English First Zhulebino, Moscow. Tatiana Shepelenko, Ljuba Sicheva and Tatiana Brjushkova, Higher School of Economics, Moscow.
David Willis. Susan Hutchison. Kirsten Holt. Tanya Whatling. Laila Meachin. Howard Smith, Clare Dunlop, Clare Waring and Andrew Mitchell, Oxford House, London. Garth Cadden, Lefteris Panteli and Vicky McWilliam, St Giles College, London. Sarah James, Sarah Lurie, Karen Mathewman, Chris Wroth, Olivia Smith, Sue Clark, Alan Greenslade-Hibbert, King's School of English, Oxford.
Sara Fiorini, CEFETI Centro de Linguas, São Paulo. Neide Silva and Maria Helena Iema, Cultura Inglesa Pinheiros, São Paulo. José Olavo de Amorim and Amini Rassoul, Colégio Bandeirantes, São Paulo. Maria Antonieta and Sabrina Teixeira,

Centro Britânico, Perdizes, São Paulo. Loreliz Kessler, Unilínguas, São Leopoldo. Marli Zim, Acele, Porto Alegre. Luciane Duarte Calcara, Britannia, Porto Alegre. Magali Mente, Lingua Lindóia, Porto Alegre. Maria Higina, Cultura Inglesa Savassi, Belo Horizonte. Eliane Peixoto, Green System, Belo Horizonte. Adriana Bozzolla Vieira, Britain English School, Belo Horizonte. Roberto Amorin, ICBEU Centro, Belo Horizonte.
Patrícia Brasileiro, Cultura Inglesa Casa Forte, Recife. Eleonor Benício, British Council, Recife. Roseli Serra, Cultura Inglesa Madalena, Recife. Alberto Costa, Cultura Inglesa Olinda, Recife. Glória Luchsinger, English Learning Centre, Recife. Angela Pougy Azevedo and Márcia Porenstein Toy Centro, Rio de Janeiro. Julian Wing, British Council, Rio de Janeiro. Karla Koppe, Colegio Tereziano, Rio de Janeiro. Márcia Martins. Ricardo Sili and Janine Barbosa, Cultura Inglesa, Rio de Janeiro.
Ágnes Tisza, Ring Nyelvstúdió, Budapest. Katalin Nemeth and Edina Varga, Novoschool, Budapest. Szilvia Hegyi, Mack Alasdair, Eva Lukacsi and Katalin Jonas-Horvath, Babilon Language Studio, Budapest. Nikolett Pozsgai, Európai Nyelvek Stúdiója, Budapest. Krisztina Csiba and Anett Godó, Oxford Hungária Nyelviskola, Budapest. Zsuzsanna Tóth and Szilvia Fülöp, H-Net, Budapest. Judit Csepela, TIT Globe, Budapest. Judit Volner and Rita Erdos, Dover Nyelvi Centrum, Budapest. Ildikó Tóth and Piroska Sugár, Katedra, Budapest. Katalin Terescsik Szieglné and Magdolna Zivnovszki, London Stúdió, Budapest. Agota Kiss and Gabriella Varga, KOTK, Budapest. Rita Lendvai and Judit Szarka, Atalanta, Budapest. Péter Gelléri, Tudomány Nyelviskola, Budapest.

The author and publishers would like to thank the following for permission to reproduce their material:
Story on Gemma Burford Enolengila © Gemma Burford Enolengila, granted with her kind permission.

The author and publishers would like to thank the following for permission to reproduce their photographs:
Alamy/M Lebed pp7(t), Photofusion 18(t), J Greenberg 31(tr), D&J Heaton 53(F), Popperfoto p53(G), S Bisserot p60(c), H Elofsson 60(b), J Renston 68, J Smith 69, B Lawrence 100(D), Images RF 100(F), National Motor Museum 106(car), N Pitt 109 (lm) J Weidel 109(mr), M Dyball 110(tr); American Express p106; Anthony Blake/C Stebbings p62; A Motiva p6(A); G Burford p7(D); Bridgeman p86(A); Cartoonstock/C Fumier p16; Corbis/R Nowitz pp6/7(B), Hulton Deutsch 18(b), B Kraft 19(bm), R Folkks 19(bl), C Trotman 19(br), R Holmes 28, R Cummins 51, K Su p52(A), 79, L Manning 82(l), B Krist 86(A), F Cevallos 86(C), C Savage 86(E), S Lupton 90(b), C Panchout 92(l), S Sands 92(m), T Stewart pp96(B), 100(B), Chip East 100(A), Sea World of California 100(E), R Ressmeyer 106(computer), Bettmann pp116(mr), (ml), S Bianchetti 116(m), Corbis 116(r); Corbis R F pp 22(t), 22(br), 22(b) 56 (burger), (chips), (pizza), (crisps), (cookies), (eggs), 61(coffee); Freemantle Stills Library p88; Getty Images/C Close pp32, (m), (b), J Hunter 52(D), R Schultheiss 53(E), P Webster 60(E), S Kushner 82(r), M Gilbert 96(A), C Baker 109(l), Hulton Archive pp8, 40(tl) 43(l); Harper Collins p19(t); Hard Rock Café p57; Imagestate RF pp 52(dolphin), 122(globe); Impact Photos p109(r); John Cole p50; Kobal pp41(t), 41(b); Lonely Planet/A Evrard pp30/31, GV der Knijff 31(b); Mary Evans pp43(r), 16(l); Magnum/S McCurry p120; Oxfam p123; Panos Pictures/J L Dugast pp52(D), M Luiza p60(D); Photodisc RF pp12(m), 56(donut), (hot dog), (ice cream); Picture Disk/Teen Spirit pp12(t), 12(br); Press Association/EPA pp78, 100(C), 101, 117, AAP 92(r); Rex Features pp22(bl), Sipa pp52(B), 97, Rex pp66(l), 66(r), 67, KMLA 96(r); Ronald Grant Archive pp17(l), 17(r), 40(b), 41(t), 41(b), 86(f), 90(tl); Science Photo Library/A Pasieka pp76(l), 76(r), C Butler 76(m), R Darkin 77; D Tolley p26; Topham pp56, 60(A), 90(tr), D Porges 86(D), UPPA pp10(t), 96(C), P A pp10(b), 86(G), Image works pp12(bl), 46, 96(D).
London Underground map reproduced with kind permission of Transport for London.
Commissioned photographs by Haddon Davies pp 36, 82 (t), 106 (items a-k), 107, 108, 128, 130, 132.

Printed and bound in Spain by Edelvives

2009 2008 2007 2006 2005
10 9 8 7 6 5 4 3 2 1